"DISCOVERY" IN LEGAL DECISION-MAKING

Law and Philosophy Library

VOLUME 24

The titles published in this series are listed at the end of this volume.

BRUCE ANDERSON

Newcastle Law School,
University of Newcastle upon Tyne, U.K.

"DISCOVERY" IN LEGAL DECISION-MAKING

KLUWER ACADEMIC PUBLISHERS

DORDRECHT / BOSTON / LONDON

A C.I.P. Catalogue record for this book is available from the Library of Congress

ISBN 0-7923-3981-9

Published by Kluwer Academic Publishers,
P.O. Box 17, 3300 AA Dordrecht, The Netherlands.

Kluwer Academic Publishers incorporates
the publishing programmes of
D. Reidel, Martinus Nijhoff, Dr W. Junk and MTP Press.

Sold and distributed in the U.S.A. and Canada
by Kluwer Academic Publishers,
101 Philip Drive, Norwell, MA 02061, U.S.A.

In all other countries, sold and distributed
by Kluwer Academic Publishers Group,
P.O. Box 322, 3300 AH Dordrecht, The Netherlands.

Printed on acid-free paper

Printed in the Netherlands

Contents

Preface

Preface

This book deals with a central problem throughout the legal profession - a solution to the problem is sought and reached in some basic form. At the centre of this problematic is the question indicated by the title: "What is the nature of "discovery" in legal decision-making?" In the final chapter that problem and the solution reached will be seen to have ramifications throughout the entire field of legal practice and theory. However, the focus of the argument is maintained first to specify adequately the particular manifestation of the problem in a variety of legal fields and secondly to arrive at a precise basic solution to this range of problems. The presentation of the solution is not dictated by the norms of clarity and coherence, but by the dynamics of the struggle to reach the solution and by aspects of the problem available to various sub-groups within the legal profession - theorists, judges, arbitrators. So, I begin from a relatively familiar zone, discussions of discovery in legal theory before moving to more unfamiliar territory.

This book is not a thorough survey of problems and writings on discovery. Rather, the strategic selection of problems and assessment of solutions across the first four chapters represents four aspects of the problem. Those chapters invite the reader to rise to the sense of occurrence of a single problem in a variety of contexts. Chapter One aims to present a representative sample of those legal theorists who have a reflective interest in the discovery process. I begin by describing the context in which legal theorists have discussed discovery, particularly the debate between the legal realists and legal positivists. Then, in an anecdotal fashion, I present recent reflections of legal theorists on aspects of the decision-making process. But this is only the first step in collecting the materials that would be relevant to a coherent explanation of the process of discovery. Chapter Two presents reflections on discovery that have emerged in the context of scientific pursuits. I investigate the processes involved in decision-making that are understood and explained by using an analogy between science and law and then turn to Cognitive Psychology.

In Chapters Three and Four, I take further steps to collect materials relevant to our problem and its solution. I turn from reflective considerations to analyse spontaneous efforts to solve legal problems. In Chapter Three, I discuss discovery in a case on abortion. Chapter Four explores the actual process of decision-making performed by an arbitrator solving a problem. These two chapters raise fundamental problems about discovery, expression, and introspection that, as yet, cannot be addressed. Taken together, the random collection of materials in these four chapters indicate that there is required a shift in context to deal coherently with the entire problematic of discovery in legal decision-making.

The central chapters of the positive presentation are Chapters Five to Seven where, within the context of the problematic generated by the previous chapters, the reader is invited to a technique of self-attention that will hopefully lead the reader to a discovery of self-discovery. The result of these chapters is to provide the reader with a plausible interpretation of the various facets of discovery. Chapter Five introduces the perspective of Bernard Lonergan, a philosopher and theologian, who studied decision-making in various fields. Chapters Six and Seven are an elementary presentation of, and application of, Lonergan's view of discovery in problem-solving. Chapter Six deals with discovery in theoretical problem-solving and the topic in Chapter Seven is practical problem-solving. Finally, Chapter Eight will bring this structure of relations to bear on the problems raised, and hints indicated, in Chapters One to Four. The chapter concludes with an indication of the broader solution within the various fields of legal interest.

Before going any further I want to thank the people who helped me with this project: Beverley Brown for carefully reading and generously commenting on my work, Zenon Bankowski and Neil MacCormick for reading and encouraging my efforts, Philip McShane for scrutinizing the the manuscript and contributing to the discussions in Chapter Eight, Glenn Anderson for telling me about his experience as an arbitrator which I examine in Chapter Four, and Donald and Helen Anderson and Jean Read for their moral and financial support. I am also grateful for the financial support I received from an Edinburgh University Scholarship, the Richard Brown Memorial Scholarship, and Edinburgh Law Faculty Grant, the University of Newcastle upon Tyne Staff Travel Fund, and the Newcastle Law School.

1

The Problematic Nature of Discovery and Justification*

1 Introduction

Contemporary studies of legal reasoning are primarily concerned with analysing how judicial decisions are *justified*. They stress the logical, rational, "objective" nature of the process of legal justification.[1] Legal theorists who study legal reasoning in this context accept that there is, and should be, a "rigid" distinction between the process of discovery (how a judge "actually" reaches a tentative decision) and the process of justification (how a judge publicly justifies a decision).[2] The "actual" process followed by a judge to invent or discover a solution to a case is a distinct and independent process that is considered relatively unimportant compared to the process of publicly justifying a judicial decision by supporting reasons and arguments. These theorists assert that the proper subject matter of their investigations is legal justification, not discovery. Some theorists even claim that the process of discovery cannot, even should not, be analysed by legal scholars. They classify the discovery process as a psychological, not a legal, matter that should be left to psychologists.[3]

Psychologists, however, have not filled the gap assigned to them by legal theorists. Psychologists have not investigated the discovery process in law. In Jerzy Wroblewski's opinion, "The psychology of judicial decision-making is relatively the least developed field of research concerning judicial decision-making. So far as concerns the psychology of judicial decision-making, there is little available except for some reconstruction and some general psychology combined with discussion of the case material; there is nothing amounting to a special form of empirical research."[4] Joxe Bengoetxea[5] seems to doubt whether the discovery process can be studied at all. He claims that "the insight or 'intuitive faculty' [a type of Gestalt switch or structural-contextual comprehension of the case and the legal solution that ought to be given] "...is difficult to control and analyse because it is a necessarily postulated element."[6]

Nevertheless contemporary legal theorists, however focused on justification, do not entirely ignore the process of discovery. The process of discovery involves the emergence of judicial "hunches" or "insights". Hunching, the psychological process of discovering or inventing a possible solution to a case, is portrayed as an activity that is not subject to conscious control. Hunching is a non-rational, non-logical and unconscious activity. Not only are hunches/insights themselves "subjective" in the sense that their emergence is non-systematic, but they are also said to be "subjective" in the sense that their emergence depends on factors such as bias and prejudice- especially mood, personality, background, education and experience.[7] Hence hunches must be tested and justified by the rational, logical and conscious process of legal justification. What a judge "actually" thinks about when reaching a decision is one thing, but its public legal justification is another independent and more important matter.

However, accounts of legal reasoning have not always been dominated by analyses of legal justification. Legal theorists have not always presumed that there is a "rigid" distinction between discovery and justification. And jurists have not always claimed that the "actual" process followed by a judge to reach a decision is either unimportant, arbitrary and non-rational or that it cannot and should not be studied by legal theorists. The American legal realists, especially Jerome Frank, John Dewey, Oliver Wendell Holmes and Karl Llewellyn, investigated what they called the judging process - ie. the actual process followed by judges to reach their decisions. They believed that understanding how judges reached their decisions would lead to wise decisions and candid legal reporting. They did not create a "rigid" distinction between discovery and justification. Instead the judging process included both the operation of thinking (discovering and testing solutions to cases) and the oral and written expositions of the results of thinking. By contrast to modern legal theorists, in the realists' opinion, the mental activities that precede the public exposition or justification of a decision are a significant part of a decision. Although they stressed the non-logical and non-rational nature of hunches and intuitions, hunches were not presented by them as arbitrary and irrational acts of discovery or invention.

I begin by examining how contemporary accounts of legal reasoning have come to be pre-occupied with the process of legal justification and have mis-represented and ignored the "actual" decision-making process. First, I describe the method used by the realists to investigate judicial decision-making and present their explanation of the decision-making process. They portrayed decision-making as a conscious and deliberate problem-solving process, a structure more complex than the legal positivists' "rigid" distinction between discovery and justification would suggest. Secondly, I trace how discovery and justification have come to be considered distinct and independent processes. I argue that contemporary legal theorists have responded to the debate between the legal formalists and the realists by creating a "rigid" distinction between discovery and justification. In this form of resolution the realists' overall project and their novel contributions have been mis-represented and ignored and legal reasoning has come to be defined in terms of the "logic" of legal justification. Thirdly, I analyse contradictions between the realists' explanation of hunching and testing in legal decision-making and the modern legal positivists' version of discovery and justification. I claim that before asserting that discovery and justification are independent processes and that public legal justification is the crucial aspect of legal reasoning that the "actual" judicial decision-making process should be thoroughly investigated.

The discussion of the problematic nature of discovery and justification in legal theory mentioned above sets out the context in which the judicial decision-making process has been analysed and discussed. Contemporary legal theorists holding diverse positions - legal positivists, critical legal scholars, and post-modernists - have published reflections on decision-making. I collect the reflective efforts of a representative sample of those legal theorists who discuss aspects of the process of legal decision-making.

2 The Realists' Investigation of the Judging or Decision-Making Process

2.1 The Critical Program: The Realists' Response to Legal Formalism

Contemporary legal theorists do not explain the work of the realists as an investigation of the judicial decision-making process or as part of an analysis of the discovery process. Rather, the realists' writings are commonly understood as a critique of legal formalism where this is taken to imply (1) that judges use deductive techniques to decide cases, (2) that judges' legal opinions are accurate descriptions of how judges reach decisions, and (3) that legal certainty and predictability are ideals that judges should strive to reach. Consequently, many legal theorists have understood the work of Frank and Dewey as a response to legal formalism and have stressed the role of the legal realists in this debate.

American legal realists such as Holmes, Llewellyn, Frank, and Dewey criticised the decisions of judges who were committed to a deductive or quasi-deductive method of deciding cases. In their opinion, to decide cases logically would be equivalent to mechanical decision-making and would lead to undesirable results. According to Frank, the rules of law are treated by formalists as if they are settled once and for all and are applied impartially and inflexibly. The problem, as Frank[8] understands it, is that it is difficult to achieve justice in particular individual cases and novelty and creativity are not permitted in judicial decision-making for fear that the law would be uncertain and unpredictable. In Dewey's opinion, the belief that "ready-made antecedent universal principles" are a key part of reasoning is the chief obstacle to the type of thinking required for intelligent social reforms and social advance by using law.[9]

Realists also rejected the claim that formalism was a correct description of legal decision-making. Many legal realists criticised theorists who described the judging process as deductive or quasi-deductive. Such formal descriptions[10] of legal reasoning were thought not only to misrepresent the judging process and promote the illusion and myth of legal certainty, but also to mask judges' biases and prejudices that can affect their work. Holmes, for example, describes the major factors in the judging process which are not examined by legal formalists and asserts that the logical form has had a limited function in decision-making. For Holmes, experience - the needs of the time, moral and political theories, public policy, and the prejudices judges share with others - has had more influence on the determination of rules of law than logic.[11]

Holmes also sums up the legal realists' criticisms of the use of the logical form to present legal decisions insofar as the logical form masks other elements in the decision-making process. In his opinion, "behind the logical form lies a judgment as to the relative worth and importance of competing legislative grounds, often an inarticulate and unconscious judgment, it is true, and the very root and nerve of the whole proceeding"[12]. The point is that different logical justifications could be used to justify conflicting outcomes. Hence the indeterminacy of formal decision-making leaves open the question of substantive elements being the real determinants of the decision.

According to Frank, how a judge reaches a decision was described by the formalists as "the judge begins with some rule or principle of law as his premise, applies this premise to the facts, and thus arrives at his decision."[13] For Frank, this description was "a dogma based on inadequate observation" and was closely tied to illusions and myths such as legal certainty, predictability, and the claim that law is completely settled.[14] He also thought the formalists ignored the critical role of the judge or jury as a fact-finder and that a multitude of elusive factors are involved in fact-finding which gave the judge or jury a creative role and made it hard to predict what a judge or jury will decide.

Frank believed that the dogma or illusion of predictability and legal certainty can lead to numerous harmful consequences such as disrespect for law insofar as formalised legal argumentation portrays lawyers as a profession of rationalizers that appear to be a guild of professional hypocrites.[15] In addition, such beliefs in predictability and certainty result in concealing rather than disclosing what the law is and in attempting to mechanise law and "reduce it to formulae in which human beings are treated like identical mathematical entities."[16] Frank claimed that the clear thinking of judges is hampered because they are compelled to "shove their thoughts into traditional forms, thus impeding spontaneity. . . tempting lazy judges to avoid creative thinking" and, instead, to find "platitudes that will serve in the place of robust cerebration"[17].

Dewey claimed that mechanical logic and abstract forms in written legal decisions are used to assume that a decision is impersonal, objective, and rational, and give an illusion of certitude which masks the vital process of reaching a decision. He also wrote that the desire for maximum possible stability and regularity of expectation in legal decisions conflicts with practical realities and, in fact, results in increased practical uncertainty and social instability. In addition, understanding and portraying rules as immutable, antecedent, and necessary sanctifies old rules and decisions, widens the gap between social conditions and the principles used by the court, breeds irritation and disrespect for law, and contributes to alliances between the judiciary and entrenched interests.

Both Frank and Dewey agree that judgments are neither dictated by legal rules and principles nor reached according to syllogistic reasoning. In Frank's opinion, rules and principles ". . .do not and cannot completely control [a judge's] mental operations and it is therefore unfortunate that either the judge or the lawyers interested in his decision should accept them as the full equivalent of that decision."[18]

2.2 The Constructive Programme: The Realists' Investigation of The Judging Process

Among legal theorists, the legal realists came the closest to identifying the process of discovery or the "actual" decision-making process when they wrote about "puzzling" and "brooding" which led to "hunches" or "intuitions". Their use of judges' reports about how they reached their decisions can be considered an attempt to create a method to study the mental activities involved in decision-making. Jerome Frank and John Dewey, stated that activities such as puzzling and brooding preceded the hunches and intuitions which led to judgments that were subsequently presented in the appropriate form as ratiocinations to or justifications of the decision.

2.2.1 Research Aims

The legal realists (especially Frank and Dewey) believed that by understanding the judging process the multiplicity of factors that affect judicial decision-making could be identified and that undesirable elements such as bias and prejudice could be controlled. The results of this part of their project were obtained by examining what they considered the "actual judging process" in law and in this work they were aided by studies about the judging process completed by psychologists.

The person who wrote most comprehensively about the judging process was Jerome Frank. His goals were to reform trial methods that in his opinion were "hopelessly antiquated" to "inject more reason and more justice into its daily workings" by examining the "non-rational" and "non-idealistic" elements in court-house government.[19] He wanted judges to recognise and to acknowledge the necessary existence of human and personal elements in themselves in order to address the possible effects of biases and prejudices when hearing law suits.[20] Frank believed that wise decisions would be achieved through self-knowledge. According to Frank, a judge, like everyone, will have habits and pre-judgments since "interests, points of view, and preferences are the essence of living."[21] In addition, a judge will have acquired social value judgments and many unavoidable personal prejudices which may be unconscious and may interfere with a judge's fairness at a trial. Frank believed that "The concealment of the human element in the judicial process allows that element to operate in an exaggerated manner. . ."[22] For Frank, ". . .the judge, through self-scrutiny, can and should prevent the operation of this class of biases."[23] This type of self-knowledge is especially important and needed in a judge, according to Frank, because a judge is peculiarly exposed to emotional influences in a court room.

Frank was also convinced that judges can perform their job of balancing conflicting human interests and determining which of several opposing individual claims the law should favour in order to promote social well-being if judges have accurate knowledge of the methods they employ to reach decisions.[24] He asserts that, to do their job well, judges need as clear a consciousness of their purpose as possible and that "the pretence, self-delusion that when they are creating they are borrowing" or merely applying the commands given by an external authority will diminish their efficiency. Moreover, judges must learn the virtue, the power and practical worth of self-authority and not rely on a non-existent guide.[25] To reach this end he wants to disclose, not conceal, the process of exercising discretion, applying abstract rules in cases, and making law. Moreover, Frank claims that "[t]he honest, well-trained judge with the completest possible knowledge of the character of his powers and of his own prejudices and weaknesses is the best guaranty of justice."[26]

2.2.2 Methodology and Results

The realists wanted to understand the judging or decision-making process by examining how it occurs. The foundation of Frank's position is his method of studying the judging process. His approach was to ask judges how they reached their decisions. Evidence for his results were the self-reports of judges such as Judge Hutcheson. Frank's method was neither grounded on assumptions about the role of logic nor guided by values such as legal certainty or predictability. Dewey, like Frank, claims he studies how people think, rather than simply considering "the relations of consistent implication which subsist between the propositions in which his finally approved conclusions are set forth. . ."[27]

Five elements that comprise the judging or decision-making process can be identified in the realists writings: (1) brooding and puzzling about the facts of a case and asking "What is the just solution in this case?", (2) achieving a tentative hunch or intuition about what is just in the case, (3) checking or testing the hunch or intuition against both the relevant laws and legal principles and against what is considered to be the wise solution in this case and other similar cases that may arise in the future, (4) reaching a judgment, decision or solution, and (5) presenting or expounding the judgment, decision or solution in the time-honoured fashion. Frank's position is that judgments "in most cases are worked out backward from conclusions tentatively formulated."[28] The realists called the judging process "backward reasoning" by contrast to the formalists' explanation of decision-making which begins with premises from which a conclusion is subsequently worked out.

According to Dewey and Frank, understanding the decision process in terms of logic misrepresents how decisions are actually reached. Dewey thinks that "logical justification implies the prior and given existence of particulars and universals"[29] and that such a view implies that for every possible case, there is a fixed antecedent rule already at hand; that the case in question is either simple or unambiguous, or is resolvable by direct inspection into a collection of simple and indisputable facts. Rather, as Frank states, judging begins the other way around ". . .with a conclusion more or less vaguely formed; a man ordinarily starts with such a conclusion and afterwards tries to find premises which will substantiate it. If he cannot, to his satisfaction, find proper arguments to link up his conclusion with premises which he finds acceptable, he will, unless he is arbitrary or mad, reject the conclusion and seek another.[30] Dewey and Frank[31] claim that, although mathematicians, farmers, lawyers, and merchants deal with different subjects and materials, the course of the operation and the form of the procedure to investigate, accept, reject, and justify their conclusions are similar.

2.2.3 Puzzling and Brooding

Dewey's description of thinking resembles Frank's analysis of the judging process in that the starting points of the judging process are questions about particular concrete cases. Dewey writes that "...thinking actually sets out from a more or less confused situation, which is vague and ambiguous with respect to the conclusion it indicates, and that the formation of both major premise and minor premise proceed tentatively and correlatively in the course of analysis of this situation and of prior rules."[32] Frank quotes from Judge Hutcheson's self-analysis of the judging process in order to explain backward reasoning by writing that Hutcheson puzzles over all the available material and broods over the issue and seeks the answer to the question "What is the just solution to this particular case?"

2.2.4 Hunches

For Frank, the most significant element in the judging process is the hunch or intuition of the judge. Judge Hutcheson says he waits for the feeling or hunch which is "that intuitive flash of understanding that makes the jump-spark connection between question and decision."[33] A hunch is an answer to the question "What is the just solution to this particular case?" For Hutcheson, the hunch depends on intuition because he thinks that "The vital motivating impulse for the decision is an intuitive sense of what is right or wrong in the particular case. . ."[34] In Frank's opinion, examining the process of hunching in reaching decisions is important to understanding the legal process because "if the law consists of decisions of the judges and if those decisions are based on the judge's hunches, then the way in which the judge gets his hunches is the key to the judicial process. Whatever produces the hunches makes the law."[35] Frank identifies the hunch producers as the rules and principles of law, political, economic, and moral prejudices of the judge, and the judge's personality and entire life-history which reflect his temperament, education, environment, and personal traits.

Although Dewey's and Frank's explanations of reasoning are similar in general structure they offer different explanations of the more specific processes whereby solutions to legal disputes are actually reached. For Dewey, solving a legal dispute involves two activities: (1) "sifting the evidence" which comprises determining what are the important data in a case and thereby arriving at the facts and (2) "selecting the rule" that is applicable to the case. These two operations are in functional correspondence with each other in that observation supplies the facts of the case and the proposed rules direct observation, thereby influencing the selection of the relevant facts.[36]

Frank, however, claims that, because Dewey does not investigate fact-finding in trials, Dewey's explanation of decision-making over-simplifies the fact-finding process. Frank argues there is more to fact-finding than "solving the double-jointed problem of selecting the relevant facts and the relevant legal rule."[37] He claims that Dewey writes as if the facts can be directly observed and are waiting ready-made before a trial begins and that the task of judges is merely to pick and choose the relevant facts. The "facts", Frank asserts, do not exist before the trial begins. Indeed, the facts are unknown and unknowable until a judge announces the decision; the facts are the judicially determined facts.[38]

Frank portrays fact-finding in trials as a complex and problematic process. Fact-finding comprises the activities of (1) determining facts, in the sense of determining what occurred, and then (2) selecting some of the facts as relevant to the problem that must be solved. The first stage involves reaching inferences that are not ready-made or given. However, reaching such inferences is a problematic activity due to human factors. For example, the trial judge's task of assessing the reliability of witnesses' observations can be influenced by factors that can be hidden from scrutiny and cannot be easily controlled. These factors include defective observations by witnesses, witnesses who lie, the prejudices of judges, inattentive judges, incompetent lawyers, and the unavailability of evidence that might be relevant. Further, a trial judge has wide discretion to believe or disbelieve any part of a witness's testimony. In the second stage, the trial judge's task of selecting the relevant facts is also problematic. Not only does this activity depend on the factors named above, but a trial judge also has the discretion to select the relevant facts from any part of conflicting testimony.[39]

2.2.5 Checking/Testing Hunches

In Frank's opinion, the proper use of rules and principles is to check tentative conclusions. The judge tries to link by formal logic his own tentative conclusion with the acceptable and more general point of view of the rule or principle. If he does not discover any link he is forced to re-consider "whether his tentative conclusion is wise both with respect to the present case and with respect to possible implications for future cases."[40] Dewey's opinion is similar. For Dewey, legal rules and principles "are working hypotheses needing to be tested by the way they work out in application to concrete situations. . ."[41]

2.2.6 Reaching a Decision and Presenting the Decision

Frank quotes Hutcheson to illustrate and affirm the distinction between the activity of hunching and other activities. Hutcheson separated hunching from the judgment, decision or the solution itself and also distinguished between the judgment itself and its public exposition - the apologia or ratiocination for that judgment in which the judge explains and encases the judgment. Hutcheson states that once he has reached a judgment, he ". . .enlists his every faculty and belabors his laggard mind, not only to justify that intuition to himself, but to make it pass muster with his critics. Accordingly, he passes in review all of the rules, principles, legal categories, and concepts which he may find useful, directly or by analogy, so as to select from them those which in his opinion will justify his desired result."[42]

Like Frank, Dewey distinguishes between reaching a decision or solution and the presentation of the decision, but uses the term "search and discovery" when he describes the process of reaching a decision. Dewey contrasts "search and discovery" with exposition. He calls arriving at a conclusion "search and discovery" since "the situation as it exists is more or less doubtful, indeterminate, and problematic with respect to what it signifies."[43] Search and discovery "unfolds itself gradually and is susceptible of dramatic surprise. . ."[44]. In contrast to "search and discovery", exposition, for Dewey, implies a definitive solution has been reached.

In these accounts, the public justification of decisions is related to the judging process and to the written presentation but the precise role and status of public justification in the judging process is unclear. For example, Frank writes that one of the chief uses of rules and principles is to enable judges to give formal justifications-rationalisations of the conclusions at which they otherwise arrive.[45] His statement implies that formal justifications occur in oral or written presentations, but there is no indication in his writings that the primary function of oral or written decisions is justification or that public justification is the most significant feature of legal reasoning. Hutcheson's self-report suggests he justifies his decision to himself and then writes it down. In Dewey's opinion, the purpose of the exposition "is to set forth grounds for the decision reached so that it will not appear as an arbitrary dictum, and so that it will indicate a rule for dealing with similar cases in the future."[46]

Frank and Dewey distinguish between the elements involved in the process of reaching a decision and the presentation of the decision. However, the elements of the judging process, which include both the method of reaching and presenting a decision, are closely linked. But the exposition of a decision, which includes arguments concerning why the decision is justified, is but one aspect of the decision-making process, not the major constituent or the primary function of the process. Frank and Dewey only mention briefly that the presentation or exposition sets forth the grounds of the apologia, ratiocination, or justification. They ascribe a limited function to public justification to the extent that justification is only one of a number of aspects of decision-making and as such is a distinct issue from the actual judgment and the written presentation of that judgment.

Frank's and Dewey's work can be understood as an attempt to understand the proper role of logic in decision-making. Their distinction between the judgment as a non-logical activity and the written presentation of the judgment helps explain why decisions can be presented in a logical form. Although Frank asserts that the judging process is not deductive, and that the written decision does not describe how the judging process actually works, he thinks that legal opinions ". . .are written in conformity with the time-honored theory. They picture the judge applying rules and principles to the facts, that is, taking some rule or principle (usually derived from opinions in earlier cases) as his major premise, employing the facts of the case as the minor premise, and then coming to his judgment by processes of pure reasoning."[47]

Dewey also distinguishes between thinking and the syllogism. In his words, ". . . while the syllogism sets forth the results of thinking, it has nothing to do with the operation of thinking."[48] Dewey believes that syllogisms can play a limited role in justifying legal decisions insofar as they present the results of thinking and are the means by which judges account to others for their conclusions. Thus, for Frank and Dewey, syllogisms can play a role in presenting decisions.

However, Frank and Dewey differ regarding the extent of a trial judge's capacity to spell out the grounds for a decision. In Frank's opinion, it is impossible for even the most articulate and lucid trial judge to translate the qualitative experiences that are part of decision-making into a discursive or logical form. In his opinion, no verbal symbols can do justice to the fulness and richness of a trial judge's unique composite reaction to conflicting testimony that may be affected by the judges emotional responses to witnesses, lawyers, and litigants. For Frank, then, the report of a judicial decision is necessarily partial and inadequate.[49] By contrast, Frank's interpretation of Dewey's writings on this issue is that after the judge has a hunch, a logical analysis can begin that will clarify the judge's reasoning and expose its roots to other people.[50]

2.2.7 Summary and Implications

The realists portrayed the judging or decision-making process as a dynamic problem-solving process involving various conscious and deliberate mental activities. They named activities such as (1) puzzling, (2) hunching, intuiting, (3) checking and testing the solution, (4) judging or deciding, and (5) presenting the judgment as all playing a role in the judging process. Despite the fact that some of these activities are little more than names, the realists created the basis for further investigations into the nature of these activities and the relations among them.

One of their most important results was the identification of the judicial hunch or intuition. Frank identified the hunch with the discovery or invention of solutions to legal problems. The hunch was the key element in the realists' explanation of the functions of, and relationships among, the other constituents of the judging process which include puzzling, testing, deciding and expressing the decision. Although the realists did not explain hunches in detail, the acknowledgment of hunching and intuitions provided the realists with an alternative to the primacy ascribed by jurists to deductive methods of decision-making and descriptions of decision-making that were deductive. Although the realists' method of investigation did not amount to much more than the assertion that they were studying how judges actually think by examining self-reports and asserting that hunches were the creative elements in the decision process and claiming that the decision process involved a non-logical process, they nevertheless initiated an important line of research into the role of non-logical and logical process in law in that hunches occur in response to brooding and puzzling. Their results also raise questions about the relationship between how legal decisions are reached and how they are presented, including both how hunches are presented in a decision and whether hunches play any role in the presentation of decisions.

Unfortunately the term "hunch" seems to suggest that the process of hunching is mysterious and cannot be analysed. Neither the legal realists' method of studying decision-making nor their results have been used or developed by modern jurists. Hunches and intuitions have not been studied in contemporary analyses of legal reasoning. Indeed, I shall argue, the nature of the judging process itself has been distorted and ignored by subsequent jurists. This state of affairs may exist because the realists themselves used their awareness of the importance of the judging process in a negative way to undermine the claims of their formalist opponents. But, there are other explanations. Although the realists distinguish between puzzling, hunching and testing hunches in the decision process, their innovations have been responded to in the form of a debate about the process of discovery and the process of justification which obscures many of the realists' arguments, novel contributions, and even their overall project to understand and to promote wise decision-making and candid legal reporting.

It is necessary to examine these later developments - in the form of contributions by Wasserstrom and MacCormick - as they define the current context in which questions about "hunches" and "discovery" are posed. Wasserstrom reformulates the legal realists' description of formalism by retreating from the claim that logic or deduction describes the actual way judges reach decisions. In so doing, he creates a clear distinction between the process of reaching a judicial decision and the process of legally justifying it. MacCormick also supports the clear distinction between discovery and justification. His work represents a modified formalism that recognises that substantive elements play a role in the process of justifying legal decisions.

3 Searching For the "Rigid" Distinction Between Discovery and Justification

Modern legal theorists neglect the "actual" decision-making process and assume that the public legal justification of decisions is the key activity in legal reasoning. This state of affairs is a consequence of considering discovery and justification to be separate processes. In this section, I trace the search for the distinction between the process of discovery and the process of justification in the writings of Wasserstrom and MacCormick that has led to the failure to develop the legal realists' project of understanding the "actual" judicial decision-making process.[51]

3.1 Richard Wasserstrom

Wasserstrom's search for a clear distinction between the process of discovery and the process of justification can be understood as a response to the legal realists' criticisms of legal formalists who described or proposed an essentially deductive or logical decision-making procedure. Wasserstrom calls such a view the deductive theory. Wasserstrom's account of the deductive theory, in fact, represents an important modification or qualification of the formalism, attacked by realists, that claimed the judging process is logical and that written decisions accurately describe how a decision is reached. The distinction between discovery and justification, in Wasserstrom's opinion, helps explain the disagreements between jurists who emphasize deduction in judicial decisions and jurists, like Frank, who criticised their theories for being inaccurate and for impeding clear thinking about the judging process. Wasserstrom says that the critics of the deductive theory say that "the deductive theory is an inadequate, quite inaccurate account of the way in which courts really have decided cases."[52] However, in his opinion, neither the characteristics of the deductive procedure nor the reasons for its rejection have been clarified in respect to the use of logic in the decision process.[53] He admits that "alternative expositions [of the decision process] have been hinted at", but thinks that they have not been developed.[54]

Wasserstrom considers the work of Hutcheson and Frank as two undeveloped alternatives to the deductive theory. According to Wasserstrom[55], Frank's position is that a hunch or intuition of what is the just solution in a case is not the determinative factor by which a judge decides a case. Instead, he argues, Frank believes that it is a judge's personality which is the key to understanding the way in which cases are decided. Hence the decision-making process employed in a case can be explained only by referring to the individual traits of the judge. Hunches, then, depend on the judge's personality. Wasserstrom argues it is wrong to base a criticism of the deductive theory on the idea that the key aspects of decision-making are "feeling, emotion, sensory experience, or unanalysed personal predilection."[56]

But Wasserstrom's account of Frank's position amounts to an over-simplification of Frank's point of view in that Wasserstrom states that personality traits stimulate hunches and are the sole elements that influence the decision that is made. By contrast, Frank wrote that legal rules and principles also influence the emergence of hunches. Indeed, Frank's point is that, if judges could identify or account for their personality traits, legal decisions would be wiser and more candid. A hunch is only one of the five elements (which include puzzling and brooding, checking and testing hunches, reaching a decision, and presenting the decision) involved in the decision-making process. Hunches are therefore not the only element in the decision-making process.

Wasserstrom also singles out Holmes' statement (quoted above) that a judgment regarding the relative worth and importance of competing legislative grounds lies behind the logical exposition of a judgment as an example of the perspective which portrays legal decisions as determined by judges' personalities. Wasserstrom criticises this point of view by contrasting it with the notion that good or persuasive reasons are the best that can be required to support propositions.[57] He argues that many philosophers, including the realists, confuse the question of whether an argument is formally valid with the question of whether there can be good reasons or persuasive reasons for believing a proposition to be true or false. Wasserstrom wants to explicitly distinguish between the process of selecting and evaluating the contents of the propositions, which involves presenting persuasive reasons that support propositions, and the use of formal logic to test the relations between premises that have been selected. Hence he thinks that statements such as Holmes' above and Frank's criticisms of the deductive theory are mistaken if they infer an inherent arbitrariness of the judicial decision process from the limited utility of formal, deductive logic.

Although Wasserstrom acknowledges that it makes little sense to describe the judicial decision process as completely deductive and that a judge's opinion is not an accurate report of the decision process, he claims that it makes even less sense to insist "that for this reason courts could not (and should not) employ a procedure or set of procedures that permits of some kind of reasoned justification for the judicial decisions reached by those courts."[58] He proposes that deduction can be used to test the validity of legal arguments.

This representation of Frank's position also is a simplification. Frank did, in fact, advocate the use of logic to check the relation between legal rules or principles and potential judgments. Hence both Wasserstrom and Frank seem to identify the use of logic in testing decisions. Also there is no evidence in Frank's writings that justifying a decision does not require reasons to be given.

Wasserstrom solves the problem concerning the legal realists' response to the formalists, as he understands it, by concluding that the formalists and Frank are describing two distinct processes or "procedures that must be followed before a decision is made or accepted."[59] The realists are describing the process of discovery and the formalists are describing the process of justification. The process of discovery is concerned with "the manner or procedure in which a decision or conclusion was reached" - the factors that led to, or suggested, the decision such as a judge's hunches, emotions, and personality.[60] On the other hand, questions concerned with the process of justification inquire about whether a given decision or conclusion is justifiable or justified and ". . .the manner in which the conclusion was to be justified."[61] The process of justification involves searching for and testing premises or arguments that substantiate a legal conclusion. An explanation of the way in which a conclusion or decision was reached is distinct from an account of the procedure a judge employed in "testing" it and does not always "respond to the question of whether the conclusion is in fact justifiable."[62] In other words, he rejects the interpretation of formalism in which the syllogism describes the actual process of decision-making. From Wasserstrom's point of view, the realists were attacking too crude a version of formalism. All that really matters, to Wasserstrom, is how the decision is justified.

Wasserstrom insists that, before judges render a decision, they must be able to justify it. Hunches and intuitions do not count as justifications for a binding judicial decision. They are aspects of the process of discovery. Hence, the decision must be tested to determine if it is justified. For Wasserstrom, there are two procedures (discovery and justification) that might be followed before a decision is made or accepted.[63]

The judicial opinion, then, is a report of the justificatory procedure employed by a judge. Wasserstrom claims that, from this point of view, the judge's reliance upon rules of law and rules of logic and "the kind of reasoning process that is evidenced by the usual judicial opinion is more suggestive of a typical justificatory procedure" than a discovery process. His evidence that such a justificatory procedure exists is the assertion that "some judges have thought they must be able to establish a formally valid relationship between the decision and certain more general premises, and to be able also to give good reasons for the premises so selected."[65]

Wasserstrom states that his description of the process of justification does not conflict with Frank's description of how decisions are reached and that it corresponds, in fact, to Frank's description of how a decision is checked. According to Wasserstrom, the legal realists' arguments are probably correct if the decision process is understood or equated with the process of discovery which he describes as a report of why or how a judge "hit upon" the decision. Remembering that, according to Frank, judging of all kinds begins ". . .with a conclusion more or less vaguely formed; a man ordinarily starts with such a conclusion and afterwards tries to find premises which will substantiate it. If he cannot, to his satisfaction, find proper arguments. . .he will, unless he is arbitrary or mad, reject the conclusion and seek another."[66]

Wasserstrom illustrates and supports the distinction between discovery and justification in law by introducing a "scientist who has discovered a vaccine which purportedly provides complete immunization against cancer. . ."[67] This scientist ". . .informs the scientific community that he hit upon this particular chemical combination. . .by writing down 1,000 possible chemical combinations on separate pieces of paper, putting them all into a big hat, and pulling out one of the pieces at random."[68] This activity is the process of discovery. But whether the vaccine works is not known. It is a subsequent question whether the scientist's claim is in fact justifiable. This vaccine must be empirically tested to determine if it immunizes people against cancer. "How the scientist happened to select the formula is one question" and "[w]hether this formula is an effective vaccine, whether the conclusion can be empirically validated, is quite a different [question]."[69] It does not matter how the vaccine was discovered or selected for testing. The relevant question is whether the vaccine, in fact, works.

Although Wasserstrom did recognise and did seek to develop aspects of the process of discovery his method of analysis is different from the legal realists' approach. It consists of attempting to reconcile the debate between formalists and legal realists by constructing two analytical categories - discovery and justification - based on relegating the non-deductive aspects of decision-making to the process of discovery. He is not engaged in an empirical study of how a decision is reached. His method is to identify the opposing positions in a debate, to comment on them, and then to settle the debate by creating two classifications or categories, arguing that the debate has arisen, at least partly, from realists mistaking formalist claims about the role of logic in justification for claims that logic describes the whole decision-making process. By using this technique he explains and justifies his interest in justification and portrays justification as the primary or more significant process in the decision process.

Wasserstrom concentrates on the critical project of the legal realists and downplays their constructive aims and results. Frank names five activities to be part of the judging process, whereas Wasserstrom claims that only two processes constitute the decision process. Frank's analysis includes (1) puzzling and brooding about the case, (2) having a hunch or intuition, (3) checking and testing the hunch or intuition, (4) judging or reaching a decision or solution, and (5) expounding the decision or solution, but Wasserstrom identifies only (1) the process of discovery and (2) the process of justification. In his explanation of the decision process, Wasserstrom relegates hunches to a minor role relative to the process of justification. But, according to Frank, hunches are the source of legal decisions and play a vital role in the decision process. For Frank, the justification of a decision is simply one aspect, feature, role, or purpose of the written decision, not the primary part of the decision process. The outcome of Wasserstrom's analysis is to reduce the five elements of the decision-making process named by the realists to two categories and to ignore one category, discovery, and to make the other category, justification, the key process in legal reasoning.

3.2 Neil MacCormick

Neil MacCormick's explanation of the process of justification can be understood as an affirmation and development of Wasserstrom's response to the legal realists' methodology and results on behalf of an extended formalist positivist perspective. It is an "extended" perspective insofar as he recognises some of the limitations of formalism as pointed out by the realists, and hence he accounts for the presence of substantive elements in legal decision-making. His analysis is shaped by his interpretation of legal realism, his own legal-political theory, and his understanding of science.

MacCormick affirms Wasserstrom's distinction between discovery and justification.[70] He shares Wasserstrom's view that justification has the more significant role in legal reasoning relative to the process of discovery and directs his attention to investigating legal justification. A number of factors that support the distinction between discovery and justification can be identified in MacCormick's work. His interpretation of legal realism is one reason for his distinction between discovery and justification. He writes that "what prompts a judge to think of one side rather than the other as a winner is quite a different matter from the question whether there are on consideration good justifying reasons in favour of that side rather than the other side."[71] He identifies the study of the process of discovery with the legal realists who, in his opinion, have studied "what prompts judges to think of one side as a winner. . ." and associates the process of justification, in contrast, with the study of "good justifying reasons" in favour of one side rather than another.[72] The separation of discovery and justification answers the claim of the simplified version of legal realism that justifying reasons are so vague and indecisive that they are always compatible with a decision no matter what it is. The line of solution to this problem taken by MacCormick is to analyse the process of justification in law in order to determine whether the process of argumentation as a process of justification simply consists of justifying reasons that do no more than cloak decisions made on other grounds.[73]

MacCormick examines two types of legal justification, namely (1) first-order justification and (2) second-order justification. In first-order justification, decisions are justified if they can be deduced from a major premise formulating a valid rule of law and a minor premise formulating the facts proven by the relevant legal procedures and rules of evidence. Thus first order justification could lead to the situation so often stressed by realists that rival rulings in a case could both be formally justified and as such be legally valid. To address that situation MacCormick analyses second-order justification. Second-order justification involves testing rival universal rulings or norms in order to decide which one to accept as legally valid. Judicial decisions are justified if they fulfil a set of general requirements or conditions. The logical and probable consequences of the legal rulings are evaluated in the particular case and in other imagined cases in terms of public good, justice, common sense and convenience. The legal ruling must also be consistent with other valid and binding rules of law and be coherent with the legal principles in the legal system. If a ruling satisfies these tests of consequences, consistency, and coherence it is said to be legally justified.

MacCormick's book, **Legal Reasoning and Legal Theory**, is important in that he openly acknowledges the political aspects of his approach. (Such political concerns have, of course, been at work from the outset in the debates between formalism and realism but often they are left unstated.) His theory can be understood as a way of coping with challenges or problems posed by a liberal democracy concerning the function and role of law, namely how to limit judicial discretion and to maintain the separation of powers between the legislature and the judiciary. Not only are deduction and legal justification methods to constrain judicial discretion, they are also methods to control the arbitrary and irrational factors that influence the formulation of rulings. The realists' talk of hunching represents a threat to the rule of law model in that hunches are seen as arbitrary, irrational, unpredictable, subjective, and the root of unauthorised innovation. Hence, MacCormick presents his account as a description and a prescription concerning how arbitrary and irrational factors in the discovery process are contained and should be contained and how unsystematic and unauthorised judicial decisions are constrained and should be constrained.[74] Because the problem is the arbitrary power of judges there seems to be a fear of anything that looks arbitrary, irrational, or uncontrollable.

To the extent that his theory responds to these challenges or solves these problems, his account of legal justification is not only presented as a description of legal justification, but also as a prescription for a "sound justification procedure."[75] He ". . .argues for what [he sees] as good procedures of decision-making and justification."[76] Indeed, his theory amounts to a defence of current judicial practice which he apparently believes lives up to the prescription.

Nevertheless, questions about the extent to which these political concerns affect and distract from an uncommitted and comprehensive investigation of legal decision-making can be raised. In particular, one can ask about the extent to which the clear distinction between discovery and justification is a solution to problems about how to constrain the discretion of judges and how to control the arbitrary and irrational factors that may affect legal decision-making rather than an investigation devoted solely to understanding the nature of discovery and justification. The process of discovery is portrayed as the psychological part of decision-making that must be "constrained" or kept under control by an independent process of justification.

MacCormick uses his understanding of discovery and justification in science to illustrate and support the distinction between the process of discovery and the process of justification in law. Discovery and justification, he asserts, are separate processes in science. "Insights" or sudden flashes of illumination are part of the discovery process. The process of discovery is exemplified by Archimedes' "blinding flash of insight" which occurred when the water overflowed as he got into the baths. In law, the various arguments presented by lawyers to a judge are analogous to scientists' "flashes of insight". Flashes of insight, however, must be justified.[77] They could be true or false. Deciding whether an insight is true or false involves testing and proof which are part of the process of justification. Similarly, a judge must test legal arguments and rulings in order to decide whether or not they are legally justified.

MacCormick draws an analogy between Popper's version of "scientific justification" and "second-order legal justification" in order to explain and support his analysis of "testing" in second-order justification. MacCormick explains the analogy between testing in science and second-order justification in the following way. He argues that ". . .just as scientific justification involves testing one hypothesis against another and rejecting that which fails relevant tests second-order justification in law involves testing rival possible rulings against each other and rejecting those which do not satisfy relevant tests. . ."[78] The relevant tests are whether or not the hypotheses/rulings (1) make sense in the world and (2) make sense in the context of the system. Whether a scientific hypothesis makes sense in the real world depends on whether the experimental evidence supports it; by analogy, whether a ruling makes sense in the world depends on whether an evaluation of the consequences of the ruling supports it. Whether a scientific hypothesis makes sense in the system depends on whether it is compatible with other relevant theories; by analogy, whether a legal ruling makes sense in the system depends on whether it is consistent and coherent with the existing legal system.

Testing in science is used as a way of understanding and legitimating the "rigid" distinction between discovery an justification in law. By identifying science with law, the prestige of science in the academic community helps bolster and enhance the attractiveness of MacCormick's account of discovery and justification and helps fix justification as the crucial process in legal reasoning. The analogy between science and law also helps quell doubts about the absence of limitations and constraints on judicial decision-making. Judicial decision-making is not out of control, but is "scientifically managed".

The current state of affairs in which legal theorists who neglect the actual decision-making process and, instead, examine public legal justification has emerged from Wasserstrom's and MacCormick's search for a distinction between discovery and justification. This distinction, in turn, rests on Wasserstrom's mis-representation of the realists' methods and results, analogies between science and law, and his attempt to reconcile the realists' and formalists' positions. For MacCormick, the distinction between discovery and justification rests on a crude version of realism, his attempt to describe and to prescribe how the discretion of judges is, and should be, constrained, and analogies between science and law.

4 Contradictions Between The Realists' and Positivists' Accounts of The Decision-Making Process

The persuasiveness of contemporary legal theorists' claims that there is a rigid distinction between discovery and justification, that the process of justification is the key activity relative to the process of discovery, and that the process of discovery need not be studied is diminished if the realists' explanation of decision-making is compared with the legal positivists' position. Indeed such a comparison reveals that before making such claims, the "actual" judicial decision-making process should be thoroughly examined.

Although the realists' writings about the judging process and the positivists' explanations of discovery and justification are similar in some respects, a comparison of their work also reveals contradictions in their accounts of judicial decision-making. First, both the realists and positivists identify puzzling and hunches/insights as aspects of the "actual" decision-making process. However, the realists' account of the judging process and the legal positivists' version of the process of discovery compete as explanations of the "actual" decision-making process. Secondly, the realists and positivists both claim that hunches/insights must be tested and justified. However, for the realists, the "actual" activity of privately testing hunches is part of the decision-making process, whereas the positivists do not examine how a judge privately tests an outcome or legal ruling. Rather, they draw a clear distinction between discovery (which for them is the "actual" decision-making process) and justification (the public process whereby a decision or legal ruling is supported by reasons and arguments) and are solely concerned with analysing the public justification of decisions and rulings.[79]

To be more specific regarding the similarities in explanations of the decision-making process, both the legal realists and legal positivists identify a creative moment or act, called a hunch or insight, as the key element in the decision-making process. The realists define a hunch as an intuition of what is just in a case. An insight, the equivalent to a hunch, is the name positivists give to the creative moment in the discovery process. Finally, the legal realists and legal positivists claim that hunches and insights are tentative and hence they must be tested or justified before they are accepted.

However, the realists' version of the judging process competes with the positivists' account of the process of discovery as an explanation of the "actual" judicial decision-making process.[80] The legal realists' version of the decision-making process includes both the process of discovering tentative solutions and the process of checking and testing them. Both discovery and testing are elements comprising the "actual" process whereby a judge reaches a legal decision and subsequently expounds it. By contrast, legal positivists define the process of decision-making solely in terms of the process of discovering tentative outcomes such as insights and legal rulings. In other words, for positivists, "decision-making" and the "process of discovery" are different names for the same activity. For the realists, not only does the "actual" decision-making process include (1) puzzling and brooding and (2) having a hunch, but it also includes (3) testing the hunch, (4) reaching a solution or decision and (5) expounding the solution or decision. But the positivists define the "actual" decision-making process in terms of only two activities (1) puzzling and (2) having insights.

Legal realists and legal positivists offer conflicting descriptions of the nature of the inquiry that leads to hunches/insights. The realists' and positivists' portraits of the decision-making/discovery process and the factors that influence the emergence of hunches and insights contradict each other. The legal realists treat the process of discovering hunches as a conscious and deliberate problem-solving activity. The judge puzzles and asks questions about a case in order to discover a just solution to it. This search for a solution and the hunch itself are not treated as if they are essentially arbitrary or irrational activities. Although a hunch may be influenced by factors such as a judge's personality traits, the crucial factors that stimulate hunches, according to legal realists, are legal rules and principles and a judge's experience deciding cases. These factors are not treated as arbitrary or irrational.

In marked contrast to the realists, positivists stress that the emergence of judicial insights depends primarily on "subjective" factors such as personalities and emotions which they consider to be essentially arbitrary and irrational influences. Moreover, they characterise the process of discovery that leads to insights as an essentially arbitrary and irrational process in the sense that it is a psychological process that cannot be studied by using the rational and logical methods used by legal positivists. While Wasserstrom recognises that the process of discovery can form a regular pattern, and in that sense be "logical", he characterises the act of hunching as irrational.

Unfortunately, the confusion about what the process of judicial decision-making entails cannot be addressed by simply comparing and contrasting the differences among legal theorists and then resolving them. In my opinion, the "actual" process of decision-making itself must be investigated in greater detail if these conflicts between the realists' and positivists' versions of the judging process and the process of discovery are to be resolved.

Compatible views on testing and justification can be detected in the realists' and positivists' writings. Realists and positivists agree that hunches/insights must be tested. They claim that both logical deduction and procedures which are not strictly logical are used to test and justify tentative outcomes. Legal realists claim that one method of testing a hunch is by comparing it to legal rules and principles to determine if the tentative solution can be deduced from the rule or principle plus the circumstances of the case. Similarly, in first-order justification logical deduction is used to justify outcomes in cases. If the outcome can be deduced from a valid rule of law or legal principle plus the requisite set of facts stated by the rule or principle, then the outcome is said to be legally justified.

Legal realists and legal positivists also identify testing or justifying procedures that involve evaluations that are not strictly logical. Legal realists claim that what a judge thinks to be just and wise in a particular case and in similar future cases is a crucial factor in checking and testing judicial hunches. Similarly, the non-logical justification procedures identified by legal positivists include tests of whether proposed legal norms are coherent with valid rules and principles of law and an evaluation of whether the consequences of legal rulings make sense in the world in light of justice, common sense, public benefit, and convenience.

Despite these similarities regarding the necessity of, and procedures of, testing hunches and insights, the realists study the "actual" testing process performed by a judge whereas the positivists do not. The realists examine testing in the context of the decision-making process. Testing is part of the judging process. By contrast, the positivists do not consider that an investigation of how a judge privately tests a proposed outcome or legal ruling is an important part of legal reasoning. Instead the legal positivists make a definite distinction between the process of discovery whereby a judge discovers a tentative outcome or legal ruling and the process of justification whereby outcomes and rulings are publicly legally justified. Indeed, discovery and justification are distinct and independent processes that must be studied by different methods. Positivists stress that the process of justification is not part of the decision-making process in the sense that the public justification of an outcome or legal ruling is a process that is "rigidly" distinct from the "actual" decision-making process and is not necessarily related to questions about what a judge thinks about when testing an outcome or ruling. Their view is that legal justification begins where the process of discovery ends.[81]

Legal realists and legal positivists differ in their assessments of the importance of investigating the "actual" decision-making process. Realists do not treat puzzling, brooding, and having hunches as less important or more important than checking and testing tentative solutions or expounding them in public. By contrast, legal positivists claim that studying the process of public justification is the more crucial project compared to investigating the decision-making process. The effort to find out how a judge "actually" reaches a decision is less important than determining whether the decision, reached by whatever means, is legally justified. Hence the legal positivists study legal justification and neglect the "actual" process that leads to hunches/insights and ultimately to decisions.

Before accepting the opinions of either group, it seems necessary to thoroughly investigate the "actual" judicial decision-making process. Perhaps, as the realists argued, such a project will even lead to wiser judgments and more open and candid legal reporting. At the very least, we will learn more about an interesting and neglected aspect of legal reasoning. The place to begin, it seems to me, is with recent reflections on discovery and legal decision-making.

5 Recent Reflections on "Discovery" in The Judicial Decision-Making Process

Although we have come to associate the judging process with the American Legal Realists, other legal theorists have discussed aspects of the decision-making process in a variety of contexts. The following presentation of decision-making is not intended to be a comprehensive analysis of recent writings about the nature of discovery in the judicial decision-making process. Rather, my selection of legal theorists with a reflective interest in discovery is simply a representative sample and my discussion of their work will not be detailed. My aim is to present reflections on aspects of discovery in judicial decision-making such as discovery procedures, weighing reasons, the ground of judgment, and types of judgment and to summarise the various methods that have been used to investigate judicial decision-making.

5.1 The Process of Discovery - Zenon Bankowski

As part of an essay defending the use of the jury, Bankowski analyses notions of truth and fact-gathering. He challenges the position that there is a clear distinction between discovery and justification. Two lines of argument can be identified which support his claim. His first argument is terminological. It is concerned with when something can be properly called a discovery. Stated simply, a discovery is something that has passed the relevant tests. His second argument is concerned with the relationship between discovery and justification. In his view, discovery and justification are not independent processes.

Bankowski's point about the use of the term "discovery" is that something cannot be called a "discovery" until it has been justified. Something counts as a "discovery" only if it has passed the appropriate tests. Thus mistakes are not discoveries. In other words, a discovery is a "justified truth". It is wrong either to call a new drug that has not yet been tested a "discovery" or to call the outcome of a legal case that has not yet been justified a "discovery". The new drug or the outcome of the case do not count as discoveries unless they satisfy the relevant tests. For Bankowski, just as part of the process of discovering a cure for cancer is to show that the particular drug actually works, part of the process of a jury discovering whether an accused person is guilty involves testing and showing that the events form a coherent picture, ie. showing that the events "fit together".

Bankowski directs his criticism of the use of the term "discovery" at Wasserstrom who uses the term to cover only those factors involved in reaching hypotheses or tentative legal decisions. Thus, on Wasserstrom's view, discovery is independent from the process of justifying scientific hypotheses or legal decisions. Nonetheless, in Wasserstrom's analysis, discovery and justification are related insofar as the process of justification guides the procedures and evaluates the conclusions of the discovery process. By contrast, Bankowski argues that Wasserstrom's version of discovery ". . .artificially curtails the notion of discovery."[82] Bankowski is emphatic that ". . .discovery includes justificatory activity."[83]

Bankowski states that his version of what counts as a discovery fits in more readily with our ordinary way of speaking about scientific research than Wasserstrom's explanation of discovery in science. According to Bankowski, if a scientist presented a conclusion to the world ". . .we assume that part of the process of discovery is showing that it actually works. . ."[84] ". . .and we would assume that this was part of the process of discovery."[85] Bankowski claims that "Wasserstrom is equating the stage of the choice of hypothesis with the whole process of scientific discovery."[86] Hence ". . .it is straining language to demarcate [the act of choosing an hypothesis] as discovery and the rest as justification."[87]

Bankowski's point about when the term "discovery" should be used is important in distinguishing simplified versions of legal realism from the accounts of legal realism presented in this chapter. The simplified versions claim that judges decide cases the way they personally desire and then rationalize their decisions or make up justifications to support them. Such decisions, by implication, are merely "discoveries" that are not necessarily related to legal rules or principles and have not been subject to legally authorized testing or justification. Indeed, the justifications given are considered to be merely camouflage for the "real" reasons for the decision. But this version is not the position of Frank or Dewey who both claimed that judges checked and tested tentative conclusions against legal rules and principles in the judging process.

The terminological point is also important in requiring linguistic precision. Unless one espouses a simplified version of legal realism, one should not speak about "discovery" as constituting the judging or decision-making process unless one also includes testing. At the same time, in the decision-making process, the activities of puzzling and hunching which lead to tentative conclusions should be distinguished from the activities involved in testing the tentative conclusions, just as the realists have argued.

Bankowski's second argument is that discovery and justification are not two clearly distinct processes. In Bankowski's words, "Discovery cannot be independent from justification: one cannot separate the two. Discovery includes justificatory activity."[88] Discovery and justification are inter-related in that what counts as a discovery is partly determined by the procedures of discovery which, in turn, depend on the procedures of justification adopted in that particular situation.[89] Like Wasserstrom, Bankowski implies that justification or truth-certifying procedures guide the process of searching for tentative hypotheses and legal decisions.

He argues against a form of the correspondence theory of truth whereby the "truth" or "facts of a matter" correspond to some independent reality which is used to measure the truth or falsity of a statement. The criterion of "truth" is not whether particular facts or events correspond to what "really happened". On the contrary, he argues that knowledge of the "truth" or "facts of a matter" is inexorably linked to the methods used to apprehend it. Thus, the procedures of discovery and justification one uses affect what one discovers.

The discovery of the "truth" or "facts of a matter" depends on both the method of searching for what subsequently counts as a discovery and the criteria or tests used to certify that a discovery has been made. For example, scientific truth depends on the particular method used to discover a hypothesis and satisfying the particular criteria used to test it. Similarly, whether a jury finds an accused person guilty depends on the trial process and the laws of evidence and procedures that are used to construct and to test rival "coherent" stories about what occurred. In Bankowski's own words, "the way we set about finding the truth will also determine in part the truth we get..."[90]

The inexorable links between the procedures used to search for and to certify or justify a discovery, plus the links between the truth-certifying procedures and what ultimately counts as a discovery, lead Bankowski to the conclusion that different methods of discovering the "truth" or "facts of a matter" can exist that are not necessarily incompatible. Particular procedures of discovery and truth-certification are specific to different systems, institutions, or modes of life. For example, the conclusion of a police investigation that "X did it" is the endpoint of a particular method of discovering what happened. The verdict of a jury that "X is guilty" is the endpoint of a different procedure for discovering what happened. The two conclusions are the outcomes of different methods of discovery.

However, they are not competing "truths" or rival explanations of what "really happened". The particular method of discovery adopted is influenced by a mixture of political, moral, and pragmatic criteria.[91] For example, the discovery and truth-certifying procedures used by the police are influenced by the desire to apprehend as many law breakers as possible. In contrast, the discovery and truth-certifying procedures adopted in the context of a trial depend, in part, on the need to produce secure verdicts.

5.2 Decision-Making as Classification - Karl Llewellyn

Karl Llewellyn portrays judicial decision-making as the exercise of situation-sense. He writes about aspects of judicial decison-making in the context of the two styles of reasoning - the formal style and the grand style - he has detected in American case law. Here "style" refers to the manner of thought exhibited in judicial opinions rather than to their literary style. . .[92] The formal style of reasoning stresses the literal application of rules to facts and shuns the social context. By contrast, the grand style stresses the reason or principle behind the rule and is concerned with policy. A judge who exhibits the grand style in his opinions must possess "situation-sense" which according to Twining ". . .appears to involve "true understanding" of the facts and "right evaluation" of them."[93] In Twining's opinnion, "this key concept is also one of the most obscure."[94] Situation-sense has been interpreted in different ways. "Clark and Trubeck assume situation-sense must be each judge's personal intuitive feel for the facts. . ."[95] Lasswell implies that "situation-sense involves the ability to classify correctly any fact-situation into a set of established categories."[96] Twining suggests situation-sense is the faculty of making sensible interpretations of situations. Situation-sense helps judges discover the right answer to every case. But in Twining's opinion, the ". . .exhibition of situation-sense involves two steps: (1) the formulation of principles or policies such as expressing the relations between manufacturers of defective products and consumers of them and (2) the classification of the facts into a general-fact-situation which depends on a grasp of, for example, commericial practice.[97]

5.3 Weighing Reasons - Steven Burton

A key part of Steven Burton's explanation of a possible and desirable form of adjudication, namely judging in good faith, comprises a discussion of how judges weigh reasons. In his book, **Judging in Good Faith**, Burton is concerned with how we, as observers, might understand judging from a judge's point of view.[98] In doing so, he presents his "good faith thesis" and his "permissible discretion thesis". The good faith thesis is that "the legitimacy of adjudication. . .depends on respect for the reasons, not agreement of results, in cases." The judge's duty is to act on "reasons provided by the law and not on reasons excluded by judicial duty or the law's standards."[99] Judicial decision-making is legally constrained in that judges can weigh only legal reasons. For Burton, "law appears as a set of reasons for action."[100]

The "permissible discretion thesis" is that ". . .judicial discretion is compatible with the legitimacy of adjudication in a constitutional democracy."[101] The extent of the discretion of judges emerges as a problem when judges have to decide a case and the law provides two or more outcomes. More specifically, the problem "arises when legal standards have less than absolute force and provide reasons with incompatible implications for action."[102] Deliberation is required. The reasons for action must be weighed - the pros and cons - whether consciously or not.[103]

Burton's project is "an effort to develop and defend a practicable and attractive ethic of judging in a judicious spirit."[104] An analysis of the reasons for decisions and reasoning are a crucial part of this effort. He identifies different kinds of standards - legal rules, moral principles, promises, relational obligations, and personal desires. Facts are simply the circumstances of a case. He identifies different types of reasons - legal[105], moral[106], promissory, relational and personal reasons. He defines reasons as facts plus a prescriptive standard of conduct. "A reason for action marries plain fact with abstract standard."[107] "A legal reason simply involves plain facts made relevant by a legal standard. . ."[108]

The key characteristic of reasons is that they have force. Each reason for action has some force. A reason is not absolute. Each reason is only one reason that is weighed together with other competing reasons.[109] "[L]egal reasoning includes a gauging of the weight of legal reasons invoked by the context of action."[110] A reason with enough force can tip the balance of pros and cons in a close case.[111] Despite Burton's statement that "weight is a metaphor that has seemed immune to clarification"[112] he examines the procedure of weighing reasons in detail. How, then, are legal reasons combined, how are they weighed? His first step is "to conceive of weighing as the gauging of the relative normative force of the reasons that properly enter judicial deliberations.[113]

His next step is to answer the question "What gets weighed?" "What is it that judges weigh - legal standards in the abstract or concrete reasons for action?"[114] His answer is that general standards get weighed in the context of the circumstances of a particular case. In other words, reasons are weighed. Facts themselves are not weighed; they are inert. Weighing abstract principles or general standards would ignore the facts of cases and would lead to decisions that are ideological, formalistic, and injudicious. Facts should not be divorced from general standards. "Judges balance concrete reasons for actions in cases, at the mid level of abstraction combining facts and standards, rather than plain facts or abstract standards."[115] The factual part of a reason provides concreteness and the standards part of a reason provides the weight - the "felt" normative force of a reason.[116] (Weight, then, is a property of reasons.) According to Burton ". . .the best understanding is that judges weigh reasons for action under the circumstances of each case."[117]

The next step is to answer the question: "What are the grounds for the weight of a decision?" Burton's answer is that "the best way to describe the grounds of weight is to say that they are 'internal to the congeries of reasons in a case'."[118] What this means is that all the relevant reasons in a case are first identified before any weight is assigned "because the importance of a legal reason ebbs and flows depending on the congeries of reasons in which it is embedded. . ."[119] The weight of a particular legal reason is a function of the weight of the other relevant legal reasons. In this way the grounds of weight are internal to each case.

Burton supposes that each judge has an 'action threshold' which is the amount of normative force sufficient to move the judge to act dutifully. He claims the supposition is plausible for two reasons: First, a judge's duty to settle disputes "...constrains a judge to distribute some minimum amount of force over the legal reasons in a case."[120] If the weight given to all the legal reasons by a judge was minimal, a judge would be acting casually. Secondly, a judge's duty "to act dispassionately constrains a judge not to distribute more than the minimum amount"[121] of force. If a judge assigned too much weight to the legal reasons, he would be injudicious by exceeding his 'action threshold'. "Accordingly, the weight of each legal reason would be a share of the amount of normative force at the action threshold."[122] A judge seeks to give each relevant legal reason a proportional share of weight. "The goal is a ratio of weights in deliberative equilibrium at the action threshold."[123] Burton describes the process of weighing reasons as follows: "the judge proceeds by gauging the weight of each legal reason in turn while standing on the ground provided by the other relevant reasons, as one might rebuild a boat plank by plank while at sea - not by a series of deductive inferences resting on an ultimate foundation. . . Deliberations would continue on this basis, by successive adjustments, until total normative force is distributed at the action threshold, the judge is comfortable stopping, and judicious action ensues."[124]

Burton stresses that weight is qualitative, not quantitative, and is a matter of proportionality among the total relevant reasons. The process of assigning the relative weight to each legal reason, then, is the act of balancing. According to Burton, "we should conceive of the grounds of weight as a ring of relevant reasons impinging on a decision. . ."[125]

5.4 The Ground of Judgment - Robert Alexy

Robert Alexy[126] presents his reflections on the judicial decision-making process in the context of his search for the grounds of the legitimacy of judicial decison-making. He discusses the importance of value judgmens in law and investigates how they are rationally justifiable in the legal context. Value judgments are required in situations in which the decision in a case does not follow logically from empirical statements (statements of fact) plus a legal norm which cannot be completely justified by referring to accepted rules of legal method. In other words, a value judgment is required when legal norms, doctrines, or precedents do not dictate a unique answer. In such cases the decision-maker has discretion. He must make a choice between competing solutions in order to determine what ought to be done or what may be done or what cannot be done. This choice or decision ultimately is pronounced as the judgment in the case.

In such situations one solution is given preference over another. Alexy states that "Giving preference . . .involves a judgment that the chosen option is in some sense the better one, and to this extent there is a value judgment[127] as the basis of the decision."[128] The application of law requires value judgments, not just the logical subsumption of facts by legal rules or principles. In fact, Alexy claims that law cannot proceed without value judgments. Value judgments are decisive factors in legal decision-making.

Alexy's project in his book, **A Theory of Legal Argumentation,** is to explain where and to what extent value judgments are required, how value judgments relate to legal arguments and legal dogmatics, and whether value judgments are rationally justifiable. To this end he poses the question What are the criteria for value judgments? Who guides the decision-maker? Is it the value judgments of the community at large or a specific group? The problem, as he sees it, is how to identify what the value judgments of a group are. It may not be sufficient justification for a legal decision. Or is it one's own convictions or those of legal experts that are the criteria for value judgments? None of these alternatives is acceptable to Alexy. He claims what is required is a model which takes account of commonly held convictions/values, the results of prior legal discussions, and leaves room for criteria of correctness (criteria for evaluating whether or not legal statements/assertions are rationally justifiable).[129]

For him, the crucial question becomes "What does it mean to decide rationally in the framework of a valid legal order?" His answer is that legal reasoning takes place in special forms, according to special rules, and under special conditions. He argues that this conformity to conditions, criteria and rules constitutes the rational character of legal reasoning. For Alexy, if a discussion is in accord with special rules (such as the canons of interpretation and the rules for applying precedents that he outlines) and is in accord with forms of legal argumentation (such as analogy, argumentum e contrario, argumentum a fortiori, argumentum ad absurdum which he expresses in the form of valid logical inferences) then the result yielded can be called "correct". "The rules and forms of legal discourse thus constitute a criteria for the correctness of legal decisions."[130]

5.5 *Ethical Judgment - Costas Douzinas and Ronnie Warrington*

In their book, **Justice Miscarried - Ethics, Aesthetics and the Law**, Costos Douzinas and Ronnie Warrington claim there are serious problems in both legal practice and legal theory. Judicial decisions are often unjust and legal theory portrays justice as extraneous to the legal system. Their "project is to articulate a theory of ethical action upon which a practice of justice can be built"[131] which does not make the mistakes of legal positivism, semiotics, critical legal studies identified by post-modern deconstruction. Their claim is that if the law is not founded on just, ethical principles it is not acceptable.[132] It is in this context that Douzinas and Warrington analyse aspects the process of judicial decision-making, particularly the criteria of judgments, practical judgments and aesthetic judgments.

They turn to the philosophy of alterity to begin their construction. This "philosophy of the other" forms the basis of their call for the re-creation of the notion of justice. To be more specific, they use Levinas' argument that "the other" must always be considered prior to an ethical decision, a demand that precedes any thought of self. "The other, for us, is always what comes first in any ethical system. The other though never fully knowable, always precedes, surprises and above all calls upon us to consider her before ethical or legal decisions are taken."[133] "The demand of the suffering other is the non-essential essence which the legal system needs to recognise in order to merit its necessary but currently absent claim to do justice."[134] "[O]therness is an essential unknowable 'demanding' our attention, respect and love. . .and this non-demanding demand precedes our own consideration of self-preservation and of being."[135] In this philosophy, "the other can never be reduced to the self or the different to the same."[136] Indeed, "the concern for the other is innate, it needs no excuse or justification, it allows no choice and asks to be acted upon immediately."[137] "The ethics of alterity is unequivocal; the sense of responsibility, the 'internal' point of view speaks to me and commands me, the 'should' and 'should not' that lie at the base of all law come from the proximity of one for another, from the fact that we are involved and implicated as we are faced and addressed by the other."[138] Law, on the other hand, "seems to forget the difference of the different and the otherness of the other."[139]

An investigation of the tradition of casuistry is relevant to Douzinas' and Warrington's argument that the philosophy of alterity should guide judicial decision-making because it takes "account of the specific context of the unique individual and holds the view that "universal laws can only achieve justice if they give way to the uniqueness of the individual who comes before the law."[140] Casuistry stresses the individuality of each case. The process of judgment, in this tradition, is not simply the application of abstract principles at whatever cost. "Casuistry is simply the process of the application of universally known and tested moral principles to individual instances."[141]

A central position of their book is that the casuistical 'basis' of the common law, and the traditions that lie within both forms of reasoning, allows for the possibility of recreating a form of ethical decision-making, and a radical rewriting of our notions of justice."[142] Douzinas and Warrington endorse, and want to develop, a secular form of casuistical reasoning in law. According to them, the common law already has the resources for "turning to a form of decision-making which is fully cognisant of the needs of the other, as well as the requirements of principle."[143]

They note the similarities between the reasoning processes - the working procedures - of casuistry and the common law in general and in a modern case. They both follow previous authorities/precedents, both appeal to conscience/equity, and both casuistry and the common law principles, by themselves, do not solve specific problems; both demand attention to details. Such a secular form of casuistry, aware of the call of the other and treating the other in acceptable ways, is their starting point. Discussions of the decision-making process are presented in this context.

A crucial problem they identify is that discussions of justice itself arise in the context of a problem in law, namely that "legal authorities proliferate in a pluralistic, under-regulated manner without the false solace of universal reason or principle that modernity promised, and that this pluralism injects decisions with the sense and urgency of ethical responsibility. But at the same time the only principle capable of universalization is that of personal freedom."[144] To cope with this state of affairs the line of solution they propose is that law should adopt principles from the traditions of practical wisdom (the Aristotelian tradition) and reflective aesthetic judgment (the Kantian tradition). For Aristotle, practical judgments "have a timely circumstantial character and depend on a full and detailed understanding of the factual situation."[145] What can be borrowed from this tradition is Aristotle's notion of epieikeia, the idea that universal laws may not do justice in a particular case. In such circumstances, justice requires practical judgment to go beyond the application of rules. "[T]he Aristotelian practical judgment is pre-occupied with the specificity of the situation and with the perception, understanding, and judging of the singular as singular."[146] Douzinas and Warrington affirm that this notion of prudent practical judgments takes account of the context, but the problem with Aristotle's account of practical judgment is that it is predicated on a teleology that does not exist today and cannot be recreated.[147] The problem is that today there is no shared universe of values to guide practical judgments.

Douzinas and Warrington then evaluate Kant's notion of practical judgment. For Kant, practical judgments subsume the particular under the universal law. But such a conception of practical judgment does not provide a shared universe of value - the good life. In accord with the philosophy of the other, they write that ". . .the good can only be defined according to the needs and demands of the other, the person in need, but also the self-defining autonomous person whose request asks for the reawakening of the sensitivity to singularity inherent in the sense of justice as dike."[148] Hence they turn to reflective (aesthetic) judgments to help them revitalise justice and ethics in law.

They argue that reflective (aesthetic) judgment is suited to the type of justice and ethics they desire in law. It takes account of the unique features of each case and the relation between universal and particulars. Rather than paraphrasing what they mean by aesthetic judgment it is best to quote them on the topic:

> Aesthetic judgments make a claim to universality, but their law is unknown, indeed non-existent; it is active in its application and yet always still to come and be formalised. The appeal to the universal makes a promise of community, of a sensus communis, and that appeal differentiates aesthetic judgments from contingent or idiosyncratic preferences and tastes. But the community remains virtual; aesthetic judgment alludes to its existence but this republic of taste can never become actual. These strict preconditions and qualities necessarily make the aesthetic judgment a judgment of pure form, uncontaminated by considerations of need, interest, desire or use. While everyone should be able to experience the pleasure of the feeling of beauty in confronting the aesthetic object, the subject cannot formulate the concept or the law that her judgment implies and thus make it accessible to others. Aesthetic judgments are examples in search of their rule, subjective and individual yet in the service of the undetermined universal. As the universal law and the community they imply cannot be actualised, they are only an idea present in each judgment which carries 'the promise of its universalisation as a constitutive feature of its singularity'. . .The aesthetic community is in a continuous state of formation and dissolution; it is the precondition and horizon of judgment but each judgment passed marks the community's end.[149]

According to them, applying such ideas in the legal context would mean that "modern legal phronesis must move between the norm and the event in the same way that reflective (aesthetic) judgments find in each particular the mark of an undetermined universal."[150] Further, "if there are criteria of justice, they are only momentary, they arise at the point of their application, as the just decision must be both regulated and without regulation. These criteria are local, partial and concrete . . ."151

6 Methods of Investigating The Discovery Process

As I mentioned above, legal theorists have considered the discovery process to be a very difficult subject to study. Wroblewski offers a plausible explanation for the lack of knowledge about the discovery process. In his opinion, "the psychological material is, as a rule, far less accessible than the case material, especially if the latter is published."152 The range of data that can be studied is also limited. External observation of judicial decision-making is technically difficult - and discussions among judges and judges' personal opinions that could be relevant to their decisions are held secret in order to promote the prestige of the decision. Further, the method of studying how decisions are reached is restricted to introspection. This method, however, "narrows the research to the self analysis of the decision-maker."153 Despite these obstacles and pessimistic sentiment, legal theorists have set out to investigate the discovery process using various methods.

6.1 Self Reports

Judge Hutcheson154, mentioned earlier in the chapter, described the judging process in terms of brooding about the case, having a hunch, and then searching for the legal rules and principles that would support his hunch reflected on the judging process by writing what he called "self-reports".

6.2 Idealized Judging

Steven Burton, also mentioned above, presents what he calls a practical understanding of adjudication. He writes about "judicial action understood with regard for the actor's standpoint in real-world circumstances,"155 in contrast to a "strict observer's standpoint". Yet, he notes his view is an ideal version of what judges are trying to do, not what they necessarily do. In other words, he presents a description of how judges should act - how they can, and should, adjudicate.

6.3 Imaginary Judges

Max Radin studies how judges think in order to advise clients. In his opinion, by knowing how judges think, lawyers will more accurately predict what judges will think about their case thereby enabling the lawyers to give good advice to their clients and to suggest the type of situation, that is the categories the judge can use as the basis of a judgment in their favour. For Radin, "[lawyers'] business is prophesy."156

Radin discusses the judicial process by imagining a judge named Zurishaddai Perkins who knows everything - all the decisions that have been handed down in his jurisdiction, all the statutes in the jurisdiction, the principles of justice, the fundamental ideas of morality, and the eternal differences between right and wrong. This judge is given an imaginary dispute between a grocer who sold and delivered goods to a purchaser and the purchaser who has not paid for them.

How would Judge Perkins decide this case? Radin claims that the judge decides the case by calling up a generalised situation from within his mind. The relevant generalised situation in this case is "the situation of a person bargaining for actual wares, agreeing to pay a certain amount for them and carrying them off on a promise to pay at a future time."[157] This generalised situation, like all generalized situations, carries with it regulations including the rule that under these circumstances the purchaser owes the seller the agreed value of the goods, and ought to pay it. Standard transactions and their regulations such as the ones relevant to this situation are familiar and get into his mind because of his experience as a citizen and lawyer. The decision is reached when ". . . the whole transaction is dropped into its proper category, like a nickel in a slot-machine, - and, click! out comes the decision at the bottom!"[158]

What the judge does not do to reach a decison is to search his mind for the principles of justice, until by a process of classification, subdivision and analysis comes upon a principle that exactly fits the situation. And a judge does not use the personalities and financial means of the plaintiffs to decide the case.

But most cases are more complex. In such cases a number of generalised standard situations are called up into their mind. The category into which to place the judgment does not leap into his mind at once. There may not be a click and a judgment. In these cases, the judge selects the category (the generalised type of conduct) that seems to him to lead to a desirable result. In this task, judges reach judgments in the same way as everyone else does. Judges proceed by ". . .working their judgment backward, from a desirable conclusion to one or another of a stock of logical premises. . ."[159] In other words, judges work backward from a desirable result to a category or type of situation that calls for the preferred outcome. Such a process is a conscious activity. Principles and statutes are used to help judges place a case in a category insofar as ". . .'principles' are not principles at all but aggregations of type transactions, schematised to make them easier to carry in one's memory."[160] A statute helps a judge in that "[i]t describes a general situation. It is a picture of which the outline is not solid steel, but rubber, or - shall we say? - a wreath of smoke."[161]

Radin concludes his analysis by writing "It is an undoubted fact that the chief purpose courts fulfil in giving us not merely a judgment but a classification of the judge by types and standards, is to make it easy for us to find out how they think.

6.4 Imaginary Cases

Duncan Kennedy[162] describes the process of legal reasoning from the point of view of a judge in a case in which, initially, the judge's preferred outcome seems to conflict with the outcome stipulated by the law - "how-I-want-to-come-out" versus "the law". Kennedy places himself in the position of such a judge in a specific imaginary situation and imagines how he would consider the case in order to reach a decision. The imaginary situation is that unionised bus drivers are on strike and obstruct a street so that non-unionized drivers cannot drive by. The bus company who employs the drivers seeks an injunction and "Judge" Kennedy must decide whether or not to grant the injunction. The problem, as he portrays it, is that he sympathises with the workers and would like to develop the law in favour of workers in general. However, his perception is that a legal rule stating that there can be no interference with the owner's means of production during a strike covers the case and would lead to a decision that is against the workers.

Kennedy portrays judicial decision-making as a process of bridging a gap between "the law" and his intuition of of the justice of the situation ("how-I-want-to-come-out"). He begins the decision process by experiencing an initial perception, an intuition that the law is unfair to a particular group, the bus drivers. He stresses he cannot tell what the solution to the problem will be until he has reached his decision. The law, he argues, does not supply a ready-made solution to the problem. Also, he is not convinced that when there is a conflict between "the law" and "how-I-want-to-come-out" that he must always follow the law. His point is that a judge is neither bound to follow the law nor free to do what she wants. A judge must "work" to achieve an outcome. The law does, however, constrain this complex and ambiguous decision-making process. The constraining influence of the law is evident when he tests his intuition of the just outcome in the case by developing the best possible arguments for and against his intuition. He considers re-categorizing the case, policy arguments, and relevant lines of cases.

He claims his arguments and conclusions are constrained by law in that he wants to legalize his position, to back up his preferred outcome with an argument that to do otherwise would violate the law. He also feels constrained in that if he does not follow the law his power or legitimacy as a judge would be jeopardized. Further, he is constained insofar as he wants to avoid an appeal court reversing his decision.

"Judge" Kennedy does not reach a decision in his imaginary case. He states the outcome "depends on the circumstances"[163] which, for him, is the size of the gap between how he wants the decision to come out and the relevant rule that governs the case. The conflict in the case, then, is between the judge changing the law and the risk this innovation presents to the judge's credibility and the amount of work required to legally justify such a development. He does, however, give us five alternative decisions: (1) He could go along with the law, but would have to explain this obedience, that is, his willingness to act as an instrument of injustice. (2) He could withdraw from the case, but he would have to justify begging off and getting some one else to do his dirty work. (3) He could decide against the injunction on the basis of what the law should be, but he would have to state who authorised him to take the law into his own hands. (4) He could decide against the injunction on the basis of implausible legal argument, but this would be a bad faith argument, and hence dishonest. (5) He could decide against the injunction on the basis of fact findings he knows to be false, but this would be an extreme measure. It is evident, then, that Judge Kennedy feels neither completely bound by law or free to do as he pleases.

7 Conclusion

This chapter may be viewed as an effort to identify those legal theorists who have
had a reflective interest in the discovery process. I began by describing the context in
which discussions of discovery in judicial decision-making have taken place, particularly the debate between the realists and legal positivists. I suggested that the
process of discovery has been mis-represented and neglected by legal theorists and
traced how this situation emerged. Next I presented the efforts of diverse legal theorists whose analyses of aspects of the decision-making process formed part of their
studies. Finally, I presented a sample of the methods legal theorists have used to
study discovery.

This chapter, however, is only the first step in collecting the contributions of
those people who have an interest in the discovery process. It was limited to a representative sample of legal theorists and anecdotal presentations of their work. It is
not intended to be a comprehensive analysis of discovery in legal decision-making.
Rather it is part of a larger effort to collect the materials that would be relevant to a
coherent explanation of the process of discovery. It is even premature to attempt a
summary of the aspects of the discovery process that have been identified in this
chapter. Further, I am not yet in a position to identify all the relevant elements. In
fact, the following three chapters continue my efforts to collect the materials relevant to understanding the dynamics of the discovery process in law.

Chapter Two (like Chapter One) is an effort to identify those writers who have a
reflective interest in the discovery process. Reflective efforts to understand the discovery process can be considered to be more coherent there than in Chapter One
insofar as I present these reflections in the context of scientific pursuits regarding
decision-making. In Chapters Three and Four, I move from "theory" to "practice".
In those two chapters, I turn to spontaneous efforts to solve actual legal problems. In
the legal context there is a spontaneous discovery or decision-making process operating that seems to be successful. Legal problems are solved by judges, not legal theorists. Such spontanesous efforts follow the Latin maxim *Solvitur ambulando*. They
are *solved by walking*, not by talking!

---

* The first part of this chapter is based on my article *The Case for Re-Investigating The Process of Discovery*, 8
  Ratio Juris (1995, 336–358. I am grateful to Blackwell Publishers, Oxford, for permitting me to include por-
  tions of that article in this chapter.
1 For example, see R. Wasserstrom, **The Judicial Decision**, (London: Oxford University Press, 1961); N.
  MacCormick, **Legal Reasoning and Legal Theory**, (Oxford: Clarendon Press, 1978); R. Alexy, **A Theory of
  Legal Argumentation: The Theory of Rational Discourse as Theory of Legal Justification**, (Oxford:
  Clarendon Press, 1989); J. Bengeotxea, **The Legal Reasoning of The European Court of Justice**, (Oxford:
  Clarendon Press, 1993). J. Bengoetxea captures this point of view when he states that "Justification domi-
  nates (is at the centre of) the structure of judicial activity in the application of law." Edinburgh University PhD
  Thesis, 1989, 29.
2 Various terms have been used to express the distinction between the process of discovery and the process of
  justification. They include: discovery and justification, the context of discovery and the context of justification, the psychological process/context of explanation and the context of justification, the process of decision

and the logic of justification, motive and reason, the psychology of judicial decision-making and the justification of a decision, the process of heuresis of decisions and the process of justification.

3 For example, William Twining writes that the factors that actually influence judicial decision-making ". . . require an answer based on acceptable psychological theory. The question is essentially a psychological one." **Karl Llewelleyn and The Legal Realists**, (London: Weidenfeld and Nicolson, 1973). Jerzy Wroblewski, however, states that efforts to study decision-making would be worthwhile. He seems to suggest that knowledge of decision-making would aid justification when he writes that if one could understand the real psychological processes of decision-making, the administration of justice could be improved if ways were found to make psychological processes more uniform. Understanding the role of psychological processes could yield methods for shaping judicial attitudes in desirable ways. **The Judicial Application of Law** (Dordrecht, The Netherlands: Kluwer Academic Publishers, 1992), 16.

4 ibid., 14-15.

5 **The Legal Reasoning of The European Court of Justice**, 118-19.

6 ibid., 118-9.

7 For example, Steven Burton writes that the psychology of judging is concerned with the exercise of discretion based on personal or political preferences or interests or felt identification with the parties. **Judging in Good Faith**, (Cambridge: Cambridge University Press, 1992), 44.

8 J. Frank, **Law and The Modern Mind**, (London: Stevens & Sons, 1949), 118-119.

9 J. Dewey, *Logical Method and Law*, 10 *The Cornell Law Quarterly*, (1925), 27.

10 These descriptions were formal in the sense of (1) passing tests of validity and (2) having a universal form.

11 O.W. Holmes, **The Common Law**, (Boston, 1881), 1.

12 O.W. Holmes, *The Path of Law*, 10 **Harvard Law Review**, (1887), 466.

13 **Law and The Modern Mind**, 101.

14 ibid., 101.

15 ibid., 118.

16 ibid., 118.

17 ibid., 130.

18 ibid., 131.

19 ibid., xxv.

20 ibid., 138.

21 ibid., xix.

22 ibid., xx.

23 ibid., xx.

24 ibid., 121.

25 ibid., 121.

26 ibid., 138.

27 *Logical Method and Law*, 18.

28 **Law and The Modern Mind**, 101.

29 *Logical Method and Law*, 22.

30 **Law and The Modern Mind**, 100.

31 K. Llewellyn wrote that psychologists say that a person reaches a decision either by ". . .sudden intuition - a leap to some result that eased the tension; or else it was one of successive mental experiments as imagination developed and passed in review various possibilities until one or more turned up which had appeal. In any ordinary case a reasoned justification for the result represented a subsequent job, testing the decision against experience and against acceptability, buttttressing it and making it persuasive to self and others." **The Common Law Tradition**, (Boston: Little Brown, 1961), 11.

32 *Logical Method and Law*, 23.

33 **Law and The Modern Mind**, 103.

34 ibid., 104.

35 ibid., 103.

36 J. Dewey, **How We Think**, (London: D.C. Health & Co., 1933), 120-126.

37 J. Frank, *Modern and Ancient Legal Pragmatism. John Dewey & Co. vs. Aristotle: I & II*, 25 **Notre Dame Lawyer**, 1950, 463.

38 ibid., 460.

39 ibid., 254, 467-468.

40 **Law and The Modern Mind**, 131.

41 *Logical Method and Law*, 26.

42 **Law and The Modern Mind**, 104.

43 *Logical Method and Law*, 24.

44 ibid., 24.
45 **Law and The Modern Mind**, 130.
46 *Logical Method and Law*, 24.
47 **Law and The Modern Mind**, 103.
48 *Logical Method and Law*, 22.
49 *Modern and Ancient Legal Pragmatism. John Dewey & Co. vs. Aristotle: I & II*, 495.
50 ibid., 493-495
51 I discuss MacCormick's position on the distinction between discovery and justification because, of contemporary legal theorists, his writings on the subject are the most comprehensive and persuasive.
52 **The Judicial Decision**, 16.
53 ibid., 14.
54 ibid., 20.
55 ibid., 21.
56 ibid., 24.
57 ibid., 24.
58 ibid., 24.
59 ibid., 25.
60 ibid., 27.
61 ibid., 25
62 ibid., 25, 30-31.
63 ibid., 25.
64 ibid., 28.
65 ibid., 29.
66 **Law and The Modern Mind**, 100.
67 **The Judicial Decision**, 25.
68 ibid., 25.
69 ibid., 26.
70 **Legal Reasoning and Legal Theory**, 16.
71 ibid., 16.
72 ibid., 16.
73 ibid., 6.
74 ibid., 77.
75 ibid., 100.
76 ibid., 77.
77 ibid., 15.
78 ibid., 103.
79 Z. Bankowski, on the other hand, challenges this position. He makes two points: (1) Something can be properly called a discovery only when it has passed the relevant tests. (2) Discovery and justification are not two independent processes in the sense that the discovery of the "truth" or "facts of a matter" depends on both the method of searching for what subsequently counts as a discovery and the criteria or tests used to certify that a discovery has been made. *The Jury and Reality*, ed. M. Findlay & P. Duff, **The Jury Under Attack**, (Edinburgh: Butterworths, 1988).
     There is a third area of similarity and difference between the realists' and positivists' positions, namely justification, which is outside the concerns of this paper. The realists and positivists both recognise that legal justification is an important part of legal reasoning. However, the realists stress the rhetorical nature of the exposition of a decision, whereas the positivists present a detailed analysis of legal justification that examines its rational and logical nature.
80 The legal realists do not explicitly use the terms "discovery" or "process of discovery" to describe the judging process. But legal positivists define the "process of discovery" as the subject-matter of the legal realists' studies, namely how a judge reaches a decision.
81 Although legal positivists do not treat the process of justification as part of the "actual" process whereby a judge reaches a decision, they do not deny that there may be some overlap of testing in the decision-making process and the public legal justification of a decision. But in their opinion, how a judge actually tests and justifies a legal decision to oneself in private is independent from the process of public legal justification that ultimately determines which rival legal ruling is accepted which, in turn, determines the outcome of a case. Hence questions about the mental processes that comprise the decision-making process such as how a judge actually tests and justifies an outcome to oneself are irrelevant to their project. Instead legal positivists direct their efforts to understanding and explaining why and how a legal decision is publicly justified irrespective of what a judge actually thought about when testing it.

82 Z. Bankowski, *The Jury and Reality*, ed. M. Findlay & P. Duff, **The Jury Under Attack**, (Edinburgh: Butterworths, 1988), 13.
83 ibid., 13.
84 ibid., 13.
85 ibid., 13.
86 ibid., 13.
87 ibid., 13.
88 ibid., 9.
89 ibid., 13.
90 ibid., 21.
91 ibid., 22.
92 **Karl Llewelleyn and The Legal Realists**, (London: Weidenfeld and Nicolson, 1973), 210.
93 ibid., 217.
94 ibid., 217.
95 ibid., 218.
96 ibid., 218.
97 ibid., 222-223.
98 S. Burton, **Judging in Good Faith**, (Cambridge: Cambridge University Press, 1992), 69.
99 ibid., 36-7.
100 ibid., xv.
101 ibid., xii.
102 bid., 50.
103 ibid., 38.
104 ibid., xvi.
105 Legal reasons are those reasons that judges are permitted by law to consider.
106 A moral reason involves facts made relevant by a moral standard.
107 **Judging in Good Faith**, 28.
108 ibid., 39.
109 ibid., 29.
110 ibid., 29.
111 ibid., 42.
112 ibid., 51.
113 ibid., 51.
114 ibid., 51.
115 ibid., 59.
116 ibid., 54.
117 ibid., 54.
118 ibid., 55.
119 ibid., 55.
120 ibid., 57.
121 ibid., 57.
122 ibid., 57.
123 ibid., 57.
124 ibid., 57-8.
125 ibid., 61.
126 R. Alexy, **A Theory of Legal Argumentation: The Theory of Rational Discourse as Theory of Legal Justification**, (Oxford: Clarendon Press, 1989).
127 The term value judgment has numerous meanings. According to Alexy, "The expression of value judgments can be used to designate either the actual giving of preference or the judgment that a particular alternative is the better one, or the rule of preference underlying this judgment (and thereby the preference)... Many use the expression to mean all these and more at the same time." **A Theory of Legal Argumentation**, footnote on page 6.
128 **A Theory of Legal Argumentation**, 6.
129 He says he understands legal reasoning as a linguistic activity - an activity concerned with the correctness of normative statements.
130 ibid., 294.
131 C. Douzinas and R. Warrington, **Justice Miscarried - Ethics, Aesthetics and the Law**, (London: Harvester Wheatsheaf, 1994), 17.
132 ibid., 19.

133 ibid., 19.
134 ibid., 19.
135 ibid., 20.
136 ibid., 64.
137 ibid., 170.
138 ibid., 171.
139 ibid., 171.
140 ibid., 21.
141 ibid., 127.
142 ibid., 96.
143 ibid., 130.
144 ibid., 179.
145 ibid., 180.
146 ibid., 181.
147 ibid., 182.
148 ibid., 182.
149 ibid., 181-82.
150 ibid., 182.
151 ibid., 185.
152 J. Wroblewski, **The Judicial Application of Law,** ed. Z. Bankowski and N. MacCormick, (Dordrect: The Netherlands, Kluwer Academic Publishers, 1992), 14.
153 ibid., 14-15.
154 J. Hutcheson Jr., *The Judgment Intuitive: The Function of the "Hunch" in Judicial Decision*, 14 **The Cornell Law Quarterly,** (1929), 274-88.
155 **Judging in Good Faith**, xvi.
156 M. Radin, *The Theory of Judicial Decision: Or How Judges Think*, 11 **American Bar Association, Journal**, (1925), 357-62 at 362.
157 ibid., 357.
158 ibid., 358.
159 ibid., 359.
160 ibid., 360.
161 ibid., 361.
162 D. Kennedy, *Freedom and Constraint in Adjudication: A Critical Phenomenology*, 36 **Journal of Legal Education** (1986), 518-562.
163 ibid., 558.

2

Investigating The Analogy Between Science and Law

1 Introduction

In this chapter, I will present reflections on discovery that will drive me forward in my search for a coherent perspective on the process of discovery in law. I continue with the anecdotal style of presentation and do not provide a selection of all the writings on discovery. So, here I present a sample of reflections on the discovery process in science, and tentatively explore the relation between natural science and law and one science itself, cognitive psychology.

A number of contemporary legal theorists, including Wasserstrom and Bankowski, have drawn an analogy between science and law in order to illustrate and support their explanations of discovery and justification in law. The analogy arose as part of Richard Wasserstrom's response[1] to a dispute, as he understood it, between the formalists and American legal realists, especially Jerome Frank, that I introduced in the previous chapter. I would suggest that these discussions about the relationship between discovery and justification in science and law are more general and gestural than explanatory. By contrast, Neil MacCormick offers what appears to be a more sustained and explicit use of the science-law analogy in his analysis of discovery and justification.[2] MacCormick uses Sir Karl Popper's explanation of scientific development, perhaps because Popper was popular at the time, to develop this analogy more extensively. The comparison MacCormick makes between Popperian science and law is concerned with two overarching analogies: *(1) that the general distinction between discovery and justification can be found in science and law* and *(2) that testing in science is a model for legal justification.*[3]

MacCormick, however, primarily focuses on the second analogy, between testing in science and legal justification. He does not examine the process of discovery in detail. The distinction between discovery and justification in science rests on Popper's claim that independent methods must be used to study each process. MacCormick transfers this idea to the legal context. The proper discipline for examining the process of discovery in science and law is psychology, whereas the process of justification in science and law is studied from the point of view of the logic of testing. Hence studying how legal rulings are discovered is not directly relevant to investigating the process of legal justification. Testing in science, then, can be compared directly to legal justification. The first part of this chapter is about that analogy. The second part of this chapter, however, turns to the findings of cognitive psychologists on the topic of discovery.

You might be surprised that I discuss legal justification in this chapter. After all, the book is supposed to be about discovery in legal decision-making, not justification. At this early point in the investigation it would not serve any purpose to explain in detail why I have included justification. For the moment, it is sufficient to say that in later chapters it will become evident that aspects of testing and justification are, in fact, part of a creative process of reaching decisions. In this chapter, I am merely collecting further reflections on the discovery process that have emerged in the context of scientific methodology. I am not seeking an integration of accounts to form a coherent explanation of the nature of discovery in legal decision-making.

Insofar as MacCormick's analysis of legal justification goes beyond a general and gestural invocation of science in law, it presents an opportunity to investigate the processes involved in legal reasoning that are understood and explained by using this analogy between Popperian science and law. However, if the analogy is taken seriously, it turns out that the analogy is rather weak. Perhaps MacCormick did not intend the analogy to be taken so seriously, but it is disappointing to discover that the analogy has a floating quality.

My focus, then, is on how MacCormick invokes Popper's explanation of scientific testing in **Legal Reasoning and Legal Theory**. However, the analogy between scientific testing and legal justification depends on understanding discovery and justification in both science and law as distinct and independent processes. Hence I will briefly discuss the discovery - justification analogy before analysing more fully the scientific testing/legal justification analogy.

2 The Discovery - Justification Analogy

MacCormick draws an analogy between science and law concerning the independence of the process of discovery and the process of justification. The analogy is between a scientist's discovery that must be justified by empirical tests and a judge's choice of one side as the winner which must be justified by good reasons. MacCormick uses the example of Archimedes' discovery of specific gravity to help understand the discovery process in law and to make the point that discovery and justification in both science and law are distinct and independent processes. He writes that

> Archimedes may indeed have discovered his celebrated principle in a blinding flash of insight resulting from the overflowing of his bath due to his own immersion therein[4]. . . But many a flash of insight has been rudely brought to earth when relevantly tested. What justified Archimedes, or anyone else, in believing that bodies immersed in fluids receive an upthrust equivalent to the weight of the fluid displaced, is that it can be proved experimentally (which for those who follow Sir K Popper means that many instances of experimental evidence have corroborated it, and none falsified it. . .[5]

Turning to the legal context to complete the analogy, MacCormick writes

> Likewise, what prompts a judge to think of one side rather than the other as a winner is quite a dif-

ferent matter from the question whether there are on consideration good justifying reasons in favour of that rather than the other side.[6]

Although MacCormick does not spell out this analogy in greater detail, further use of the science-law analogy to illustrate and support the clear distinction between discovery and justification can be detected if Popper's and MacCormick's writings are compared. Popper's book, **The Logic of Scientific Discovery**, is primarily devoted to the logic of 'justification'.[7] The logic of scientific knowledge is concerned with answering questions about how new theories and hypotheses are tested and justified. It is concerned with the logical examination of scientific statements that have been formulated and presented for logical analysis and testing. Popper stresses that

> The initial stage, the act of conceiving or inventing a theory, seems to me neither to call for logical analysis nor to be susceptible of it. The question how it happens that a new idea occurs to a man - whether it is a musical theme, a dramatic conflict, or a scientific theory - may be of great interest to empirical psychology; but it is irrelevant to the logical analysis of scientific knowledge. This latter is concerned not with questions of fact (Kant's quid facti?), but only with questions of justification or validity (Kant's quid juris?). Its questions are of the following kind. "Can a statement be justified? And if so, how? Is it testable? Is it logically dependent on certain other statements? Or does it contradict them?"[8]

Popper sharply distinguishes between discovery and justification in the sense that "the process of conceiving a new idea" is independent of "the methods and results of examining it logically."[9] This distinction is based on his claim that different methods must be used to study how hypotheses are discovered and how hypotheses are tested. How new ideas and scientific theories occur and the reconstruction of the processes involved in the stimulation and release of an inspiration are, in his opinion, the concerns of empirical psychology, not his discipline - the logic of knowledge. Questions about the discovery of new ideas and inspirations cannot be answered by logical analysis. Popper claims "there is no such thing as a logical method of having new ideas, or a logical construction of this process"[10] because "every discovery contains an irrational element, or a creative intuition, in Bergson's sense."[11]

MacCormick transfers Popper's clear distinction between discovery and justification in science to law. In both fields the process of discovery provides tentative formulations - hypotheses and legal rulings - that must be subsequently tested by an independent "objective" testing or justifying process. A scientist's flashes of insight and the "subjective" psychological factors that prompt a judge to chose one side as a winner must be tested before accepting them. Scientists require experimental evidence in order to test insights and judges require good justifying reasons in order to justify decisions. Having acknowledged this distinct zone, MacCormick focuses on testing.

3 The Scientific Testing/Legal Justification Analogy

I begin by explaining that MacCormick's science-law analogy *cannot* be between scientific testing and what MacCormick calls first-order justification. Next I examine the nature of the *correspondence* between scientific testing and second-order justification. Finally, I investigate various *differences* between scientific testing and second-order justification that call into doubt the suitability of using the science-law analogy to help us understand legal reasoning.

3.1 Scientific Testing/First-Order Legal Justification

Popper distinguishes two stages of scientific testing. MacCormick distinguishes two stages or types of legal justification. MacCormick compares Popper's model of testing in science with justification in law. An analogy between the initial steps in scientific testing and first-order justification is, however, not to be expected. The first steps of Popper's explanation of scientific testing are in a different realm than first-order legal justification. Testing a scientific theory or hypothesis is performed (1) by deducing predictions from a theory or hypothesis which will, in turn, (2) be subject to empirical tests. Consider the hypothesis that "Smoking causes lung cancer." The first step would be to deduce a prediction such as "Of 100 people, there will be a positive correlation between smoking more than 2 packs of cigarettes per day and the number of people in the sample who have lung cancer." This prediction is deduced from the hypothesis. The second step would be to empirically test how many of the 100 people have lung cancer. These are the two key stages involved in Popper's explanation of testing in science.

More specifically, the initial stage of scientific testing consists of four activities: (1) deducing predictions from theories or hypotheses, (2) comparing these predictions to each other to determine whether the logical relations among predictions are equivalent, whether the predictions are compatible with each other, and whether the theory is internally consistent, (3) determining whether or not the theory is testable in the sense that the predictions can be empirically tested, and (4) judging whether, if the theory passes the requisite tests, it would be a scientific advance compared to a rival theory.[12] In the second stage of testing Popper envisages competing theories or hypotheses being tested to determine which one is better corroborated by experimental results, which one can predict new phenomena that its rival cannot predict, and which one is more capable of explaining the success of the rival theory or hypothesis. This initial part of Popper's account of scientific testing could be considered a test of the testability of the theory or hypothesis in the sense that it is concerned with whether or not the theory or hypothesis can be and should be tested. If the theory or hypothesis is not testable it would be rejected.

MacCormick's book, **Legal Reasoning and Legal Theory**, explores the potential and limitations in the deductive application of rules. MacCormick calls the process of legal justification, to the extent that it is purely deductive and logical in character, first-order justification. First-order justification consists in testing whether the relationship between a valid rule of law, legal facts, and a proposed legal decision is a valid deductive inference. A decision is legally justified if it can be logically deduced from a valid rule of law plus the existence of the relevant operative facts which are stated in the rule of law. For example, the following decision would be legally justified:

In any case, if goods sold by one person to another have defects unfitting them for their only proper use but not apparent on ordinary examination, then the goods sold are not of merchantable quality. [valid rule of law]

In the instant case, goods sold by one person to another had defects unfitting them for their proper use but not apparent on ordinary examination. [relevant operative facts]

Therefore: In the instant case, the goods sold are not of merchantable quality. [outcome or decision][13]

You might expect the science-law analogy to be between *predictions* deduced from a theory and *decisions* deduced from a rule of law. It would follow, then, that *testing predictions* would be analogous to *testing legal decisions*. Hence the plausibility of the analogy might seem to rest on understanding the *legal syllogism* as the method of deriving predictions, just as predictions in science are *logically deduced* from theories and hypotheses. But this is not the case. MacCormick does not draw the analogy this way. Popper wants to test a theory by deducing predictions and then testing those predictions. But MacCormick wants to test outcomes (the analogue of predictions) by determining whether they can be deduced from the rule of law (the analogue of theory).

One clear important difference between the first steps of testing in science and first-order justification is evident. In Popper's first stage of testing (ie. before empirical testing), predictions are tested to determine their relations among each other and whether or not they are testable. The predictions must still be subject to empirical testing. By contrast, a legal decision, derived by logical deduction, is not subject to further testing. It is said to be legally justified.

But the key difference is that, in science, empirically testing the predictions will test the theory. By contrast, in first-order justification the particular decision in a case is not deduced in order to test a rule of law; the rule of law is taken to be legally valid before the decision is deduced. There is no question at all that one could end up concluding that a rule of law is not valid. To draw such an analogy would be like saying that "Smoking causes cancer" because the prediction that there will be a positive correlation between smoking two packs of cigarettes a day and the incidence of cancer can be deduced from the statement "Smoking causes cancer". In first order justification, deduction is used to test whether the particular decision in a case is legally authorised. The legal syllogism is used to determine whether a particular outcome can be deduced from a single valid rule of law plus the requisite factual situation stipulated by the rule.

Further, in the first stage of scientific testing, *deduction* is used to draw predictions from rival theories in order to empirically test which of the competing theories should be accepted, whereas in first-order justification deduction is *not* part of testing the rival interpretations of a rule of law or rival rulings, for each version of a rule or a ruling has a corresponding decision that is part of a syllogistic justification. That is why legal rulings are rivals.

Thus there is no analogy between the first steps of testing in science and first-order legal justification. In science, predictions are deduced to determine if the theory or hypothesis is testable, whereas if a legal decision can be deduced from the law plus facts it is said to be justified. Predictions in science are tested in order to test whether or not a theory or hypothesis is falsified, whereas decisions are not tested in order to test whether a rule of law is valid. Predictions are not tested by deduction, whereas decisions are tested by deduction. In fact, first-order justification is not part of the science-law analogy. Hence the analogy between science and law drawn by MacCormick is between *testing rival scientific hypotheses* and *justifying rival legal rulings* (rival interpretations of a rule of law or rival legal rulings) in second-order justification.

Deductive justification in first-order legal justification, however, has a number of well-known weaknesses. The same decision can be derived from different rules of law and, on the other hand, opposite decisions can also be obtained by deductive reasoning. As the realists emphasised, the problem of formalism as a test is that rival decisions can easily survive. Hence, deductive subsumption in some cases, by itself, does not seem to be a sufficient test of legal justification. It is due to these weaknesses of first-order justification that, while first-order justification is necessary, it is not always sufficient on its own to justify a decision.

Due to these weaknesses, especially the possibility that rival versions of a valid rule of law may compete for acceptance or the possibility that rival rulings may compete for acceptance as a legal warrant, other factors must be examined in order to determine whether or not a decision is legally justified. If first-order justification is not sufficient by itself to justify decisions that involve such problems, it is due to the fact that "substantive" elements operate in an uncontrolled way. For MacCormick, the key issue that must be addressed is how such elements function, and how they are controlled in legal reasoning.

3.2 Scientific Testing/Second-Order Legal Justifiction

In MacCormick's opinion, the judges' evaluation of such "substantive" factors is not some whimsical irrational activity that leads to arbitrary outcomes, but rather the process is controlled through various requirements or processes known collectively as *second-order legal justification*. A legal ruling must be a *universal* proposition in the sense that the present case must be treated in the same way as similar cases that occur in the future would be treated. Also, the ruling *must make sense in the world*. The consequences of rival interpretations of a valid rule of law or rival rulings are identified and evaluated in the particular case and in other imagined cases in terms of, for example, public interest, justice, common sense and expediency or convenience. The interpretation of a ruling or the particular ruling itself that is chosen take place in the context of a legal system. Hence the constraint by the legal system placed on the judgment whether or not to accept a rule as law is that the interpretation or ruling must *must make sense in the legal system* as a whole. To be more specific, a ruling must be consistent with other valid and binding rules of law in the sense that the ruling does not conflict with other rules of law. The ruling must also be *coherent* with the legal principles in the legal system in that the ruling does not contradict directly, or by analogy, general principles. Second-order justification comprises two key elements: "[1] . . .consequentialist arguments and [2] arguments testing proposed rulings for consistency and coherence with the existing legal system."[15]

I will identify the main points of *correspondence* between scientific testing and MacCormick's account of second-order legal justification. I will examine the analogies MacCormick draws between (a) scientific hypotheses and legal rulings as rivals, (b) the requirement in science and law that hypotheses and rulings must make sense in the "real" world and (c) the same requirement in regard to the system. I develop this analogy by comparing predictions deduced from scientific theories to consequences derived from legal rulings.

MacCormick compares the legal problem of *rival interpretations of a legal rule or rival rulings* to the situation in science described by Popper of *rival scientific theories or hypotheses.* A ruling is like a hypothesis. Both rulings and hypotheses are portrayed by MacCormick as rivals that must pass tests if they are be accepted. He writes

> ... just as scientific justification involves testing one hypothesis against another, and rejecting that which fails relevant tests, so (I shall argue) second-order justification in the law involves testing rival possible rulings against each other and rejecting those which do not satisfy relevant tests...[16]

For example, the following two hypotheses are rivals: either "Smoking causes lung cancer" or "Smoking does not cause lung cancer." Legal rulings are rivals in that they *compete for acceptance*. For example, the ruling that "It is the law that manufacturers owe a duty of care to consumers of their products" competes with the ruling that "It is not the law that manufacturers owe a duty of care to consumers of their products." In science, if the relevant tests are satisfied, one is justified in accepting one hypothesis rather than another and in law, if the appropriate tests are passed, one is justified in claiming that one interpretation or ruling is legally justified and therefore the outcome that follows ought to be given.

MacCormick draws a general analogy between *scientific hypotheses* and *legal decisions* in that hypotheses and legal decisions must make sense in both the world and in the context of the legal system. He notes that

> ... from the point of view of the logic of justification there are two points of contact: [1] that legal decisions deal with the 'real world' as do scientific hypotheses, and [2] that they do so not in vacuo but in the context of a whole corpus of 'knowledge' - in this case, the whole corpus of the normative legal system, rather than a corpus of descriptive and explanatory theory.
>
> To put it crudely, legal decisions must make sense in the world and they must also make sense in the context of the legal system. In our problem cases, they must be based on rulings which make sense in the context of the legal system.[17]

He develops these two analogies between testing rival theories and testing rival rulings (1) by explaining the analogy between the requirement that a hypothesis must fit a *general theory* and the requirement that a legal ruling must be consistent and coherent with the *legal system* and (2) by suggesting that *empirical testing* and *consequential arguments* are analogous. Let us examine each analogy in more detail.

MacCormick explicitly develops the general analogy between the requirement that a ruling *must make sense in the legal system* and the requirement found in Popper's first stage of testing that a hypothesis *must make sense in the system or body of knowledge*. To be specific, MacCormick claims that

> ... these points about consistency and coherence have their analogues in the Popperian theory of scientific reasoning, in that a particular hypothesis has to fit with a general theory...[18]

Not only does the process of testing hypotheses depend on previous scientific knowledge, but new hypotheses arise only in the context of scientific knowledge. MacCormick stresses that problems are noticed, questions are considered important, and explanations are judged relevant only in the context of a body of knowledge. Even new discoveries involve extrapolation from what is already known.

> [T]he interpretation of the evidence necessarily involves the use of assumptions which themselves belong to scientific theory...To be technical about it, testing always involves reliance on 'auxiliary hypotheses' which are themselves, in a given experiment, taken for granted; though they can themselves be direct objects of experimentation also - in which case other auxiliary hypotheses will be involved.
>
> So we are never testing out scientific hypotheses in vacuo; we are always and necessarily testing them in the context of a body of theory with which they are compatible, and taken together with which they make sense. What is more, with the possible exception of revolutionary discoveries on the grand scale of a Newton or an Einstein, the making of 'discoveries' - the flash of insight which reveals a new explanatory hypothesis [eg. the shape of DNA molecules] - takes place within a body of scientific knowledge.[19]

When the legal context is investigated we notice that the requirements of consistency and coherence depend on the assumption that

> [t]he basic idea is of the legal system as a consistent and coherent body of norms whose observance secures certain valued goals which can intelligently be pursued altogether.[20]

Following this line of reasoning, a ruling that directly conflicts with any part of the system will be rejected. In MacCormick's words, a ruling "...may not be adopted if it is contradictory of some valid and binding rule of the system."[21] Moreover, a ruling which conflicts with any general part of the system will be rejected.[22]

MacCormick illustrates the requirements of consistency and coherence by discussing the legal ruling in the *Donaghue v Stephenson* case, namely that "Manufacturers owe a duty of care to consumers of their products." This ruling cannot conflict with existing rules of law. MacCormick notes that Lord Atkin distinguished this ruling from the rulings in precedents such as *Dixon v Bell* and *Langridge v Levy* so that there was no conflict.[23] The ruling must also be coherent with general principles of the legal system. MacCormick explains that in *Donoghue v Stephenson* the ruling is supported by the settled general principle "... that there can be no [delictal] liability save where the defender owes the pursurer a duty to take care."[24] Further, he argues that Lord Atkin's neighbour principle[25] is coherent with the principles of the legal system in the sense that it is a general principle that not only covers specific cases giving rise to a duty of care, but it also expresses the underlying common purpose of a set of specific rules...[26]

In summary, both hypotheses and rulings must make sense in the system. A scientific hypothesis which must make sense in the context of general theory is analogous to a legal ruling which must make sense in the context of a legal system. Hypotheses must be compatible with, or fit with, other theories and hypotheses. A legal ruling must be "consistent with the pre-established body of law in the strict sense of not directly conflicting with any already authoritative and un-distinguishable rule."[27] Further, a ruling also "has to fit with the general principles of the system [ie. the pursuit of some policy or value such as the safety of consumers], whether principles already formulated or newly developed on the basis of analogical arguments."[28]

MacCormick suggests that there is an analogy between *empirical testing* and *consequential arguments* by first describing scientific justification and then considering consequential arguments in legal justification. He claims

> There is a profitable analogy to be drawn here with the Popperian theory of scientific justification: for Sir Karl Popper, the logical element in scientific discovery is the logic of testing. The scientist frames an explanation of a certain range of phenomena, which is in rivalry with other possible explanations of the same phenomena. The process of experimentation is a process of testing two rival hypotheses as explanations; for a relevant experiment is such that it can falsify one or other of the predictions about its outcome which the scientist derives from the two rival hypotheses. No theory can ever be conclusively proved true by such a procedure; but if one theory is corroborated while a rival is falsified by such experimentation, we are justified in adhering to the former rather than the latter.[29]

In other words, if a theory is corroborated it makes sense in the world. Turning to the legal context, and thereby presenting the legal equivalent to empirical testing, MacCormick writes

> . . . I suggest that second-order justification is concerned with 'what makes sense in the world' in that it involves *consequentialist arguments* . . .[30][Consequentialist argumentation] considers the consequences of making a ruling one way or the other to the extent at least of examining the types of decision which would have to be given in other hypothetical cases which might occur and which would come within the terms of the ruling.[31]

Typically, consequential arguments involve answering the questions "What does this or that ruling imply, and what will it probably bring about?"[32] If the answers to these questions are acceptable the ruling makes sense in the world. For example, in the *Donoghue v Stephenson*[33] case, where a woman became ill due to a snail in her ginger beer, the consequences of the potential legal ruling that "Manufacturers do not owe a duty of care to consumers of their products" were identified and tested. Not only would the plaintiff not have a remedy against the manufacturer of ginger beer in this particular case, but if any consumer in the future was injured as a result of consuming bottled beer or chocolates, or as a result of using medicine, ointment, soap, cleaning fluid, or cleasing powder[34] they, also, would not have a remedy.

MacCormick, however, does not explicitly state that there is an analogy between *empirical testing* of hypotheses and *consequential arguments* to test rulings. Rather, this comparison must be made by the reader. The link MacCormick identifies is that hypotheses and rulings must make sense in the world. Presumably, *evaluating the acceptability of the logical and probable consequences* of legal rulings in light of their justice, common sense, public benefit and convenience is analogous to *testing predictions by performing experiments* and comparing them to observable experimental results.

The analogy between *empirical testing* and *consequential arguments* can be made even more specific. For Popper, the key to testing hypotheses is to deduce predictions from them and then to test the predictions by comparing them to experimental results. If a prediction does not agree with the observed situation, then the theory or hypothesis is shown to be false and is said to be falsified. Whether or not a prediction turns out to be acceptable, therefore depends on whether the experimental results contradict the prediction. If the prediction turns out to be acceptable or corroborated, that is not falsified, then the theory has passed the test. It has proved its mettle by past experience. For the time being there is no reason to discard the theory. There is always the possibility of future negative experimental results which could overthrow the current theory.[35] A theory, then, is not and cannot be tested directly. Only specific predictions are tested by experiments and practical applications. The question of the falsifiability of theories is reduced to the question of the falsifiability of predictions. For example, the hypothesis that "Smoking causes lung cancer" would be tested by deducing predictions and then empirically testing them. One prediction that could be deduced is "There will be a positive correlation between smoking 2 packs of cigarettes per day and the number of people with lung cancer in a group of 100 people." This prediction, then, would be empirically tested as part of the process of determining whether or not the hypothesis is falsified.

Although it is not stated by MacCormick, the analogue to *predictions* in law is presumably the *consequences* which are derived from legal rulings and subsequently tested. The consequences of accepting a ruling that "Manufacturers do *not* owe a duty of care to consumers who use their products" would be evaluated in light of, for example, the public interest, justice, common sense, and convenience or expediency of the consequences of accepting the ruling. In the *Donoghue v Stephenson* case, the consequences of the ruling above were not desired and the ruling was not accepted. MacCormick writes that the consequences of that ruling would conflict with the public interest that the manufacturer is in the best position to secure safe use and consumption of its products; justice would not be achieved if an injured person who is not responsible for their injury is not compensated by a party who is responsible for their injury; it would be against common sense because people would not agree it is desirable for a manufacturer to carelessly injure others and to be free from liability.[36] In short, predictions and consequences are treated as analogues by MacCormick. Hypotheses are tested by deducing predictions and testing them and rulings are tested by deriving consequences and testing them.

3.3 Problems With The Scientific Testing/Second-Order Legal Justification Analogy

Despite the attractiveness of the analogies between testing in science and legal justification, there seems to be a floating quality to the analogy. This comparison suggests a superficial plausibility to the analogy between scientific testing and legal justification. If the analogy with science is examined more closely, we find that some aspects of testing in science and legal justification are very different. Furthermore, we find that some analogies between science and law have not been developed.

I now want to examine the *differences* between testing in science and legal justification, the weakness of MacCormick's analogy. Although MacCormick presents *rival legal rulings* and *competing scientific hypotheses* as analogues in that they both must be subject to a testing process before accepting one rival and rejecting the other, legal rulings and scientific hypotheses are different in an important way. Two scientific hypotheses are rivals in the sense that a scientist must decide which hypothesis is corroborated by the experimental results and which hypothesis is falsified. Legal rulings seem to be rivals in another way. Although two legal rulings are rivals in the sense that they are alternatives that compete for acceptance by a judge, there is a more significant type of rivalry that has not been noticed. Legal rulings yield opposed outcomes, rival decisions. In the *Donoghue v Stephenson* case if "Manufacturers owe a duty of care to consumers" the plaintiff wins the case. If "Manufacturers do *not* owe a duty of care to consumers" the defendant wins the case. There does not seem to be a scientific analogue in the sense that the acceptance of one hypothesis does not yield an "actual" outcome that its rival hypothesis would not.

Further, the *consequences* of each legal ruling also make the rulings rivals. In other words, if two rulings are rivals the consequences of each ruling are also rivals. However, the significant difference between science and law is that the judge must decide which consequences are preferred - those of ruling A that "Manufacturers owe a duty of care to consumers who use their products" or the consequences of ruling B that "Manufacturers do *not* owe a duty of care to consumers who use their products." To be more specific, the evaluation of the pros and cons of the consequences of ruling A competes with the evaluation of the pros and cons of the consequences of ruling B. Hence the significant rivalry between rulings is between the *results of two separate test results* - the results of the test of the consequences of ruling A and the results of the test of the consequences of ruling B. For example, if ruling A is chosen, consumers will have a remedy against manufacturers. By contrast, if ruling B is chosen consumers will not have a remedy. These consequences compete for acceptance. Further, the reasons for providing consumers with a remedy against manufacturers compete with the reasons for *not* providing consumers with a remedy.

This type of rivalry is not found between scientific predictions deduced from competing theories. The rivalry between predictions in science is settled by one common set of test results. The prediction that "There will be a positive correlation between smoking more than 2 packs of cigarettes per day and the number of people in a group of 100 who have lung cancer" competes with the rival prediction that "There will not be a correlation between smoking and lung cancer." The rivalry between these predictions is settled by one test - counting the number of people in the sample with lung cancer. But rival consequences in law that have been tested are still rivals because the test results themselves compete. For example, ruling A that "Manufacturers owe a duty of care to consumers" may be considered to be in the public interest (thought to secure the safe use and consumption of goods), but ruling B that "Manufacturers do *not* owe a duty of care to consumers" may be considered expedient (thought to limit claims that would cause gross inconvenience to the legal system). The judge must still choose which ruling to accept. In this way, the test results themselves are rivals; "public interest" competes against "expediency". The rivalry between rulings is not settled until the judge judges that one set of tested consequences is preferred to another set and chooses to accept the ruling that has those particular tested consequences. In short, the rivalry between scientific hypotheses is over which hypothesis is better supported by what, in fact, are the experimental results. But the rivalry between legal rulings remains unresolved, even after testing consequences, until a further *judgment of value* is made between which of the two sets of test results is preferred.

Again, although both hypotheses and legal rulings, and hence predictions and consequences, must be tested to determine whether or not they make sense in the world the method of testing is fundamentally different in science and law. As discussed above, predictions are tested by comparing them to actual *observable situations* by experimentation. Deciding whether to accept or reject a prediction depends on whether the prediction corresponds to observed events. By contrast, consequences are tested by examining how they are related to values such as public interest, justice, common sense, and expediency or convenience. The findings of such an analysis are then compared in order to decide which set of consequences is more acceptable and, in turn, which ruling is preferred. This type of testing amounts to a *thought-experiment*. Testing involves thinking of a case, working out the logical consequences and speculating about the probable consequences of that case and other cases and testing the consequences by thinking about them.

Further, in science the decision whether or not to accept a prediction depends on whether the *prediction agrees with the observed events*. The prediction that "There will be a positive correlation between smoking more than 2 packs of cigarettes per day and lung cancer in a sample of 100 people" depends on counting the cases of lung cancer in the sample. But in law the decision to accept a consequence rests, not on observations, but on an e*valuation of the consequences*. In science, testing predictions can be summed up by the question, "Do these predictions agree with the experimental results?" Take the smoking example. The question would be "Is a positive correlation between smoking 2 packs of cigarettes per day and lung cancer supported by the empirical evidence?" But in law the question is "Do I prefer these imagined consequences or those imagined consequences?" For example, "Do I prefer the imagined consequence of the ruling that "Manufacturers owe a duty of care to consumers", namely consumers have a remedy against manufacturers, which "scores high" on public interest (ie. this consequence has the potential to secure safe consumption)?" or "Do I prefer the imagined consequence that consumers do *not* have a remedy against manufacturers which "scores high" on expediency (ie. this consequence has the potential to limit the number of cases litigated on the issue)?" Science calls for judgments of fact, whereas law calls for evaluations.

In fact, testing in law seems to be a more personal activity than testing in science. Even in MacCormick's own terms, testing in law is evaluative and subjective. He recognises that

> Consequentialist argumentation "is intrinsically *evaluative*, in that it asks about the acceptability or unacceptability of such consequences."[37] . . . Judges characteristically refer to criteria such as 'justice', 'common sense', 'public policy', and 'convenience' or 'expediency' in weighing the case for and against given rulings . . . [Consequential argumentation] is in part at least *subjective*. Judges evaluating consequences of rival possible rulings may give different weight to different criteria of evaluation, differ as to the degree of perceived injustice, or of predicted inconvenience which will arise from adoption or rejection of a given ruling.[38]

Even the test of coherence "... involves reflection on the values of the system..."[39]

Personal evaluations seem to play a much more limited role in scientific testing than in law. Comparing and judging whether observed events, in fact, support predictions is the activity which determines whether or not a hypothesis is falsified. There is much less scope for the use of diverse criteria when engaged in these activities than when making legal judgments. The judgment whether to accept a ruling rests on evaluations and judgments of value regarding public interest, justice, common sense, and expediency which by their very nature, are more variable and "subjective" than judgments in science.

Finally, MacCormick accepts Popper's account of falsifiability and suggests that a theory or hypothesis that is not falsified is similar to a ruling that has been accepted. In Popper's model, despite the fact that a theory may be thought to be a better explanation than its rival, it is not verified in the sense of being true. It has only been shown that, so far, the *theory is not false*. One cannot say that it is true that smoking causes cancer, but one can say that the theory is not yet false. By contrast, the legal ruling ("Manufacturers owe a duty of care to consumers who use their products") which was chosen over its rival is the one that "ought to be given" and the ruling which is considered to be "just" and "right". From this perspective, the acceptance of a legal ruling is more conclusive than the non-rejection of a theory or hypothesis. One might even go so far as (as MacCormick does) to say that a valid *legal ruling is a "true statement" of the law* at that particular time and in those circumstances. On the other hand, the legal ruling could be considered as not yet falsified in the sense that disadvantages of the ruling may become evident in the future and the law may need to be modified. But these issues are not raised by MacCormick.

Although MacCormick presumably equates *predictions* with *consequences* in that both are derived from universal statements and are subject to testing, there are significant differences in the way they are derived and tested. For Popper, predictions are derived by deducing them from rival hypotheses. Predictions amount to specific statements *deduced* from universal statements. The process of deduction moves from a universal to particulars, from statements that claim to be true for any place and any time to statements that cover specific places and times. From the universal statement that "Smoking causes lung cancer" we can deduce the particular prediction that "In a sample of 100 people there will be a positive correlation between smoking more than 2 packs of cigarettes per day and the number of people with lung cancer in the group". Although MacCormick speaks of the "logical and probable" consequences of a legal ruling, consequences are not derived from a legal ruling in the same way as predictions are deduced from universal hypotheses. Consequences are not derived through syllogistic deduction. Consequences are derived through a process that involves *imagining* and *considering* the effects of the ruling in the particular case and in similar cases. The judge presumably wants to know the consequences that the legal ruling logically implies and would probably bring about in hypothetical cases which might occur and would come under the terms of the ruling.[40] In other words, consequences are understood as the outcome of inferring universal consequences from particular imagined examples. The process, then, moves from particular consequences to universal consequences. In *Donoghue v Stephenson*, the reasoning moves from the particular situation of a person becoming ill after drinking ginger beer to imagined cases in which consumers are injured by beer, chocolates, medicine, ointment, soap, cleaning fluid, cleansing powder, or bread. These cases may occur in the future and a consumer in these cases would not have a remedy if the universal ruling that "Manufacturers do *not* owe a duty of care to consumers who use their products" was accepted. Hence we move from the particular consequences that a particular plaintiff would not have a remedy to particular imagined plaintiff in each particular imagined case who would not have a remedy to the universal consequence that any consumer would not have a remedy against *any* manufacturer.

This explanation is quite different from Popper's explanation of the deduction of predictions from hypotheses. The process of deduction in science moves *from universal* to *particular*, that is, from a universal statement that claims it holds in all places and times to a specific prediction about what will happen at a particular place and time. By contrast, in law the process moves *from a particular to a universal*, that is from identifying the specific consequences of a legal ruling in the case in question to inferring the consequences in all similar hypothetical situations.

In summary, although deducing predictions from theories and hypotheses and then testing them is vital to Popper's explanation of testing, no analogous process of deduction can be detected in MacCormick's account of legal justification. Despite the fact that deduction is a crucial part of first-order justification, first-order justification is not part of the science-law analogy and deduction in first-order justification has nothing to do with deriving predictions or consequences. However, in second-order justification, where predictions are presumably analogous to consequences, it turns out (1) that predictions in science are *particular* but consequences are *universal* and (2) that predictions are *deduced* but consequences are *inferred*.

Again, Popper writes about assessing the consistency among predictions deduced from a theory or hypothesis. The aim is to determine if the predictions are logically equivalent, derivable, and compatible with each other. For example, the prediction that "There is a positive correlation between smoking more than 2 packs of cigarettes per day and the number of cases of lung cancer in the group" would be compatible with the prediction that "There will be a negative correlation between not smoking and the number of cases of lung cancer in a group of 100 people." But, for MacCormick, the logical relations among consequences (the analogues to predictions) are not tested at all. For example, the public interest is not tested against expediencey: the potential for improving the safety of manufactured products is not tested against the potential for increased litigation to adversely affect the administration of justice. Rather, the *requirement of consistency* is concerned with testing whether a legal ruling is consistent with other valid and binding rules of law, that is, whether it makes sense in the system. Thus the science - law analogy in this context actually drawn by MacCormick turns out to be between *predictions* and *legal rulings*, *not* between *predictions* and *consequences* as one might anticipate.

MacCormick's explanation of the *requirement of coherence*, according to which a legal ruling cannot conflict with valid principles of the legal system, resembles

Popper's requirement in the initial steps of testing that the relation between a new theory or hypothesis and the existing body of scientific knowledge must be examined. For Popper, spelling out the relation between a new theory or hypothesis and other scientific theories and hypotheses is a vital part of the testing process. It is part of determining whether or not a theory is testable. The requirement of coherence, on the other hand, is not part of a procedure for testing whether a legal ruling is *testable*. Instead, the test of coherence is an important part of testing whether or not to accept the ruling itself. Coherence is not a test of the testability of a ruling.

As part of the process of testing whether a new theory or hypothesis is *testable*, a new theory or hypothesis must be examined to assess whether it has any meaningful implications for the body of scientific knowledge in the sense of whether the theory or hypothesis would be an advance in understanding if it is not falsified by empirical testing. By contrast, questions about whether a legal ruling would be some sort of "advance" in the legal system are not raised by MacCormick. In fact, MacCormick does not raise questions about *testability* in the legal context. Apart from the requirement that legal rulings must be universals, he does not discuss whether there are any pre-requisites that must be satisfied before testing the consequences, consistency and coherence of a legal ruling. By contrast, for Popper, a theory or hypothesis is testable only if it has some form that can be empirically tested. Some theories such as Marxism, psychoanalysis, and astrology are so vague that opposite predictions can be deduced from them. Such theories are empirically untestable. If a theory or hypothesis is to rank as science it is essential that only one element in a set of opposites can be deduced from the theory or hypothesis.

Not only can the results of testing the consequences of two rulings be rivals, but the test of consequences and the requirement of consistency and coherence can also be rivals. This situation would emerge if the consequences of one ruling are preferred to its rival, but the ruling itself conflicted with other valid rules or principles. Here, satisfying the test of consistency and coherence would be considered more important than the consequential arguments and the competition would be settled by rejecting the ruling. However, there is no scientific analogue. Science does not have a neat method of resolving conflicts between experimental results and the body of accepted scuientific knowledge. The accepted theories may be revised or rejected. Experiments may be repeated. The experimental results may be rejected for some reason. At the very least, when this situation arises it indicates that a new problem has been discovered that should be investigated.

3.4 Conclusion

The analogy between Popperian science and law, namely, understanding legal justification as testing, involves accepting the plausibility of a comparison between the "theoretical " and "empirical" field of science and the more "practical" and "evaluative" field of law. I have indicated many points of assymmetry and lack of fit between what initially was presented as a plausible analogy between testing in science and legal justification. Some differences between testing in science and testing in law are fundamental while other differences are less significant. However, collectively they cast doubt on the appropriateness of the attempt to use testing in science as a way of understanding and legitimating the process of legal justification. The analogy drawn between science and law cannot be defended by arguing that the analogy is only meant gesturally for three reasons. First, by identifying law with science, the prestige of science in the intellectual community helps bolster and enhance the attractiveness of MacCormick's account of legal justification. In this sense, the analogy helps quell doubts about the absence of limitations and constraints on judicial decision-making. The "subjective" aspects of decision-making are not out of control, but are "scientifically managed".

Secondly, the plausibility of the analogy seems to depend on not taking the analogy too seriously. Although analogies are drawn between hypotheses and rulings, between the derivation of predictions and consequences, between the idea of empirically testing predictions and consequences, and between the body of scientific knowledge and the body of rules that constitute a legal system, the analogy breaks down at almost every point of comparison when subjected to a detailed analysis. The asymmetry between predictions and consequences and between empirical testing and evaluations of justice, common sense, etc. challenges the plausibility of comparing science and law.

Thirdly, the science-law analogy masks important aspects of legal reasoning. It suppresses the extent to which judges are personally responsible for legal decisions. To be more specific, the analogy obscures the fact that judges are ultimately responsible for evaluating the pros and cons of the consequences of a ruling; they are responsible for judging which set of consequences, in their opinion, is more appropriate than another set; and they are responsible for evaluating and judging whether or not a ruling is consistent and coherent with other valid rules and legal principles. Moreover, the focus of the science-law analogy on testing and justification hides the problem-solving tradition that is crucial to legal decision-making. The pre-occupation with the "objective" logical aspects of legal reasoning obscures the important contribution that the experiences, knowledge, values and methods shared by the legal profession play in understanding problematic situations and in discovering and inventing appropriate solutions to problems.

4 Recent Research by Cognitive Psychologists into "Discovery"

In the previous section I questioned the appropriateness of invoking Popper's account of discovery and testing in science to help us learn about legal procedures. In this section I explore the research findings and methods of cognitive psychologists on the nature of discovery. I turn to another science dealing in a general way with the same subject matter as my study in order to identify aspects of their work that may be relevant in the legal context. The legal realists' idea that the process of discovery involves having hunches as sudden flashes of intuition seems to have been borrowed from Gestalt psychologists who emphasised the importance of a sudden flash of insight when the parts of a problem fit together into a solution (or whole) which transcends the sum of the parts.[41] Also, Jerome Frank used the work of Sigmund

Freud to help explain why the legal profession was obsessed with certainty and predictability. But many important developments have occurred in psychology since the times of the early Gestalt psychologists and psychoanalysts. In the past fifteen years cognitive psychologists have directed their research efforts to learning about consciousness. Let us examine the recent work of cognitive psychologists that may be relevant to legal theorists investigating the judicial decision-making process. I proceed by briefly summarizing their research findings and their methodology - introspection.

Advanced level undergraduate textbooks in Cognitive Psychology present what for legal theorists is the discovery process or decision process under such headings as "Understanding and Inference", "Judgment and Decision-Making", "Reasoning", "Problem-Solving", and "Creativity". In fact, these textbooks regularly devote a chapter to each of these four topics. In accord with this regularity I will now summarise the recent work in cognitive psychology found in textbooks that seems to be relevant to understanding and explaining the judicial decision-making process.

4.1 Understanding and Inference

Cognitive psychologists investigate "understanding". They want to know what understanding is. In order to find out, they study how people understand sentences. They claim that the meaning of a sentence is not simply the words in a sentence. Rather, the reader of a sentence constructs the meaning of a sentence from the input plus activated knowledge.[42] Thus what we learn depends on what we already know, our background knowledge. Understanding, they stress, is an active process whereby input is supplemented with knowledge. It involves making active inferences to represent the presented information (in this example the words of a sentence) as an integrated representation. "We understand when we are able to figure out how all the information fits together to make sense - integrating presented information with previous knowledge to construct a unified representation."[43]

They explain the relation between the input and a potentially vast amount of knowledge or a whole body of knowledge in terms of the use of a general knowledge schema or general knowledge structure. A schema is knowledge about the world, not information in the world in the sense that it comprises encoded information about a type of situation. It is general in that it does not include knowledge about any exact situation, but does include how the general knowledge is related to a particular situation. Schemas are learned as we experience events. We remember events and develop schemas from noticing commonalities among particular events. Cognitive psychologists propose that the appropriate schema is triggered by key words in sentences, or related words, or by the context in which an event occurs. We also learn schemas by modifying schemas. For example, if a new event is not an instance of any schema, it may be related to a known schema by modifying the schema.

Mental models are another mental process by which we understand. They are actively constructed, often spontaneously. By contrast to schema, mental models are used to attain specific knowledge about particular situations and do not involve filling in the features of a category. A mental model, for example, would be required to understand how a thermostat works.

Medin and Ross admit that there are problems with explanations of schemas. They point out that the general description of schema is "short on details" and recognise the "vagueness" of their description. They also write that it is not clear to cognitive psychologists how schemas are implemented. Mental models also puzzle them. For them, the question "Where do mental models come from?" remains a fascinating problem.

4.2 Judgment and Decision-Making

Cognitive psychologists investigate the nature of judgment and decision-making. Medin and Ross open their chapter on this topic with the sentence "One of the hardest things about decision-making is to define it, for it is so pervasive that we could equate it with virtually all voluntary human behaviour."[44] However, they soon manage to give a definition: "Decision-making can be roughly defined as generating, evaluating, and selecting among a set of relevant choices, where the choices involve some uncertainty or risk."[45]

Cognitive psychologists want to find out how judgments and decisions are reached. The research efforts to answer this question are directed to understanding and explaining how people cope with a set of choices and ultimately make a judgment or decision. They investigate the strategies or heuristics which people adopt (1) to select the alternative that satisfies the desired goal (called effectiveness) and (2) to reduce the number of potential alternatives or choices (called efficiency). They identify four strategies or heuristics used to reduce a set of choices. First, people search through alternatives until a satisfactory choice is found. The limitation of this strategy is that the optimal choice may not be selected. Secondly, people repeatedly eliminate options that do not possess a designated feature until one option remains. Thirdly, people cluster options according to some feature, pick the most desirable cluster, and select indifferently within the cluster. Fourthly, in adaptive decision-making people examine alternatives and weigh aspects of the alternatives. Medin and Ross are surprised "how effective and efficient human decision-making strategies often prove to be."[46]

But judgment and decision-making are not always effective and efficient. Poor decisions can be made and they may have serious consequences. The arguments of Medin and Ross is that decision-making should be understood better so it can be improved. To further this aim cognitive psychologists investigate the relation between rationality and irrationality. The early view on this topic was that human thought was comprised of two distinct components - (1) a logical, rational mode and (2) an irrational, blind, emotion-laden mode. However, the view of cognitive psychologists today is that a judgment or decision is irrational if the law of contradiction is violated. In other words, a reasoning process is irrational if a person reaches contradictory conclusions on the same evidence.

Cognitive psychologists do not understand the logical rational mode of thought and the irrational affective mode as distinct and independent processes. The current view is that ". . .normal cognitive processes frequently give rise to non-rational by-products that are associated with systematic misperceptions of other individuals and groups."[47] To put it simply, "human rationality is not segregated from the processes that lead to cognitive biases."[48] The authors then name and give examples of such strategies or heuristics that can lead to poor judgments and decisions. It is worth briefly summarising them. People may adopt the availability heuristic and make a judgment based solely on what can be brought to mind. People may base a judgment on a solo or token member of a group. People may adopt a representative heuristic and judge an event as likely to occur if it represents typical features of its general category. People may adopt causal schemas and accept a prediction as likely to occur if it is consistent with what we expect. Finally, our judgments and decisions may be biased by over-confidence.

But it would seem that psychologists do not know much about judgment and decision-making. Medin and Ross capture the current state of the research on this topic by writing that ". . .we really know far less about [cognitive heuristics and biases] than we would like. So far, work in this area has the character of being more like a list of ingredients than a recipe. . . This is not a satisfying state of affairs, particularly from the point of view of improving human judgment."[49] Finally, cognitive psychologists stress that human judgment and decision-making is fallible. In psychology this is not major news. But Medin and Ross stress that ". . .it is big news in economics, stock-market forecasting, eye-witness testimony, medical decision-making."[50]

4.3 Reasoning

Cognitive psychologists want to know how we reason. Reasoning covers the topics of deduction and inductive reasoning[51] and the sites at which mistakes can be made in these two models of reasoning. Medin and Ross focus on the relation between deduction and induction. They ask whether or not reasoning by using abstract rules in a deductive model is a separate process that is more fundamental then reasoning with mental models in particular situations. They also ask whether mental models are part of deduction. Median and Ross stress that this area of research is, at the present time, "speculative".

Cognitive psychologists also study analogy. Their key point is that relational similarity is the core of analogies. Analogies are made on relational similarity, not simply on the number of similarities or on overall similarity.[52]

4.4 Problem-Solving

Cognitive psychologists study the cognitive processes associated with problem-solving. Their methods have included observing people solving problems, listening to the verbal reports when people are solving problems, and computer simulations. Their analyses of problem-solving comprise descriptions of what a problem is and investigations of the heuristics or methods used to solve problems. The features of a problem are: (1) the goal, (2) givens, that is the situation at the beginning of the problem, (3) some means (knowledge) of transforming the initial situation, and (4) obstacles or restrictions, that is there is no immediately available solution.

They offer a further refinement of the situation at the beginning of the problem by distinguishing between well-defined problems and ill-defined problems. In an ill-defined problem some aspects of the problem (such as the initial situations, the goal, the obstacles) are not completely specified.

In order to solve a problem the initial situation must be represented. The external world must be transformed into an internal representation and this representation (if incomplete) must be elaborated by memory so it can be operated on. Psychologists stress the importance of representing the problem. To understand a problem you must pay attention to crucial information and ignore irrelevant information. Their research suggests that "the likelihood of solving a problem depends on the way it is represented."[53] A good representation of the critical features of a problem ". . .allows the problem-solver to proceed with an efficient search for the solution; it does not immediately lead to a solution."[54]

The representation of a problem is operated on by selecting and applying a heuristic procedure. A heuristic or problem-solving approach guides the search for a solution so that a complete search of all possible answers is not needed. Heuristics "do not guarantee a solution, but usually allow one to have a good chance at a solution."[55] If the means-end heuristic is selected the person figures out the desired end and then figures out the means to reach that end. A problem may be divided into sub-problems or smaller problems and each sub-problem is solved by detecting the difference between the initial situation and the goal and reducing the difference between the two. Analogy can be use as a heuristic insofar as a successful solution to an earlier related problem can help the search for a solution in a new situation. Another problem-solving strategy is the simple search in which solutions are chosen at random.

4.5 Creativity

What is creativity? Cognitive psychologists define a creative solution as a discovery that must be original and relevant. They claim that creativity is related to imagination, especially flashes of insight. For Gestalt psychologists, understanding a problem involved "seeing" how all the parts fit together to form the whole. In such instances the solution to a problem suddenly enters our minds and we experience the feeling of Eureka! or Aha!

Creativity also seems to involves "seeing" problems in a new way.[56] Sometimes problems are spontaneously restructured enabling the parts to fit together in a new way leading to a new understanding. For them, the key aspect of creativity is not in the choice of the solution, but finding the "real" problem. For them, the key problem in the creative process is not finding the solution, but the problem of how best to formulate the problem. This description, however, is criticised by cognitive psychologists for its vagueness.

Psychologists distinguish four stages of creativity: (1) Preparation: knowledge is obtained about the problem and the person experiences a mental block; (2) Incubation: the problem is set aside; (3) Illumination: the solution occurs in a sudden insight; (4) Verification: the insight is checked because not all of them are correct.

By contrast, the findings of other cognitive psychologists portray creativity as incremental problem-solving, a process comprising a series of small steps rather than the springing of a solution into one's mind without warning. Background knowledge is said to be crucial to this process. For these psychologists, the key question is "Are creative products produced by a cognitive process different than those producing non-creative products?"

Medin and Ross identify other limitations of explanations of creativity. They claim that psychologists do not offer an explanation of what cognitive processes actually occur. In their opinion, psychologist offer, at best, a description of creative thinking, what it feels like. Accounts of the creative process may be unreliable and stages may overlap. In fact, many creative solutions are not documented.

4.6 Introspection

The chief method cognitive psychologists use to study cognition is called introspection. According to William Farthing, introspection is ". . .looking into one's own mind and observing its contents."[57] Introspection is ". . .observing your conscious experience." Introspection, however, is not a matter of literally looking within oneself. For Farthing introspection is a thought process or set of thought processes. The data for the process come from short term and long term memory. It is an active thought process that involves discriminating, classifying, and naming experiences - verbal thoughts, images, perceptions, feelings, intentions, and actions. Introspection is not some sort of direct inner observation. It is not a sensory process. Rather, it is mainly a matter of verbal thinking. Introspection is thinking about one's conscious experience. It can lead to a verbal description of one's conscious experience.

Farthing distinguishes between two types of introspection: (1) descriptive introspection and (2) interpretive introspection.[58] Asking and answering the question "What do I feel?" is an example of descriptive introspection. Asking and answering the question "Why do I feel this way? is an example of interpretive introspection. In interpretative introspection the questioner intends to discover the causes of his own thoughts, feelings and actions. These two processes represent two levels of consciousness- (1) primary consciousness or direct experience and (2) self consciousness or introspective self-awareness.

Introspection can involve thinking out loud, thought sampling, retrospective reports, diaries, and group questions. But all these methods, in Farthing's opinion, have limitations. Thinking out loud slows thinking. Thinking out loud can be influenced by an experimenter's presence. Verbal reports can be distorted or partial due to a person's inhibitions and censorship. Retrospective reports may be incomplete due to forgetfulness. Gaps may be filled inaccurately and the recall of events may be more orderly than the introspective experience itself. A person giving a verbal report may not be able to capture the richness of his experience in words. Further, introspective verbal reports cannot be independently verified.

5 Conclusion

It would seem that the account of the work of cognitive psychologists parallels the efforts of MacCormick's use of Popper. But my method of analysis is based on a different approach than that of MacCormick. It will appear that when we gather our clues together there is required a shift in context to deal coherently with the entire problematic of discovery in legal decision-making. At this point, however, it is too early to raise the issue in a precise way; it is a later task.[59] What I have done so far, (and what I will continue to do in the following two chapters) can be viewed profitably in the light of some of the procedures mentioned in the previous section.

The contribution that the cognitive psychologists offer are their explanations of problem-solving and creativity. They define problem-solving in terms of four elements - (1) the goal, (2) the situation at the beginning of the problem, (3) some method of transforming the problematic situation, and (4) no immediately available solution. They treat problem-solving as a conscious and active procedure when they write about the strategies or heuristics people adopt to guide and to help them solve problems. Heuristics, of course, do not guarantee that a solution will be discovered. In their discussions of creativity psychologists accept that creative problem-solving follows a formula comprising four stages: (1) preparation, (2) incubation, (3) a sudden insight, and (4) testing. They also stress the importance of the relation between the representation of a problem and the likelihood of finding of finding a solution.

Despite these important contributions which seem to be crucial to understanding legal problem-solving, psychologists consider their work to be incomplete. For example, they consider descriptions of the spontanesous representation of problems to be vague. They claim that understanding involves the use of schemas, yet they admit they do not know how schemas are modified. Introspection is another problematic topic that must be saved for later chapters. Perhaps the greatest problem with their work is that they have not discovered the relations between understanding and inference, judgment and decision, reasoning, problem-solving, and creativity. The work of cognitive psychologists examined in this chapter is more suggestive of further areas of inquiry than it is explanatory.

In light of the recent work of cognitive psychologists, the reflections of legal theorists presented in Chapter One seem to be incomplete. Legal theorists do not discuss legal problems in terms of the general features of problems or legal heuristics. Reflections on legal decision-making might benefit from analysing the dicoveries of cognitive psychologists. But this chapter is not an appropriate place to perform such an integration. Analyses of the tentative solutions offered in Chapters One and Two must remain incomplete for the time being.

The selection of available materials regarding discovery in legal decision-making must be continued. I will move from reflective considerations and their associated tentative solutions to the problem - which lawyers and judges have no respect for - to actual performance in the legal context. In Chapter Three I discuss the nature of discovery illustrated by a judge's written legal opinion concerning a controversial issue - abortion. Chapter Three adds further complex dimensions to the problem "What is the nature of discovery in legal decision-making?" It raises questions about how legal problems are solved and the relation between problem-solving and expression.

Chapter Four comprises an account of how an arbitrator resolved ·a dispute. Chapter Four, dealing with a problem contiguous to legal debate on a topic that seems to be of no deep significance (the occupation of a car), carries us forward to a perspective that is a threshold leading to the fuller context that I seek - a coherent account of the problems indicated in these four chapters. That perspective will also involve a criticism of introspection as it is presented in Chapters One and Two, but it seems best to postpone addressing these difficulties until I accumulate further illustrations of discovery in law.

1 R. Wasserstrom, **The Judicial Decision**, (London: Oxford University Press, 1961).

2 N. MacCormick, **Legal Reasoning and Legal Theory**, (Oxford: Clarendon Press, 1978).

3 ibid., 101-104.

4 ibid., 15.

5 ibid., 16.

6 ibid., 16.

7 Popper says he is describing the logical part of discovery. I have not analysed Popper's position on the clear distinction between discovery and justification. This idea, however, has been questioned by philosophers of science. See especially P. Feyerabend, **Against Method** (London: New Left Books, 1974), 165-167. For an analysis of the discovery-justification distinction in law see M.P. Golding, *A Note on Discovery and Justification in Science and Law*, ed. J.R. Pennock & J.W. Chapman, **Justification**, Nomos xxviii, 1986, 124-140.

8 Karl Popper, **The Logic of Scientific Discovery**, (London: Hutchinson, 1959), 31.

9 ibid., 31.

10 ibid., 31.

11 ibid., 31.

12 ibid., 31-32.

13 **Legal Reasoning and Legal Theory**, 25.

14 ibid., 104.

15 ibid., 107.

16 ibid., 103.

17 ibid., 103.

18 *Universalisation and Induction in Law*, **Reason in Law: Proceedings of the Conference Held in Bologna, 12-15 December 1984**, Volume One, ed. C. Faralli & E. Pattaro, Milan, 1987, 101.

19 **Legal Reasoning and Legal Theory**, 102-103.

20 ibid., 106.

21 "Of course, ostensibly contradictory precedent may be 'explained' or 'distinguished' to avoid such a contradiction ..." **Legal Reasoning and Legal Theory**, 106.

22 This criterion applies "To the extent ... that the rules are, or are treated as being, instances of more general principles the system requires a degree of coherence .... [T]he requirement of coherence is satisfied only to the extent that novel rulings given can be brought within the ambit of the existing body of general legal principle." **Legal Reasoning and Legal Theory**, 107.

23 ibid., 127.

24 ibid., 121.

25 Lord Atkin's neighbour principle is: "The rule that you are to love your neighbour becomes in law: You must not injure your neighbour, and the lawyer's question: Who is my neighbour? receives a restricted reply. You must take reasonable care to avoid acts or omissions which you can reasonabley foresee would be likely to injure ... persons who are so closely affected by [your] act that [you] ought reasonably to have them in contemplation as being so affected when you are directing your mind to the acts or omissions which are called in question." **Legal Reasoning and Legal Theory**, 125.

26 ibid., 126.

27 *Universalization and Induction in Law*, 101.

28 ibid., 101.

29 ibid., 101-102.

30 ibid., 106.

31 ibid., 105.

32 ibid., 101.

33 [1932] A.C. 562; 1932 S.C. (H.L.) 31.

34 **Legal Reasoning and Legal Theory**, 109.

35 ibid., 96.

36 ibid., 111.

37 ibid., 105.

38 ibid., 105.

39 ibid., 107.

40 ibid., 105.

41 The key difference between Gestalt psychologists and legal theorists is that legal theorists stress that insights must be tested, whereas Gestalt psychologists claimed that when we experience insight and the solution to a problem suddenly enters our minds we immediately realize that it is correct. M. Matlin, **Cognition**, (London: Harcourt Brace, 1994), 361.

42 D. Medin & B. Ross, **Cognitive Psychology**, (London: Harcourt Brace Jovanovich College Publishers, 1992), 336.

43 ibid., 336.

44 ibid., 394.

45 ibid., 395.

46 ibid., 423.

47 ibid., 408.

48 ibid., 408.

49 ibid., 415.

50 ibid., 422.

51 Reasoning by deduction involves the application of a general rule to a set of facts to reach a conclusion. On the other hand, induction involves the use of mental models which are built up from recurring events which are compiled into rules. We will return to this distinction in Chapter Eight.

52 **Cognitive Psychology**, 445.

53 ibid., 466.

54 ibid., 467.

55 ibid., 461.

56 On this topic see: A. Koestler, **The Act of Creation**; N. Hanson, *Patterns of Discovery;* S. Langer, **Feeling and Form**; B. Lonergan, **Insight**; E. deBono, **Lateral Thinking**.

57 G.W. Farthing, **The Psychology of Consciousness**, (New Jersey: Simon & Schuster, 1992), 46.

58 Farthing identifies a third more elemenary type of introspection called analytic introspection. This type of introspection leads to a description of one's conscious experience in terms of elementary sensations, presumabley for examle, "I see a red flag." "I hear the fog horn."

59 In Chapters Five to Eight, I will raise the issue in a technical fashion as presented by Bernard Lonergan in his treatment of generalized empirical method. On this topic see P. McShane, *Features of Generalized Empirical Method and the Actual Context of Economics*, **Creativity and Method**, ed. M. Lamb, (Milwaulkee: Marquette University Press, 1980), 543-570.

3

Examining "Discovery" and A Woman's Point of View as Justificatory and Rhetorical Strategies in Madame Justice Wilson's Analysis of The Right to Liberty in *R v. Morgentaler, Smoling and Scott*

1 Introduction

Lawyers, law teachers and law students, especially in Canada, often talk about how judges reach decisions in their efforts to explain the reasons for legal judgments. But, as Chapters One and Two indicate, investigations of how judges reach decisions, commonly called the process of discovery, have been unsystematic and anecdotal. Madame Justice Bertha Wilson's opinion in *R v Morgentaler, Smoling and Scott*[1], however, seems to offer a precise account of how she "actually" reached her judgment. Her analysis of the right to liberty provides an opportunity to examine, in detail, the role "discovery" plays in legal reasoning.

The *Morgentaler* case, especially Madame Justice Bertha Wilson's opinion, makes fascinating reading. Not only does her opinion mark the first time that "liberty" in s. 7 of the **Canadian Charter of Rights and Freedoms**[2] was defined by a Supreme Court Judge, but she is one of the first judges to self-consciously address so-called substantive legal issues, not simply procedural matters, in Canadian Constitutional Law.[3] But for my purposes the most interesting part of Wilson's opinion is the crucial role that "discovery" plays. She reports her analysis of liberty as a search for, and discovery of, a solution to a legal problem. This problem-solving style of presentation also plays a key role as a justificatory strategy. Further, the process of discovery is an important part of the woman's point of view that Wilson presents, and uses as a justificatory strategy, in her report.

Justificatory strategies comprising explanations of how judges reach decisions and women's points of view have not been examined in any cases I know. I examine these justificatory strategies in Wilson's analysis of the right to liberty in *R v Morgentaler*. Although Wilson's discussion of the right to liberty and her method of solving the legal problem seem to be very persuasive, after reflection, they become much less convincing. I explore this state of affairs.

2 The *Morgentaler* Case

Six years after the decision of *R v Morgentaler, Smoling and Scott*, which declared that the criminal law regulating abortion was unconstitutional, abortion in Canada is still not regulated by law. Although the Canadian Parliament has not attempted to introduce any legislation to cover abortions, provincial legislatures have attempted to regulate abortions. But such legislation in Nova Scotia, passed in response to Dr Morgentaler opening an abortion clinic in Halifax, was declared unconstitutional by both the Nova Scotia Trial Division[4], the Court of Appeal[5], and the Supreme Court of Canada[6]. Similar legislation in Prince Edward Island[7] was also ruled unconstitutional and proceedings in New Brunswick[8] are underway. Hence, *R v Morgentaler*, continues to dominate legal discussions about, and legal responses to, the abortion issue.

The *Morgentaler* case arose after three physicians - Drs. Morgentaler, Smoling and Scott - set up a clinic to perform abortions on women even though they did not have a certificate from a committee of an approved or accredited hospital which is required by s. 251(4) of the **Canadian Criminal Code**. They were indicted on the charge of conspiring with each other with the intent to procure abortions contrary to s. 423(1)(d) and s. 251(1) of the **Criminal Code**. Before the three doctors entered pleas they moved to quash the indictment or to stay the proceedings on the grounds that s. 251 of the **Criminal Code** was ultra vires the Parliament of Canada because it infringed ss. 2(a), 7, and 12 of the **Canadian Charter of Rights** and s. 1(b) of the **Canadian Bill of Rights**. The appellants and the Crown agreed that the main issue concerned s. 7 of the **Charter**. Consequently, the arguments of counsel and the judges' opinions in the case dealt with the constitutional question whether s. 251 of the **Criminal Code** infringed the right to life, liberty and security of the person in s .7 of the **Charter**.

The problem that Madame Justice Wilson must solve in this case was agreed upon and formulated by counsel for the Crown and the defence. The problem she is given to solve is *"Does s. 251 of the Criminal Code violate s. 7 of the Charter?"*[10] *"Does s. 251 of the Criminal Code which limits the pregnant woman's access to abortion violate her right to life, liberty, and security of the person within the meaning of s. 7?"*[11] Wilson's opinion is ultimately a solution to this problem; it is an answer to this constitutional question.

It is useful to summarise the aspects of the other opinions in the case that are relevant to Wilson's opinion. Chief Justice Brian Dickson states in his opinion that, in order to answer the constitutional question, "it is sufficient to investigate whether or not s. 251 meets the *procedural standards* of fundamental justice."[12] He emphasises that the job of the Court is not to solve the abortion issue, but simply to measure the content of s. 251 against the **Charter**. Although s. 7 of the **Charter** states that "Everyone has the right to life, liberty, and security of the person", Dickson answers the constitutional question solely in terms of the right to security of the person. He defines a breach of security of the person as state interference with bodily integrity or as serious stress imposed by the state.

Dickson answers two questions, (1) *"Does s. 251 infringe the s. 7 right to security of the person?"* and (2) *"Is the infringement of security of the person in accord with the fundamental principles of justice in the procedural sense?"* His answer to the first question is that the right to security of the person is breached for two reasons: One, forcing a woman to carry a foetus to term unless she meets certain criteria unrelated to her own priorities and aspirations by a threat of criminal sanction is a profound interference with a woman's bodily integrity. Two, the result of the delay in obtaining abortions caused by the mandatory procedures of s. 251 is a higher probability of complications and a greater risk to the woman's physical and psychological health. These two reasons are concerned with procedural issues.

Dickson's answer to the second question *"Does the breach of security of the person comport with the principles of fundamental justice in the procedural sense?"* is that the objective of the legislation is valid, but that the means to balance the competing interests of the woman and the foetus are not "reasonable and demonstrably justified" because the procedures and administrative structure of s. 251 are unfair and arbitrary. Consequently, they defeat the legitimate objective of protecting the life of the woman. He argued that, according to the Canadian criminal justice system, a defence should not be illusory or so difficult to attain as to be practically illusory. He points out that abortions are not available in some hospitals because the legislation requires that each hospital must have four doctors who can perform abortions; some hospitals are not accredited and so are automatically disqualified from performing abortions; the requirement that a province must authorise a hospital to perform abortions restricts the number of hospitals that can perform abortions; and that s. 251(4) fails to provide an adequate standard for abortion committees to decide whether a woman qualifies for an abortion. Thus, in his opinion, s. 251 infringes the right to security of the person and the principles of fundamental justice in the procedural sense guaranteed by s. 7 of the **Charter**.

In a similar opinion, Justice Beetz agrees with Dickson's analysis of the procedural requirements of security of the person and with the decision that s. 251 infringes the right to security of the person. Like Dickson, Beetz says that the means, ie. the rules and procedures in s. 251, are not reasonable and demonstrably justified because they are not rationally connected to the legitimate objective of the legislation which is to protect the foetus, and to the ancillary objective, which is to protect the life and health of the pregnant woman.

3 "Discovery" as The Style of Wilson's Analysis of The Right to Liberty

Wilson does not immediately provide an answer to the question - *Does s. 251 of the Criminal Code violate s. 7 of the Charter?* Her solution is neither derived by simply deducing an outcome from a valid rule of law plus the relevant operative facts, nor is it simply a matter of testing the consequences, consistency, and coherence of rival universal legal rulings, nor is it a matter of presenting a solution and supporting it by reasons. Rather, she describes an elaborate problem-solving process that ultimately leads to her solution to the constitutional problem. Wilson's opinion highlights the process of discovering a solution, not the process of justifying an outcome already identified. It is this topic, Wilson's description of her process of discovery, her own problem-solving process, that is the focus of my investigation. I examine "discovery" in the context of Wilson's analysis of the right to liberty.

The style or form in which Wilson presents her decision is that of a process of discovery. She presents her opinion as a search for a solution to a problem, a search for an answer to the question - *"Does s. 251 of the Criminal Code violate s. 7 of the Charter?"* Her ultimate goal is to solve this problem. In conventional terms, her opinion can be considered a description of a discovery process which includes both discovery and testing procedures.

Although questions, definitions, and judgments can be identified in Wilson's text, I am not attempting to re-construct the actual process Wilson followed to solve the problem. The questions and answers she formulates in her text could be a partial re-construction of her own problem-solving process, but at most her text describes the broad outline of the actual process she followed. It would be impossible for her, or me, to identify all her questions and answers in such a complex problem-solving process.

Wilson's method of solving the constitutional problem - *"Does s. 251 of the Criminal Code violate s. 7 of the Charter?"* - is comprised of three stages. *First*, she specifies her version or interpretation of the problem. For her, the problem is whether a woman can be compelled by law to carry a foetus to term. *Secondly*, she devises and follows a strategy or method to discover a solution to this problem. She must discover the meaning of the right to liberty in the context of the abortion issue. The meaning can be discovered by considering the purpose of the **Charter** in general and the purpose of the right to liberty in particular. She follows that method in order to answer that question and discovers that: (a) the purpose of **Charter** rights is to achieve human dignity; (b) the right to liberty *". . .guarantees to every individual a degree of personal autonomy over important decisions intimately affecting their private lives"*[13]; and (c) in the context of the abortion issue, the right to liberty *". . .gives a woman the right to decide for herself whether or not to terminate her pregnancy."*[14] *Thirdly*, she answers the constitutional question by judging that s. 251 violates the right to liberty in s. 7.

Let us trace her account of the process of discovery in more detail. Wilson begins by asking *"Does s. 251 of the Criminal Code violate [a woman's] right to life, liberty, and security of the person within the meaning of s. 7 of the Charter?"* She re-phrases this question as *"Does s. 251 of the Criminal Code which limits the pregnant woman's access to abortion violate her right to life, liberty, and security of the person within the meaning of s. 7?"* Her general strategy to answer these questions is to search for definitions of the right to life, liberty, and security of the person in s. 7. In particular, she wants to know *whether liberty or security of the person gives a woman the right to decide whether to have an abortion*. This question provides her search for the meanings of liberty and security of the person with a further degree of precision.

Wilson further narrows down her search from "life, liberty, and security of the person" to "liberty" by arguing that current definitions of security of the person do not and cannot answer a particular question.[15] She begins by examining security of the person. She agrees with Dickson's and Beetz' definition of security of the person that security of the person covers threats to the physical and psychological security of a pregnant woman. But, in her opinion, both this definition of security of the person and this interpretation of s. 7 are limited. This interpretation of s. 7 does not answer the question *"Whether a legislative scheme that does not pose a threat to the physical and psychological security of the person of the pregnant woman would be valid under s. 7?"* Her point is that s. 7, which includes liberty and security of the person, may encompass more than physical and psychological security. This unanswered question is used to demonstrate the relevance of liberty to the problem and the inadequacy of the current definition of security of the person.

Her method of addressing this issue is to ask *"What is meant by the right to liberty in the context of the abortion issue?"* To answer this question she asks *"What is the purpose of the **Charter** in general and the purpose of the right to liberty in particular?"* Her answer is that the purpose of **Charter** rights is to achieve human dignity.

Her next move is to present three increasingly specific definitions of the purpose of the right to liberty. One, *the right to liberty covers the right to make fundamental decisions without interference from the state*. Two, *"the right to liberty grants to the individual a degree of autonomy in making decisions of fundamental importance."* Three, *"the right to liberty guarantees to every individual a degree of personal autonomy over important decisions intimately affecting their private lives."*

Then she asks *"Does the decision of a woman to terminate her pregnancy fall within this class of protected decisions?"* The answer is that she has "no doubt that it does"[16] cover a woman's decision to terminate her pregnancy. She presents evidence in support of her judgment. The decision is a special type of decision that comprises the totality of a woman. A man cannot understand the situation. And the right to reproduce is part of a woman's dignity.

She goes on to re-state her key question *"What is the meaning of the right to liberty in the context of the abortion issue?"* She answers it by defining the right to liberty. For her, the right to liberty *". . .gives a woman the right to decide for herself whether or not to terminate her pregnancy."*[17] This is Wilson's fourth and most specific definition of the right to liberty.

She returns to answer her overarching constitutional question *Does s. 251 of the Criminal Code violate s.7 of the Charter*? Wilson's judgment is "Clearly it does."[18] The reasons she gives in support of this judgment are that (1) the purpose of s. 251 is ". . .to take the decision away from women and give it to a committee"[19]; (2) ". . .the committee bases its decision on criteria entirely unrelated to [a pregnant woman's] own priorities and aspirations"[20]; and (3) letting a committee decide whether a woman should be allowed to *terminate* or continue her pregnancy are equal violations of a woman's right to personal autonomy in decisions of an intimate and private nature because "both arrangements violate the woman's right to liberty by deciding for her something that she has the right to decide for herself."

4 "Discovery" as Both a Justificatory and a Rhetorical Strategy

Wilson uses her account of how she reached her solution to the constitutional problem to persuade the reader to agree with her opinion. This justificatory strategy has
been used by other judges, especially in Canada, but it has not been analysed. What
is especially interesting about the strategy in this case is how Wilson uses questions
and answers for her own purposes. However, I begin by identifying conventional justificatory strategies used by Wilson before turning to consider the discovery process
as a justificatory strategy.

Within the rubric of her account of the discovery process outlined above Wilson
offers the reader a sample of conventional justificatory strategies that would likely
be accepted by the legal community as sufficient to authorise her decision. These
justificatory strategies are found in most legal opinions. She cites authorities and
defines terms according to authorised methods. For example, she cites American
cases to support her definition of the right to liberty. And she quotes Neil
McCormick, a legal philosopher, to provide and support her interpretation of liberty. She uses the method spelled out by Chief Justice Dickson in *Big M Drug Mart* to
define and to support her definition of the right to liberty.[22] Wilson also follows the
conventional method for analysing the outcome of cases in which an **Charter** right
may or may not conflict with specific legislation. Typically, the right is defined in
some general way that is relevant to the legislation and then the pertinent legislation
is evaluated in light of the newly defined **Charter** right. In this case, Wilson defines
the right to liberty in the context of the abortion issue, examines s. 251 of the
Criminal Code in light of her newly formulated definition of the right to liberty, and
judges that s. 251 violates the right to liberty in s. 7 of the **Charter**.

But by far the most remarkable aspect of how Wilson justifies her solution is how
she uses the structure of the discovery or problem-solving process in an effort to persuade the reader to agree with her opinion. To be more specific, she uses the structure of the problem-solving process as a method of persuading the reader to agree
with, assent to, or accept her way of solving the constitutional problem. In fact, her
line of solution, and her ultimate answer to the constitutional question seem to be
very persuasive.

Aristotle's investigation of rhetoric[23] - the study of the available means of persuasion - can be used to help understand how Wilson uses the discovery process as a justificatory strategy. For Aristotle, each rhetorical technique[24] that a speaker adopts
to lead an audience to the desired judgment can be understood in terms of three
means of persuasion - (1) the character of the speaker, (2) arousing emotions in the
audience, and (3) the logic of the argument. The speaker could present herself in a
favourable light. Aristotle claimed we trust a speaker who is wise and of good will.
Hence we are more likely to agree with what we are told or to do what we are advised
by such speakers. The speaker could also attempt to arouse emotions in an audience
in order to facilitate the desired judgment. The explanation is, for example, if an
audience sympathises with the speaker's point of view or if an audience is angry
about an opponent's argument the audience is more likely to make the judgment

desired by the speaker. Aristotle argued that we trust logical arguments. If the speaker can show the truth or apparent truth of what is said it will help persuade the audience to reach the desired judgment. Let us examine the extent to which these three means of persuasion can be detected in Wilson's description of her discovery process.

4.1 The Role of "Discovery" in Portraying Wilson in a Favourable Light

Wilson's description of how she reaches her solution to the problem, asking questions and answering them, reads as her personal search for a solution. She is candid and open about how she solves the problem. Wilson writes about how *she* understands the problem, about *her* concerns for women. Presenting her opinion as a discovery or problem-solving process reveals her sensitivity to the problem in that she acknowledges a very serious and complex practical problem. Moreover, she affirms the human aspect of the problem; the problem involves the totality of women's lives.

She does not treat the problem as a narrow legalistic issue abstracted from human living. Rather, she faces the relevant controversial issues head on. She does not take the more conventional legal route to a solution by restricting her analysis to security of the person and procedural matters. She prefers to define the right to liberty and to address the substantive issues. She seems to be a sensitive, wise, and open-minded judge who grasps the "real" issues in the case. For a judge, she seems to be brave. Moreover, she does not claim to have all the answers. Wilson portrays herself as an honest, forth-right and down to earth person who not only is telling us the inside story, but the whole story. To put it simply, Wilson is one of us. It is easy to trust and agree with the arguments and judgments of a person possessing these qualities.

4.2 The Role of "Discovery" in Evoking Emotions in The Reader

The "discovery" style of presentation is engaging to read. It is fresh and novel. My interest in the problem and its solution was provoked by Wilson's account of how she "actually" reached her decision. It is not a typical boring and narrowly legalistic report in which a rule of law is authoritatively applied to the facts and supported by a parade of precedents. I had the impression that she was taking me seriously and that I was not being coerced into agreeing with her opinion. I had the feeling I was being asked to solve the constitutional problem for myself. The report seemed to be something of a dialogue between Wilson and me with Wilson asking the questions and inviting me to answer them. After answering one question, I was very interested in what she would ask next and what its answer would be. She even assisted by answering the questions.

Wilson also seems to capture the complexity of the issues relevant to a woman's judgment whether or not to have an abortion that Dickson and Beetz do not articulate. She seems to understand the dilemma faced by women who were not permitted to judge whether or not to have an abortion and also for those women who could decide whether or not to have an abortion. I imagined that making such judgments would be very difficult.

I felt very happy about the outcome of this case. I was hoping s. 251 would be declared unconstitutional. I leaned towards her solution and agreed with her that she, indeed, had addressed the more important substantive issues, the real problem which Dickson and Beetz had side-stepped. Their line of solution did seem superficial and legalistic compared to Wilson's efforts to comprehensively deal with the problem.

4.3 The Role of "Discovery" in Presenting a "Logical" Argument

How does Wilson prove the truth or apparent truth of her argument? Wilson's argument is not "logical" in the sense of formal logic. She does not use chains of syllogisms to prove her solution is correct. Although there is no point here in rehearsing Wilson's explanation of how she solved the constitutional question it is important to stress its non-logical character. Her report comprises a complex problem-solving procedure comprised of related questions and answers that ultimately lead to a solution to the constitutional problem.

Wilson engages the reader in problem-solving insofar as the reader asks and answers questions in order to correctly understand her opinion. The reader asks questions in order to understand ideas expressed in her text and may also ask questions to understand ideas which are gestured at rather than spelled out. In both contexts, the written text provokes the reader to ask questions and to discover and test the answers for oneself. For example, the reader might ask "What is the problem Wilson must solve?" and "Is my understanding of Wilson's interpretation of the case correct?" In short, the reader's acceptance of, or assent to, her solution depends on the reader's questions and answers concerning the case.

In fact, she uses the structure of problem-solving in an effort to persuade the reader to accept her legal opinion. Wilson's general approach is to lead or guide the reader through a complex problem-solving process giving the reader the opportunity to assent to each step in her search for the solution. Stated simply, Wilson wants the reader to understand and to solve the problem in the same way as she presents the case. This approach seems to be typical of many judicial opinions and Wilson's opinion should not be understood as an exceptional case. But Wilson's strategy for doing this is very interesting.

She shapes and controls the reader's problem-solving process by leading or guiding the reader through her own particular method of solving the problem. Wilson persuades the reader to agree with her solution to the problem by asking questions and providing clues that direct the reader to consider particular aspects of the problem. Wilson provokes and creates a series of opportunities for the reader to ask questions, experience insights, and make judgments by formulating questions and answers in her text. She invites the reader to answer her questions as if they are one's own, to follow her strategy of answering them as if it is one's own, and subsequently to reach answers similar to her own. She leads the reader through her text by asking and answering questions in the same way a teacher leads a student to the desired answer to a question.

I want to examine in detail how Wilson uses questions and answers to persuade the reader to agree with her argument, in particular, that her line of solution and her ultimate solution are correct. I analyse how she (a) uses questions to *shape* and *control* the reader's formulation of the issue and (b) how she uses answers to *shape* and *control* the reader's definition of the right to liberty.

5 Shaping and Controlling The Reader's Questions: Leading The Reader to Ask The Right Questions

Wilson shapes and controls the reader's problem-solving process by presenting questions that appeal to the reader's curiosity and ability to solve problems.[25] The reader could, in principle, ask any question and seek its answer, including the questions explicitly posed by Wilson. But Wilson shapes the questions the reader asks by explicitly posing the relevant questions for the reader. With this technique she controls the reader's understanding of the case insofar as an answer is correlative to, and depends on, the particular question asked. Supplying or presenting the reader with questions to answer is an effective way to shape the reader's understanding of her decision. By explicitly providing significant questions in an orderly sequence Wilson leads the reader from one question to its answer and then to the next question and its answer until the reader comes to understand the case from her point of view.

The process of shaping and controlling the reader's questions and answers can be illustrated by examining how Wilson leads the reader to accept her formulation of the key issue or problem in the case. The way that Wilson defines the problem that must be answered by focusing on the "real" or "deeper" question illustrates a number of ways she uses questions to persuade the reader to agree with her version of the problem. Most important is the way she presents her approach and that of Dickson and Beetz as alternatives. The competing positions take different questions as the specification of the problem. The reader is presented with the choice between two different interpretations of the relevant problem to be solved. Wilson confronts the reader with the choice of either accepting the approach of Dickson and Beetz by presuming that a woman can be compelled by law to carry a foetus to term or to accept her own position which is to explicitly *ask* and *answer* the question "*Can a woman be compelled by law to carry a foetus to term?*" Dickson and Beetz presume the answer to this question in the sense that they evaluate the procedural requirements that must be met in order to have an abortion. One can infer that they first presume that the law can compel a woman to carry a foetus to term before they analyse the procedural requirements of the legislation. The reader's choice is between presuming that a woman can be compelled or to explicitly ask and answer Wilson's question "*Can a woman be compelled by law to carry a foetus to term?*" If the reader presumes the answer to the question is yes, then the problem that must be solved is the question "*Do the procedural requirements of s.251 comport with fundamental principles in the procedural sense?*" But if, on the other hand, the reader explicitly asks the question whether a woman can be compelled by law to carry a foetus to term, this question becomes the problem that must be solved. These alternatives appear exhaustive, limiting the reader's choice to these two alternatives. She rhetorically diminishes Dickson's and Beetz' approach in a series of propositions in which she repetitively characterises the alternative approach as "purely academic", "pointless", and "an exercise in futility".[26]

But how is the reader led to choose one alternative rather than another? Wilson first considers the alternative position. She agrees with Dickson and Beetz that s. 251 violates the right to security of the person. But then she contrasts their position more sharply with her own. She presents their position as limited to considering only security of the person and coping only with the contingent and immediate legislative scheme of s. 251. In contrast to her own position, their analysis does not answer the question whether a legislative scheme that does not create a threat to a woman's physical and psychological health would be valid under s.7. She suggests they do not answer this question because they do not consider the right to liberty and fail to ask if the definition of security of the person is wider. In other words, from her perspective their approach omits to ask and answer relevant questions.

She continues to denigrate their position by asserting that their definition of security of the person "begs" the central issue in the case. They are concerned with purely procedural matters. Then she presents her own position as a way to solve the limitations or deficiencies of Dickson and Beetz. From Wilson's perspective the question they do not answer is crucial. According to her, if the right to liberty or security of the person or a combination of the two confers the right to decide whether or not to have an abortion, then we must look at both substantive and procedural issues. Hence the problem that must be solved is whether the right to liberty or security of the person or a combination gives a woman the right to decide whether to have an abortion. Wilson presents the method of solving the problem by explicitly formulating three questions that "we must answer".

To summarise, Wilson introduces the problem as a choice between two alternative methods of answering the constitutional question. She shakes the foundation of Dickson's and Beetz' opinions by posing questions that their shared perspective does not, and cannot, answer, and presents their focus on procedural justice as evasive. Moreover, which interpretation of the problem to choose can only be decided by asking further questions and then answering them in turn. By identifying the relevant questions that must be answered, Wilson moves beyond Dickson's and Beetz' approach. What began as the reader's choice between two possible alternatives has been developed by Wilson into a choice between trying to discover an answer to a crucial question or ignoring the question.

By posing particular questions and answering them, Wilson *directs the reader's attention* to selected aspects of the case or the issues that she considers relevant. This technique shapes and controls the reader's questions and answers to the extent that, by asking and answering questions along the line proposed by Wilson, the reader's attention is directed toward what she considers important and away from aspects of the case that may provoke questions about other issues that she considers irrelevant. By selecting what is important to her decision, Wilson helps the reader ignore other issues. For example, questions could be raised about the circumstances in which deciding to have an abortion could be appropriate or inappropriate. She directs the reader's attention to considering the capacity or ability of a woman to decide to have an abortion and ignores questions about what factors or guidelines would be relevant to making educated, reflective individual decisions concerning abortions. This technique restricts the range of questions the reader asks about the case. In other words, she uses her questions and answers to direct the reader's attention to what she considers relevant thereby displacing other questions that may lead to understanding the case from other points of view.

6 Shaping and Controlling The Reader's Answers: Leading The Reader to The Right Definition

Wilson also *gives the reader the answers* to her questions. This practice enables the reader to check one's own answers by comparing them to her answers to ensure that the reader's answers are correct from Wilson's point of view. Providing "correct" answers, and in some instances, arguments in support of her answers amount to exerting a further degree of control over the reader's definitions and judgments in that alternative answers are not considered. In this way, the reader's answers are shaped and controlled.

Wilson's search for, and discovery of, a definition of the right to liberty illustrates how, by providing answers to questions, she shapes and controls the reader's answers thereby avoiding alternative ways to understand issues that are not in accord with her point of view. Wilson confronts the reader with the problem of how to discover an answer to the question "What is meant by the right to liberty in the context of the abortion issue?" by explicitly posing this question. There is more than one route that could be taken to answer this question and the right to liberty could be defined in a number of ways. But Wilson leads the reader to the answer by telling the reader the method to use. The method is to consider the purpose of the **Charter** and the purpose of the right to liberty. She presents the execution of this strategy as if it is the sole way to answer the question. Alternatives are not considered.[27]

The strategy Wilson follows to discover the purpose of the **Charter** is to lead the reader through a series of interpretations of the relationship between the **Charter**, liberty, and human dignity drawn from MacCormick's writings and legally authorised sources. She specifies a potentially broad and general analysis of the topic by initiating a discussion of the relationship between the individual and the state from the point of view of classical liberalism. Then she further develops this discussion by presenting various versions of the "inextricable tie" between the **Charter**, liberty, and human dignity before presenting the reader with her version of the purpose of the **Charter**. The purpose of the **Charter** is to achieve human dignity.

Her next step is to lead the reader to accept her definition of the right to liberty as the correct definition. She leads the reader to her definition through a series of definitions of liberty. Each definition is formulated more specifically than its predecessor. She begins by claiming that all the **Charter** rights express the idea of human dignity and that the **Charter** is founded on one aspect of human dignity, namely *"the right to make fundamental decisions without interference from the state"*.[28] She claims this right is an aspect of the right to liberty. This general definition of the right to liberty is consistent with classical liberal theory.

Wilson re-defines this general definition of liberty in more specific terms by simply presenting increasingly specific interpretations or definitions of the right to liberty. She states that the right to liberty ". . .*grants to the individual a degree of autonomy in making decisions of fundamental personal importance.*"[29] In that definition, she stresses the characteristics of the decision insofar as the right to liberty is concerned with protecting "*decisions of fundamental personal importance*". Wilson then takes the reader back to the general statement that the proper scope of the *right to liberty requires the state to respect personal decisions made by citizens, but does not require them to approve them,* and says that this view is consistent with American jurisprudence. She leads the reader through American cases in which, according to the right to equality and the right to privacy in the American Constitution, the state could not interfere with certain fundamental personal decisions concerned with education, child rearing, procreation, marriage, or contraception to a more specific definition of the right to liberty. Now the right to liberty is interpreted or defined by stating that the right to liberty ". . .*guarantees to every individual a degree of personal autonomy over important decisions intimately affecting their private lives.*"[30] After taking the reader through an analysis of the nature of a woman's decision whether or not to terminate her pregnancy, she presents her final definition of the right to liberty. The right to liberty ". . .*gives a woman the right to decide for herself whether or not to terminate her pregnancy.*"[31] The reader is invited to agree with her interpretation or definition because it is presented as the only plausible definition and is somehow derived or discovered by following the one and only plausible method of discovery.

More specifically, Wilson uses questions, definitions and judgments to shape and control the reader's own questions and answers about the case in order to lead the reader to understand and to solve the legal problem in the same way as she presents the case. Wilson's questions and answers play a crucial role in persuading the reader to agree with each step in the problem-solving process. Wilson wants to convince the reader that the questions she formulates are relevant and that her answers are correct. For example, when she defines her version of the constitutional problem, she raises crucial substantive questions that are not, and cannot be, answered by the competing "proceduralist" position and she does this in order to undermine the competing position. When she searches for the meaning of the right to liberty, she presents her line of questioning as the sole plausible method of discovery and her definition of the right to liberty as the correct definition. And her ultimate solution to the problem is presented as an answer that has been proven to be correct.

From the point of view of conventional analyses of legal justification, the role of discovery as a justificatory strategy might be understood as inappropriate. It is currently accepted that the process of discovery is a subjective, unconscious, irrational procedure and that proposed legal rulings must be subject to an objective, rational, logical process of legal justification before accepting them. In this way, it is argued, judicial decision-making is constrained and checked. It would follow that Wilson's use of the discovery process to justify her decision would be unacceptable. Her strategy of legal justification is personal, non-logical, and is dominated by questions and answers. So, questions concerning the adequacy of Wilson's rhetorical justification can be raised. Is her rhetorical treatment of the problem an adequate invitation to the reader to reach one's own evaluation of the problem? If her opinion was expressed in an axiomatic style would this be an adequate invitation to the reader to come to one' own justification or opinion? Or is the adequacy of her justification assumed by the legal community because she use accepted styles of legal authorization? The problem is whether or not the limitations of either axiomatic or rhetorical expression can be recognized in a sufficiently educated consciousness, that is by a person who understands not only the full context in which a problem has emerged and in which their solutions are sought, but also the manner in which a reader needs to supplement either presentation to reach adequate comprehension. Or is the problem (as current analyses of legal justification suggest) simply whether or not a decision can be expressed in a form that would be acceptable to legal professionals. In this scenario whether or not a particular decision is legally justified would be more or less assumed and a rational reconstruction of the legal opinion would follow. But these questions raise issues that are very complex and will be saved for Chapter Eight.[32]

7 A Woman's Point of View as A Justificatory Strategy

Wilson uses the uniqueness of a woman's point of view as part of her justificatory strategy. The women's standpoint she presents is created by distinguishing it from aspects of a men's point of view and aspects of classical liberalism. The women's point of view presented by Wilson comprises a special type of reasoning performed by women, special interpretations of key terms - liberty, dignity, and private - in the context of the abortion issue, and the claim that women have a right to reproduce or not. She constructs this point of view by invoking the language of Carol Gilligan on women's decision-making, citing Noreen Burrows' work on women's rights, and by re-defining the meanings of key terms in the context of the abortion issue. Surprisingly, Wilson's account of her discovery process plays a crucial role in the formulation of these aspects of a women's perspective. The discovery process captures how women make decisions and it helps manage the tensions and conflicts between a woman's point of view and that of men and classical liberalism.

From a conventional point of view, Wilson's use of the women's point of view is an effective justificatory strategy. She justifies her solution to the constitutional problem by claiming to be doing better law than Dickson and Beetz by adhering more strictly to the conventional strategies of legal justification than they do. She asks relevant questions they neglect. She addresses substantive issues, not simply procedural matters. She analyses the right to liberty whereas Dickson and Beetz do not. In so doing, Wilson follows conventional legal methodology when she defines the right to liberty in the context of the abortion issue. The outcome is justified by defining the right to liberty in the **Charter** according to the accepted method and by citing cases and legal academics. These arguments are acceptable because Wilson follows the conventional methods of justification.

The women's point of view, as a women's justificatory strategy, can be understood as complementing traditional methods of legal justification by offering an important perspective that should be considered. On this view, Wilson is offering an additional way to justify her legal judgment. This strategy is welcome. After all, the issue is abortion and Wilson contributes a relevant perspective to consider - a woman's point of view. It is women, not men who become pregnant and it is women who seem better placed to make such judgments. Also, it is women like Wilson, not men, who are in a better position to evaluate such issues. The women's point of view provides a more thorough analysis of the relevant issues than that of conventional analyses.

7.1 Women's Decision-Making

An important aspect of the women's perspective she presents is the special way that women reason. In fact, Wilson portrays the discovery process as an explanation of how women reason. Her portrait of the discovery process embodies women's reasoning. Not only does she argue that the decision whether or not to have an abortion is a women's decision, but she also portrays her own legal decision (her analysis of the abortion issue) as a woman's decision.

The decision, whether or not to have an abortion, is presented by Wilson as (1) *a special type of decision* and as (2) a woman's decision. This decision is special in that situations in which the decision is made are complex. Moreover, this decision is made in light of how a woman understands herself and her relationship to others. Wilson claims that

> This decision is one that will have profound psychological, economic, and social consequences for the pregnant woman. The circumstances giving rise to it can be complex and varied and there may be, and usually are, powerful considerations militating in opposite directions. It is a decision that deeply reflects the way the woman thinks about herself and her relationship to others and to society at large. It is not just a medical decision; it is a profound social and ethical one as well. Her response to it will be the response of the whole person.[33]

Not only is the decision whether or not to have an abortion a special type of decision, but Wilson presents it as a *women's decision*, not a man's decision. She asserts that

> It is probably impossible for a man to respond, even imaginatively, to such a dilemma not just because it is outside the realm of his personal experience. . .but because he can relate to it only by objectifying it, thereby eliminating the subjective elements of the female psyche which are at the heart of the dilemma.[34]

Presumably, her point is that this decision should be made only by women. Whether or not to have an abortion is a women's question to be answered only by women. Men cannot even understand the problem faced by pregnant women. In this quotation she also suggests that women's decision-making is superior to men and is beyond the scrutiny of men.

How does this portrait of women's decision-making work as a justificatory strategy? It might seem that the persuasive power of Wilson's strategy of portraying the decision whether or not to have an abortion as a woman's issue owes more to stifling the potential dissent of men than it does to persuading the reader to agree with her analysis of the issue. As I stated above, she implies that a woman's decision whether or not to have an abortion cannot be scrutinised by men. You might expect that such a distinctive perspective would be an ineffective justificatory strategy insofar as it conflicts with more conventional justificatory strategies. But the women's point of view is an effective justificatory strategy. What is fascinating is how Wilson uses the discovery process to manage this tension or conflict.

The tension between a distinct women's point of view and a male perspective takes a number of forms. The tension arises regarding the nature of Wilson's decision as a woman's decision. Not only is her decision portrayed as a special type that involves the whole person, but this decision is a woman's decision. Taking the discovery process as the embodiment of women's reasoning Wilson's decision is made by asking questions and searching for answers in an effort to solve real problems and to address substantive issues. It is a personal quest that engages the whole person and involves complex considerations.

Presumably, this strategy of justification would compete with conventional justificatory strategies that are dominated by logic and rules in an effort to solve what are seen as merely procedural problems. It follows then that, in contrast to Wilson's strategy, conventional strategies would be abstract, objective, and legalistic.

Women's reasoning can be understood as conflicting with men's reasoning in another way. Not only is it impossible for men to understand the dilemma, but Wilson even suggests women's reasoning is superior to men's reasoning. Men's reasoning is portrayed as incapable of adequately solving the abortion issue.

Yet Wilson's portrait of women's decision-making supports her claim that the decision whether or not to have an abortion is a woman's decision which, in turn, supports her definition of liberty in the context of the abortion issue. In other words, the portrait of women's reasoning supports her own solution to the problem. Also, her report of how she reached her decision supports this portrait. Her legal opinion is a case study of how women reason. As a woman, she is qualified to analyse the abortion issue. Further, she is authorised to use the discovery process as a justificatory strategy as that is how women reach decisions.

Presenting the decision whether or not to have an abortion as a decision that is special and is a women's decision is consistent with the way Wilson casts her own legal decision. Just as the decision whether or not to have an abortion is special because it involves complex considerations - psychological, social, medical, ethical - Wilson's legal decision is special because it involves, and recognises, complex considerations. She portrays the legal problem she must solve as complex and involving many issues - legal, psychological, social, political. Her line of solution is contextual; she does not analyse the abortion issue in a narrow legalistic fashion. She attempts to address substantive issues.

Just as the decision whether or not to have an abortion is a woman's decision, her legal decision is a woman's decision. Her account of how she solved the constitutional problem can be understood as an example of how women reason - a method of making decisions that is not performed by men. Just as a woman deciding whether or not to have an abortion faces her dilemma, Wilson explicitly addresses the substantive issue, the deeper issue, the real problem. Just as the abortion decision is oriented to solving a problem, Wilson's line of solution is comprised of a complex problem-solving procedure. Just as the abortion is a personal decision, Wilson's legal opinion is personal in that she explicitly identifies the questions and answers and the values she affirms that lead her to search for and solve the constitutional problem.

By contrast, Wilson's portrays the reasoning of her male colleagues - Dickson and Beetz - in a quite different light. Wilson suggests that women's decision-making is superior to men's decision-making and beyond their comprehension. She caricatures their opinions as being merely procedural, academic, and pointless because they fail to address the real problem, the deeper substantive issue. Since men are unable to understand and evaluate a woman's decision whether or not to have an abortion, presumably Dickson and Beetz (and by inference, other men) are unable to understand and evaluate her solution to this case. Both issues are women's issues.

The implication is that male reasoning is concerned with mere procedure rather than substantive issues, is abstract rather than contextual, is objective rather than personal, and comprises the logical application of rules rather than an intelligent problem-solving procedure.

But Wilson effectively manages these tensions by arguing that the type of reasoning used to make decisions about abortion is women's reasoning. Women's reasoning is portrayed as crucial to solving this problem. By analysing the problem from a woman's point of view, not only can her opinion be understood as more thorough analysis than that of the men - Dickson and Beetz - but the inclusion of a woman's point of view can also be understood as essential to answering the constitutional question. Because the decision affects women their voices should be, and must be, heard.

In summary, the decision whether or not to have an abortion is a woman's decision in the same way as Wilson's decision is a woman's decision. Women reason about the abortion issue as Wilson does about the constitutional problem. Women solve problems by asking questions and searching for, and discovering, solutions, and some problems are particular to them. Chapter Eight will return to the strengths and the weaknesses of this view. Our concern here, and in that final chapter, is methodological. In another context detailed consideration of the weaknesses of the contrast would be relevant, but they would distract us here from the central issue of basic procedure.

7.2 Women's Rights

A distinct women's perspective is presented by Wilson when she contrasts men's rights and women's rights. Wilson uses Burrows writings to discuss men's rights in terms of men versus the state, whereas women's rights are presented in terms of women's struggle for equality with men. According to Burrows, the struggle for human rights since the Eighteenth Century has consisted in men struggling to assert their dignity and common humanity against the state, but the more recent struggle for women's rights has been "a struggle to place women in the same position as men."[35] The consequence has been that the right to reproduce has been ignored because it is not part of the existing set of male rights. In Wilson's opinion, the right to reproduce or not is to be properly perceived "as an integral part of a modern woman's struggle to assert her dignity and worth as a human being."[36] Thus, it seems that the right to reproduce or not is both part of a woman's right to liberty and a condition or means for a woman to achieve liberty.

The claim that women have a right to reproduce or not helps support her final interpretation of liberty, namely that the right to liberty ". . .gives a woman the right to decide for herself whether or not to terminate her pregnancy."[37] That discussion introduces the idea that rights cover reproduction. Wilson subsequently specifies the general attribution of rights in the context of the abortion issue for her own purposes.

Wilson's account of women's rights can be understood as potentially conflicting with men's rights. But this tension is managed by Wilson by presenting women as being behind men in their struggle for human dignity and by the claim that reproductive rights have been ignored. Hence women are not a threat to men's pursuit of dignity via rights and she is simply contributing an insight that has been left out.

As part of her formulation of a woman's point of view Wilson uses the discovery process to present and to justify interpretations of key terms. She uses the discovery process to define "dignity", "liberty", and "private" from a woman's point of view. These key words are initially defined in accord with classical liberal notions and then re-interpreted from a women's point of view. In the liberal context, these terms are presented in terms of an individual's relationship to the state. "Liberty" is defined in terms of the line between the individual and the state, in particular protecting individuals from the state. But later she re-defines "liberty" as the right to choose whether or not to have an abortion. Initially, "dignity" is presented in terms of the state not interfering with individual choice, self-respect, contentment, freedom of conscience. But later these aspects of "dignity" (presented in terms of the individual versus the state) are transformed into a woman's struggle for her dignity. The right to reproduce or not is presented as part of a woman's struggle to assert her dignity and worth by placing women in the same position as men. She initially defines "private" in terms of the boundary between personal decisions and the state, namely protecting personal decisions from the state. But later "private" is re-formulated to cover a special type of decision - a women's decision whether or not to have an abortion. The decision is "private" also in the sense that the dilemma cannot be understand by men.

The re-interpretation of these terms is a key part of her justificatory strategy. Wilson re-interprets these terms so that they cover the abortion issue, thereby supporting her definition of the right to libery in the context of the abortion issue and ultimately supporting her judgment that s. 251 of the **Criminal Code** violates s. 7 of the Charter. "Liberty" gives a woman the right to decide whether to end her pregnancy. The right to reproduce or not is part of a woman's "dignity". The decision is a "private" decision. Her definition of the right to liberty and her judgment that s. 251 violates the right to liberty read as the inevitable outcome of Wilson's re-interpretation of these terms.

8 Conclusion

Superficially, Wilson's explanation of how she solved the constitutional problem appears to be a novel and intelligent method of legal problem-solving that yields a just solution. Yet, after closer scrutiny, we find that she ignores and suppresses relevant issues and alternative methods of discovery and problem-solving. The rhetoric of discovery turns out to be an authoritarian monologue. We read the case her way.

What makes the woman's point of view an effective part of Wilson's justificatory strategy also opens it to criticism. Much of her account of a woman's point of view has to be inferred and presumed by the reader. It is impossible to pin down her particular standpoint. Hence it is difficult to criticise her point of view because it is vague and general. Her description of the decision to have an abortion, her definition of key terms, and her explanation of women's rights are all superficial and broad. A problem, however, is her portrait of men's reasoning, namely that men cannot understand the abortion dilemma and her suggestion that women's reasoning is superior to that of men. Such claims seems over-stated and, at the very least, require supporting methodological arguments.

Wilson's perspective does not lead to a coherent position. It has weaknesses. It is rhetorically unsound. Her presentation is an inadequate invitation to arrive at one's own justification, one's own value judgments regarding the problem and its solution. If her opinion is translated into an axiomatic expression (or rationally reconstructed) her positon remains incoherent. The reasons for her solution are not evident. By contrast, a more suitable presentation could invite the reader to ask the question "What is the most suitable solution to the problem?" and to answer the question "Why is this proposed solution the most suitable?"

Finally, my analysis of Wilson's legal opinion suggests another type of self-attention that is not "looking-in", but rather identifying elements in the reader that are part of the process of searching for solutions to problems. Such self-attention would comprise reading a legal opinion in the light of one's knowledge of judging and the issues relevant to a problem to arrive at a judgment of value. Here the presentation of the decision would be understood as an invitation to follow Wilson's arguments, to evaluate her reasons and her solution, and to make a judgment of value. Discovery in law, then, cannot be understood until the reader investigates herself or himself solving problems. But a solution to these problems must be saved for later. The main aim here was to draw attention to the refreshing focus of Wilson's work, her consideration for the discovery process both in justification and communication.

Let us return to the actual performance of legal professionals. In the following Chapter we take another step towards identifying relevant elements in our problem and its solution. A particular case is discussed, this time a relatively uncontroversial case. Again, the discovery process is the central topic and the approach leads us closer to the strategy required to come to grips with the spectrum of problems raised in these chapters.

1 *R v Morgentaler, Smoling and Scott* [1988] 1 S.C.R. 161-172.
2 S. 7 of the *Canadian Charter of Rights and Freedoms* states: "Everyone has the right to life, liberty, and securi-

ty of the person and the right not to be deprived thereof except in accordance with the principals of fundamental justice."

3 The first case to explicitly state it was dealing with substantive issues was the *Re B.C. Motor Vehicle Motor Vehicle Act* (1985) 2 S.C.R. 486.

4 The *Queen v Henry Morgentaler* (1990), 99 **N.S.R.** (2d) 293 (T.D.)

5 The *Queen v Henry Morgentaler* (1991), 104 **N.S.R.** (2d) 361 (C.A.)

6 *R v Morgentaler*, [1993] 3 **S.C.R.** 463.

7 *Morgentaler v P.E.I. (Min of Health & Social Services)* (1994), 112 D.L.R. (44) 756 (P.E.I. S.C.) - under appeal

8 *Morgentaler v The A-G (N.B.) et al.* (C.F. No. F/M/24/94)

9 The **Charter of Rights** is part of the Canadian Constitution and the **Canadian Bill of Rights** is federal legislation.

10 This question and the other quotations in italics in this chapter are not underlined in Wilson's text.

11 *R v Morgentaler*, 162.

12 ibid., 53.

13 ibid., 171.

14 ibid., 172

15 Wilson does not define or interpret "life" in s. 7 of the Charter in her legal opinion.

16 ibid., 171.

17 ibid., 172.

18 ibid., 172.

19 ibid., 172.

20 ibid., 172.

21 ibid., 172.

22 In that case, Dickson advocated discovering the meaning of **Charter** rights by considering the "purpose" of the **Charter** in general and the "purpose" of the particular right in question.

23 Aristotle, **On Rhetoric**, trans. G. Kennedy (Oxford: Oxford University Press, 1991).

24 He also identified a non-artistic mode of persuasion which involves presenting the testimony of witnesses. Artistic modes of persuasion, on the other hand, are modes of persuasion invented by the speaker. For example, two common lines of argument Aristotle identified were arguments using enthymemes (conclusions with supporting reasons) and illustrations. He further identified other lines of argument, for example arguments from a previous judgment about the same or a similar matter, arguments from definitions, and arguments from consequences.

25 For a general discussion of this aspect of persuasion see G. Barden, **After Principles**, (Notre Dame: University of Notre Dame Press, 1990), 128-131.

26 *R v Morgentaler*, 161-62.

27 For example, she does not compare or explain why her interpretation or definition of liberty is more suitable than others. Remembering that in this case three doctors have been indicted, perhaps one way to answer the constitutional question would be to define the right to liberty from their point of view as a right to perform safe medical procedures when a person's physical or psychological health is threatened and she has consented to the procedure. She does not evaluate why the reasons that support the judgment that the law *should not* be used to compel a woman to carry a foetus to term are more persuasive than the reasons why the law *should* be allowed to compel a woman to carry a foetus to term. She neither explains *why* nor *how* a woman's right to decide whether or not to terminate her pregnancy leads to greater human dignity nor what she means by human dignity.

28 ibid., 166.

29 ibid., 166.

30 ibid., 171.

31 ibid., 172.

32 The problem of axiomatic and rhetorical expression had best be treated in the context of my answer to the question "What is the nature of discovery in legal decision-making?" The related problem is the connection between deductive and inductive logic.

33 ibid., 171.

34 ibid., 171.

35 ibid., 172.

36 ibid., 172.

37 ibid., 172.

4

Investigating "Discovery" in The Arbitration Process

1 Introduction

How do legal decision-makers 'actually' go about the process of reaching decisions? I began this book by presenting the reflections of legal theorists on this topic. Next I suggested that the cognitive psychologists' accounts of problem-solving would be relevant to understanding discovery in legal decison-making. Now it is time to address this issue. In my effort to answer this question I investigated 'discovery' in arbitration. I interviewed an arbitrator and then analysed his own account of how he discovered a solution to a dispute.

Legal theorists have concentrated solely on judicial decision-making and have more or less ignored other legal contexts in which people reason. They, for example, have neglected to study reasoning in the arbitration process. Yet arbitration has become an important method to resolve labour and commercial disputes. Not only are experts in particular areas employed to resolve disputes, but many people use arbitration because it is a less expensive and less time-consuming process than recourse to the judicial system. It seems that an examination of reasoning in the arbitration process is warranted.

This chapter explores the nature of 'discovery' in the arbitration process. I investigate the 'actual' decision-making process whereby an arbitrator resolved a dispute in a Canadian insurance case. His process of discovery is studied by examining the method he devised and followed to resolve the dispute. I interviewed the arbitrator and recorded his own account of how he set about to discover a solution to the problem. His account of his decision-making process revealed a pattern of asking and answering questions and of discovering relations similar to the cognitive psychologists' account of problem-solving and creativity in Chapter Two. Like the other chapters before it, the aim of this chapter is to present materials relevant to discovery in law, not to present a comprehensive and coherent solution.

2 The Dispute

The arbitrator had been asked by two insurance companies whether he would resolve a dispute between them regarding insurance benefits. He was provided with a written description of the 'facts' that the insurance companies considered relevant and a statement of what they regarded as the problem to be solved. The insurance companies agreed on the 'facts' of the case and that the problem was which company should pay Schedule B no fault insurance benefits to an injured woman. The circumstances were that two cars were parked near each other - the woman's car and an empty adjacent car. The woman was opening the trunk of her own car when a moving car hit the adjacent parked car which, in turn, hit the woman. The dispute was between the company that insured the woman's vehicle and the company that insured the adjacent car. The arbitrator's task or problem had been to judge whether Company A or Company B should pay Schedule B insurance benefits to the injured woman. The insurance companies agreed that either one of them was liable.

The companies also agreed that the key question that had to be answered in order to resolve the dispute was whether or not the woman was an occupant of her own car at the time she was injured. (The definition of 'insured person' in the **Insurance Act** R.S.N.S. 1989, c. 231 covers (a) any person who is an occupant of the described automobile and (b) the insured person if they are an occupant of any other automobile. See Appendix A.) Each company provided the arbitrator with copies of the relevant legislation - Schedule B to Part VI of the **Insurance Act** and the Claims Agreement, Insurance Bureau of Canada, Section 111, Rule 11A, of which both insurers are signatories. (see Appendix B) Company A included a list of five cases they claimed supported the judgment that they should not have to pay Schedule B benefits because, in their opinion, the woman was *not* an *occupant*, whereas Company B simply stated they were 'not responsible'. (The companies' submissions were not prepared by lawyers. The arbitrator did not hear oral arguments.)

My analysis of 'discovery' in the arbitration process begins by presenting an arbitrator's account of how he discovered a solution to the dispute. It *describes* the problem-solving process in which the arbitrator was engaged by tracing the questions he asked and answered in order to solve the problem. I then consider the nature of 'discovery' in the arbitrator's problem-solving process before briefly discussing introspection.

3 The Arbitrator's Process of Discovery

The following analysis is an examination of the structure of the lines of inquiry initiated and followed by the arbitrator in his effort to resolve the dispute between Company A and Company B. The analysis traces the method followed by the arbitrator to solve the dispute, especially the questions he asked and answered as he explicitly stated in the interview. The questions presented in this section are a selection of the questions he asked. It is impossible to reproduce every question asked and every question answered by the arbitrator in his process of discovery. He may not have been aware of all the questions he asked and answered. He even may have forgotten questions that he asked. Consequently, only what he considered to be the important questions are presented.

3.1 Searching For and Discovering The Overarching Question

The arbitrator began his discovery process by asking, what he called, the 'big question', 'What am I supposed to decide in order to resolve this dispute?' He read the documents sent to him by the companies to discover what he ultimately had to decide. Reading provoked questions such as 'What is the problem?' 'What happened?' He stated he wanted to understand the problematic situation as the companies understood it. Drawing a diagram of the cars helped him understand the situation. He also read the **Insurance Act** and the Claims Agreement and discovered that the 'big question' - the overarching question - the companies wanted him to answer was *'Who pays Schedule B insurance benefits and why?'* But he also wanted to know, accurately and precisely, what the problem was. He wanted to know, exactly, what the dispute between the two companies was about.

3.2 Searching For and Discovering A Method to Answer The Overarching Question

3.2.1 Searching For and Discovering The Key Question

The two companies offered him a method to answer the overarching question. They suggested the dispute could be resolved by determining *whether or not the woman was an occupant of her car at the time she was injured.* The companies' statements provoked the arbitrator to ask further questions - 'Is the companies' question concerning whether or not the woman is an *occupant* the "right" question?' He wanted to determine whether their formulation of the issue is the 'right' question to ask and answer in order to determine which company should pay insurance benefits.

He stated he wanted to find a method to follow in order to discover who should pay. The questions he asked himself were 'What method do I use to discover who should pay and why they should pay?' 'What rule do I follow?' 'What guidelines are there for me to use?' He drew on past experience to answer these questions. He considered that the legislation might possibly provide a method - rules and guidelines - that would help him answer the question above. So, he turned to the legislation and he discovered what the consequences of judging the woman to be an *occupant* would be and what the consequences of judging her not to be an *occupant* would be. Company A must pay the insurance benefits if the woman is an *occupant*, whereas Company B must pay the insurance benefits if the woman is *not* an *occupant*.

3.2.2 Testing The Key Question

The question proposed by the two companies as the issue in the case was tested by the arbitrator to judge whether or not, in his opinion, it was the 'right question' to ask. His investigation of the concrete situation, the **Insurance Act,** and the Claims Agreement led to his judgment that the companies' formulation of the issue was, indeed, the 'right question' to ask in order to resolve the dispute. The 'right question' - the key question - to answer was *'Was this woman an occupant of her car when* *she was injured?'* By answering this crucial and more basic question he would be able to answer the overarching question, thereby resolving the dispute.

The arbitrator also stated the questions that he did not have to answer. He did not have to determine the extent of the compensation and he did not have to formulate a general rule that would cover situations that might occur in the future. This statement raises a question concerning the extent to which the arbitration process is similar to the judging process, a topic I have not examined in this paper.

3.2.3 Searching For A Method to Answer The Key Question

The arbitrator initiated a search for a method to answer the key question 'Was this woman an *occupant* of the vehicle when she was injured?' He judged that answering his key question depended on asking a more basic question. He set out to answer the question *'What is an occupant as contemplated in the Section B provisions of the Insurance Act?'* On previous occasions, in order to answer similar questions, his method had been to search for answers in Nova Scotian legislation. So, in this case, he searched the relevant legislation - the **Insurance Act** - for an answer. But he discovered that the legislation did not provide him with an answer. The problem he identified was that occupant is not defined in the **Insurance Act**. So far, he did not know who counted as an occupant. Although he was unfamiliar with the Claims Agreement, he judged that it possibly might provide a rule or guideline that would enable him to answer his key question. But he judged that it does not provide an answer to his key question because occupant is not defined in the Claims Agreement. Because occupant is not defined in the Act or in the Claims Agreement he knew that he must continue his search for a definition or method to define occupant.

While reading the Claims Agreement the arbitrator raised questions about its relationship to the **Insurance Act**. The fact that the Claims Agreement speaks only of *pedestrians* provoked the question 'Is the Claims Agreement consistent with the **Insurance Act** which speaks only of *occupants?*' 'Is a *non-occupant* under the **Insurance Act** the same as a *pedestrian* under the Claims Agreement?' In answer to these two questions he judged that the **Insurance Act** and the Claims Agreement are consistent insofar as *non-occupant* means the same as *pedestrian*. (In other words, in this case *non-occupant* and *pedestrian* cover the same class of persons.) He also asked the question 'Does the Claims Agreement have precedence over the **Insurance Act?**' But he discovered that by answering the two previous questions he did not need to answer this question. He judged that the different terms under the **Insurance Act** and the Claims Agreement would make no difference in the test used to differentiate between an *occupant* and *non-occupant* or between a *non-pedestrian* and a *pedestrian*. The same test could be used in each context. He noted that answers to these questions also supported his previous judgment that, indeed, the key question '"Is the woman an *occupant?*" is the "right question" to ask.'

He again asked the key question 'Is this woman an *occupant?*' and continued his search for help in defining *occupant*. He stated he was searching for a rule or guideline that would enable him to judge whether or not the woman was an *occupant*. He

examined the 'Words and Phrases' Section of the **Canadian Abridgement**. There
was nothing there to help him. Next he examined the 'Words and Phrases' Section of
the **Nova Scotia Reports** which was no help. He still wanted an answer to his basic
question - *'What is an occupant?*

He repeated his key question 'Is the woman in this case, who was hit by another
car when she was opening the trunk of her car, an *occupant?*' He continued the
search for a method to answer his key question based on methods he employed in
past cases. His answer to this question was that, according to the common use of the
term, the woman would *not* be an *occupant* because she was not *physically situated in
the vehicle* when she was injured. He also re-asked the basic question, *'What is an
occupant?*' He searched for a definition of occupant in the **Oxford Concise
Dictionary.** It defined *occupant* as *one who resides or is in a place.* He interpreted this
as meaning *physically in a place.* He judged that if he accepted this definition of *occupant*, the woman would not be an *occupant.*

But he continued to search for other possible answers to the basic question. He
asked 'Is this answer appropriate?' 'Are there other ways to define *occupant?*' To be
specific, he asked 'Does *occupant* have an *extended meaning* in the common law that
is broader than the meaning of *occupant* in common usage and in the dictionary?'
He knew from his knowledge of other cases that the common law meaning of terms
sometimes differs from common usage.

To answer the question immediately above he initiated a line of inquiry. The
method he selected was to find, and to analyse, relevant case law. He asked the question 'How does the legislation of other Canadian provinces define *occupant?*' Again
he stressed he was searching for a rule, guidelines or a method to define *occupant.*
He found, read and considered a selection of cases dealing with the meaning of the
term *occupant.* He examined the cases in no particular order. He wanted to know
what the legislation of the other provinces stated. He reasoned that 'if Nova Scotia
does not have a definition of *occupant*, do the other provinces have one and, if they
do, will it help me define *occupant?*' He discovered that one other province does not
define *occupant*, but that four provinces define *occupant* in broader terms than in
common usage or the dictionary.

He identified what he called a dilemma. There are two competing ways to define
occupant - (1) according to common usage and the dictionary where *occupant* means
physically situated in a place or (2) according to an extended meaning of *occupant*
that would lead to a *broader definition* than physically situated in a place.

3.2.4 Searching For and Discovering A Method to Test The Answers to The Key Question

The discovery of two ways to define *occupant* provoked the arbitrator's question
'Which method of defining the term should I adopt?' He posed his question more
specifically as 'How do I judge, in Nova Scotia, if *occupant* means *physically situated
in a vehicle* or if it has some sort of *extended meaning?*' These questions led him to
ask himself 'Where do I start?' 'How do I answer that question?' His method was to
return to the cases in search of a method to help him judge which one of the two pos-

sible ways of defining occupant he should adopt. He analysed the relevant cases in detail. He found an Ontario case, *Kyriazis v Roval Insurance Company of Canada (1991), 82 DLR (4th) 691 (Ont Gen Div)*, in which the judge stated that in provinces that do not define *occupant* a method is used to determine whether or not a person is an *occupant*. The arbitrator noted that other provinces had dealt with exactly the same question he must answer. The judge in *Kyriazis* stated that these other provinces used a 'zone of connection test' to determine who counted as an *occupant*. The test involved assessing the degree of physical proximity between the injured person and the vehicle. A person did not have to be physically in the vehicle to be an *occupant*. It was sufficient if the person was getting into the vehicle or out of it. The arbitrator noted that *perhaps* this is a method he should adopt. In fact, he asked himself "Do I want to adopt this test?"

The method he used to test the two ways to define *occupant* was to carefully examine how the 'zone of connection test' was used in other cases and to consider judges' comments on the test. He examined the 'facts' and outcomes of each case and evaluated the strengths and weaknesses of the 'zone of connection test'. He stated the *Kyriazis* case was especially important to him. He agreed with the criticisms of the 'zone of connection test' offered in that case. The test was said to be cumbersome, subjective, imprecise and inconsistent with the plain ordinary meaning of words. He also considered that these factors were reasons for not adopting this test in his case. But, at this point, he had not yet judged which method of defining *occupant* he should adopt.

He applied the 'zone of connection test' to his case to judge whether or not the woman would be an *occupant* if he adopted the test. He asked 'What would be the consequences if I adopted the "zone of connection test"?' His answer was that the woman had less connection between herself and her car than in the cases where a zone of connection was used. He judged that even if he adopted the 'zone of connection test' the woman would be outside the zone and hence would not be an *occupant*. She was neither getting into her car nor getting out of it. She was opening the trunk of her car.

He made other discoveries as he read the cases. He discovered that, even in the cases where *occupant* is given an extended meaning by legislation, in the sense that the term covers situations wider than *physically situated in an automobile*, the courts have interpreted the term narrowly or restrictively. He discovered that courts only applied the *extended meaning* of *occupant* when they were authorised by legislation. If the situation was not covered by the literal terms of the definition, then the person was not an *occupant*. In other words, a person getting out of a car would be an *occupant* only if the legislation specified it. He judged that this discovery would be consistent with interpreting *occupant* in Nova Scotia as meaning *physically situated in an automobile*. He reasoned that, in Nova Scotia, where the legislation does not specifically extend the meaning of *occupant* to cover, for example, getting into and out of cars, then the term should not be given an *extended meaning*. He tentatively judged that the term occupant in the Nova Scotia **Insurance Act** should mean *physically situated in an automobile*.

Other factors the arbitrator considered relevant to the question "Should I define *occupant* as *physically situated in the vehicle* or adopt an *extended meaning* of the term?" was his desire not to create new rules unless it was necessary. He was reluctant to extend the definition of occupant in the absence of supporting Nova Scotian legislation. He reasoned that if the Nova Scotia Legislature wanted *occupant* to have an *extended meaning* it would have spelled it out in the legislation.

He also considered that if he adopted the definition of *occupant* as *physically situated in a vehicle* that this definition would be consistent with the outcome of cases in other provincial jurisdictions. He was also concerned, if at all possible, that his solution should be consistent with other legislation he considered relevant. By adopting the plain ordinary meaning of occupant he would be following the **Interpretation Act** which, in his opinion, directed him to adopt the plain ordinary meaning of words unless it was not appropriate to do so. An extended meaning of *occupant* would only be authorised, in his judgment, if the plain meaning of the term was not appropriate.

After considering all these factors, the arbitrator judged that *occupant* in the Section B provisions in the **Insurance Act** should be defined according to the plain ordinary meaning of the term and mean *physically situate in the vehicle*. He rejected the method of giving *occupant* an *extended meaning*. He was confident that this judgment was correct because he could not think of anything else he should consider.

3.2.5 Discovering An Answer to The Key Question

He asked himself 'Was this woman physically situated in her car when she was injured?' He remembered the facts. The woman was standing behind the car. He answered his question 'No, she was not physically in her car when she was injured.' He judged that 'The woman was *not* an *occupant* of her car when she was injured.'

3.3 Discovering The Answer to The Overarching Question

The arbitrator turned his attention to answering the overarching question - *'Which company should pay Schedule B insurance benefits to the woman*?' He judged that 'Company B must pay Schedule B insurance benefits to the woman because the woman was *not* an *occupant* of her own vehicle when she was injured.'

4 "Discovery" as A Problem-Solving Process

The arbitrator's method of discovery did not comprise the blind application of a set of rules or formula that provided him with a solution to the dispute. The solution was not the result of applying a set of rules. The arbitrator had to discover or invent a solution. Yet, although his process of discovery could not be predicted at the outset, his method was not an irrational activity. Subjectively, his questions arose spontaneously, but he did not ask them randomly hoping that the answer to one of them would hit the nail on the head thereby solving the dispute. Rather, his method was primarily a matter of systematic trial and error. It was not an irrational procedure. He attended to the relevant aspects of the materials he received, identified the problematic issues, actively sought answers to his questions, discovered intelligent solutions to problems, and critically tested the truth and suitability of his answers.

The best way to understand the arbitrator's process of discovery is to see it as a self-conscious and deliberate *problem-solving procedure*. The arbitrator was aware that he directed his attention to various aspects of the problem, knew that he asked himself questions, and knew that he must test proposed answers to questions before judging his solutions to be acceptable. He was aware that his strategy of resolving the problem is to correctly understand what the problem is and to search for a solution in legal materials. The arbitrator is an active problem-solver in the sense that he deliberately asked questions in order to find a solution to the problem, deliberately searches for answers in legal materials and tests his answers to judge their suitability.

The arbitrator's method of discovery comprised the pattern of the questions he asked and the answers he discovered that led him to a solution to the dispute. An analysis of the structure of his questions and answers reveals his method of discovery. He began by understanding and formulating an interpretation of the problematic situation. He captured the problem by posing the overarching question he ultimately had to answer - *'Should Company A or Should Company B pay Schedule B benefits to the injured woman and why?'* But the answer to this question was not immediately forthcoming. The method he initiated to answer this question was to first answer the key question 'Was this woman an *occupant* of her car at the time she was injured?' But he could not immediately answer this question. To answer that question he asked the more basic questions 'What method should I use to define *occupant*?' 'What is an *occupant*?' He searched for answers in the **Insurance Act**, the Claims Agreement, previous knowledge, the dictionary, and case law. He discovered two possible ways to define *occupant* - by common usage/dictionary or by a 'zone of connection test'. He asked 'Which method should I adopt?' He tested the 'zone of connection test'. He judged that the common usage/dictionary meaning of *occupant* is more suitable. He could now return to, and attempt to answer, the key question 'Is this woman an *occupant* of her car?' He judged she was *not* an *occupant* of her car. This answer enabled him to answer the overarching question 'Which company should pay Schedule B benefits?' He judged Company B must pay her benefits because under the legislation it must cover individuals, in situations like this one, who are struck by its insured's car and are *not occupants* of another car.

Discovering the solution to the *overarching question* depended on first discovering answers to other questions. Not only did answering the overarching question require an answer to a prior *key question*, but in order to answer the key question, prior more *basic questions* also had to be answered. Many of the arbitrator's important questions could not be answered until related questions were answered or until even more basic questions were asked and answered. The arbitrator's process of discovery comprised the emergence of relevant questions and the discovery of, and execution of, methods to answer these questions as they arose. It is this general strategy of discovery - posing a question that can only be answered after discovering and following a line of inquiry to answer more basic questions - that the arbitrator employed to resolve this dispute.

The arbitrator's questions arose spontaneously in the sense that he experienced them as 'popping into his head'. The search for an answer to the overarching question led to the emergence of a key question. The key question led to the emergence of other more basic questions. The awareness of the incompleteness of his answer or his inability to answer a question provoked another question and so on. The answer to each successive question complemented the answer to a previous question in that his successive answers became more comprehensive and accurate. It is in this fashion, by asking questions and seeking answers, that the arbitrator accumulated the knowledge that led him to discover answers to his key and overarching questions. The process of discovery, then, advances from discovering answers to simple questions to discovering a solution to a series of problems. The arbitrator's discovery process was an incremental process of discovering answers to related questions.

Solving the dispute depended on answering questions. Answers will not occur unless questions are asked. The arbitrator's answers depended on the questions he asked. His questions focused his attention on particular aspects of the problem that he considered relevant. His questions created the context in which his answers were relevant. Framing the question accurately narrowed the relation between the question and the answer by placing limits on what was considered an appropriate answer. His questions guided the inquiry toward answers to questions, toward a solution to the problem.

The successful resolution of this dispute also depended on asking the 'right' questions. A crucial part of the arbitrator's process of discovery, he says, was to discover and to formulate what he called the 'right question'. He asked a question whose answer he anticipated would be the key to solving the dispute. It was a question that went to the root of the problem, a question that captured the essence or heart of the matter. The question was '*Is the woman an occupant*?' The fact the arbitrator considered this question to be the 'right question' depended on him accurately and precisely interpreting the problematic situation. In turn, the arbitrator's interpretation of the problem depended on previous experience of similar cases, previous understanding of similar cases, and previous correct judgments regarding similar cases. In order to correctly understand the problem the arbitrator knew which factors were relevant and which factors were irrelevant in the case.

But the arbitrator's key question is not the only question that must be a 'right question'. The arbitrator's solution also depended on him asking other pertinent questions. The relevance to the problem of these questions depended on his previous knowledge. His knowledge of law, his knowledge of cases involving Schedule B benefits, and his knowledge gained by writing briefs, negotiating settlements, and arguing similar cases in court helped him formulate the 'right questions'. Where he directs his attention and the factors he considered important or relevant to solving the problem influenced the questions he asks. Knowing which factors are relevant and which factors are irrelevant in a particular situation depended on his familiarity with similar situations. By understanding the background of the problem, he knew what to expect. He knew what is and what is not problematic in the situation. In other words, knew which questions would probably help lead to the discovery of a solution and which questions probably would not. By this process, the arbitrator can solve new problems as they emerge and can follow promising lines of inquiry as he discovers them.

Not only did the arbitrator engage in a problem-solving process that led to a solution to the overarching problem, but he also made 'discoveries' throughout his problem-solving process. The arbitrator's questions and answers are relatively easy to identify. However, the precise nature of the discovery or invention the arbitrator makes in response to questions is a more difficult matter to analyse. Legal theorists have presented this topic as a search for an explanation of the link between questions and answers. Judge Hutcheson stated that in the judicial decision-making process the link or nexus between questions and answers is an 'intuition' or 'hunch'. He described a hunch as "that intuitive flash of understanding that makes the jump-spark connection between question and decision."[1] For Neil MacCormick, the equivalent of hunches are 'insights' or flashes of illumination.[2] Although both men portray hunches and insights as acts of discovery or invention they have merely named a mental activity. They did not explain in detail the nature of hunches and insights. My efforts here are gradually revealing the difficulties attendent on attempting such explanation. The key strategy will be an appropriate type of introspection, a topic to which I will very briefly turn.

5 Introspection

The method used to investigate discovery in the arbitrator's account of his decision-making process was neither to read a self-report, nor to concoct imaginary judges or cases. Rather, I asked the arbitrator questions about how he reached his decision - about the subjects he considered and the reasons for proceeding along particular lines of inquiry. We leisurely shared his questions and insights upon which I was then capable of reflecting. I did not observe the arbitrator in action solving this problem. I did not imagine his activities. I did not listen to a verbal report. And I did not create an idealized version of how to arbitrate. Rather, I reproduced the data of inquiry - the problematic situation and the search for, and discovery of, a solution. In this fashion, I was able to share the arbitrator's efforts to reach a solution to the problem. I reproduced the problem in my own consciousness and attended to the successes and failures of my own activities in my search for a solution to the problem. This revealed the key to me. My method of inquiry comprised a rhetorical and leisurely sharing of relevant insights. This method reveals a meaning of introspection that is precise and homely (not some mystery and not some activity that is unconscious).[3] Introspection, then, is a heightening of attention, not a matter of looking inward or observation.[4]

6 Conclusion

My treatment of the nature of, questioning in discovering possible relations and in testing and justifying further complicates the debate concerning the distinction between discovery and justification mentioned in Chapters One, Two, and Three. For example, in contrast to the legal realists who simply state that puzzling and brooding lead to hunches and insights, I have presented the process of discovery as a conscious and deliberate problem-solving process comprised of asking and answering questions and argued that particular types of questions demand particular types of answers and discover particular types of relations. Rather than speaking vaguely about the process of discovery and separating discovery and justification, I explicitly distinguished between two orientations or phases in problem-solving - (1) interpreting situations/solving problems and (2) testing interpretations/solutions - and illustrated that asking questions and seeking answers is the crucial activity in each context. In marked contrast to legal positivists' explanations of testing and justification, this suggests that the creative and synthetic aspects of insight constitute a significant part of testing and evaluation.

I have completed my selection and anecdotal treatment of writings about discovery and the methods used to study it. Now it is useful to summarise these diverse points of view in order to indicate the confused and incoherent nature of the writings on discovery. I began Chapter One by tracing how discussions of discovery in law have emerged in the context of a debate betweeen the legal realists and legal positivists concerning the distinction between the process of discovery and the process of justification. The realists portrayed discovery as a conscious, intelligent problem-solving process whereas the legal positivits considered hunches or insights (the crucial element in the discovery process) to be an unconscious and irrational activity that is the site of bias and prejudice in decision-making. The discovery process, they claimed, was a problem that psychologists should deal with. I ended the chapter by presenting the recent reflections of legal theorists on judicial decision-making that identified aspects of decision-making such as testing, weighing reasons, the ground judgment, equitable judgment, and ethical judgment. A coherent account of discovery in judicial decision-making was not proposed.

Continuing the presentation of reflective considerations, in Chapter Two, I analysed MacCormick's use of Popper's account of science to understand legal decision-making. Science, as described by Popper, did not seem to offer much enlightment. This analysis also raised questions about the relation between discovery, justification and expression that were left unanswered. I acted on the legal positivists' claim that discovery should be left to psychologists and presented the recent work of cognitive psychologists on the topic. I suggested that their general analysis of problem-solving and creativity could be transferred to the legal context and might help legal theorists understand discovery in law. However, this brief period of optimism could not be sustained; cognitive psychologists stressed the vagueness of their findings and the absence of an explanatory account of their subject matter.

After judging that my selection of reflective accounts of discovery in Chapters One and Two did not lead me to a coherent viewpoint on discovery, I turned to the actual performance of a judge and an arbitrator solving legal problems. The inquiry into the nature of discovery in Madame Justice Bertha Wilson's legal opinion was consistent with the problem-solving procedures identified by cognitive psychologists. Wilson described a strategy of discovery. That discussion also identified other elements that are important in the discovery process, particulary questions and answers. However, I also noted that Wilson's treatment of the abortion issue raised further complex questions about the relation between axiomatic and rhetorical expression and justification. No attempt was made to deal with these problems in that chapter; it requires the larger context to be arrived at through the following chapters.

Finally, in Chapter Four, when I investigated how a legal decision was "actually" reached by an arbitrator, I noted similarities between the cognitive psychologists' description of problem-solving and the activities of the arbitrator. The most significant finding in that analysis was a new understanding of introspection that differs from the versions presented in previous chapters. I rhetorically shared the problem-solving process with the arbitrator. This is a crucial key insight, and as you will soon see, leads me out of the confusion and incoherence of current accounts of discovery and justification in legal decision-making and enables me to tackle the questions raised in these four chapters that went unanswered. The difficulty of proceeding now is that brevity demands not the full dialogue of a pedagogical rhetoric, but some form of plausible and somewhat axiomatic presentation of results.

Appendix A: The Insurance Act

Schedule B to Part VI of the Insurance Act, R.S.N.S. 1989, c. 231 states:

The Insurer agrees to pay to or with respect to each insured person as defined in this section who sustains bodily injury or death by an accident arising out of the use or operation of an automobile:

Subsection 3 - Special Provisions, Definitions, and Exclusions of this Section states:

(1) The words "Insured Person" mean:

(a) any person while an occupant of the described automobile. . .

(b) the insured and. . .while an occupant of any other automobile. . .

(c) in subsections 1 (medical, rehabilitative and funeral expenses), 2 (death benefits and loss of income payments) and 2A (Quebec accidents) of this section only, any person, not the occupant of an automobile or of railway rolling-stock that runs on rails, who is struck in Canada, by the described automobile. . .

(d) In subsections 1, 2 and 2A of this section only, the named insured. . .not the occupant of an automobile or railway rolling-stock. . .who is struck by any other automobile. . .

Subsection 143(1) of the Insurance Act states:

Where a person who is entitled to (Section B Accident Benefits)

(a) is an occupant of a motor vehicle involved in an accident, the insurer of the owner of the motor vehicle shall, in the first instance, be liable for payment of the benefits provided by the insurance; or

(b) is not an occupant of a motor vehicle or a railway rolling stock that runs on rails and is struck by a motor vehicle, the insurer of the owner of the motor vehicle shall, in the first instance, be liable for the payment of the Accident Benefits. . .

Appendix B: Claims Agreement - Insurance Bureau of Canada

The Claims Agreement - Insurance Bureau of Canada, in which both insurers are signatories, Section 111: Interpretation, Rule 11A: Priority of Payment of Accident Benefits for Pedestrians states:

Insurers agree, where a claim for Accident Benefits in respect of a pedestrian injured or killed in a motor vehicle accident may be payable under more than one motor vehicle liability policy providing Accident Benefits, as follows:

Pedestrian struck by single vehicle

1. Where a pedestrian is struck by a motor vehicle the owner of which

(a) is insured under a motor vehicle liability policy providing Accident Benefits, the automobile insurer of the owner of the vehicle shall pay the Accident Benefits.

(b) is not insured under a policy referred to in Clause (a) but the pedestrian is so insured, the automobile insurer of the pedestrian shall pay the Accident Benefits.

1 J. Frank, **Law and the Modern Mind**, (London: Stevens & Sons, 1949), 103.

2 N MacCormick, **Legal Reasoning and Legal Theory**, (Oxford: Clarendon Press, 1978), 15-16.

3 B. Lonergan, **Method in Theology**, (London: Darton, Longman & Todd, 1971) 14, 251.

4 J.A. Fodor's statement ". . . that the central cognitive processes are not amenable to investigation: while the input systems have problem status, the central systems have mystery status; we can handle problems but mysteries are beyond us" brings out the prevalence of that obscurantist view in another context. ed. *F. Newmeyer, Linguistics: The Cambridge Survey,* (Cambridge: Cambridge University Press, 1988), Volume 3, 57.

5

Bernard Lonergan on Insight in Theoretical[1] and Practical Reasoning

1 Introduction

It is apparent that the reflective considerations of the discovery process presented in Chapters One and Two and the illustrations of the spontaneous use of the process of discovery in Chapters Three and Four do little more than name some relevant elements which constitute "discovery" in law. Identifying elements such as puzzling, brooding, hunches and intuitions does not explain how these activities are performed or how they are related. Furthermore, the tendency of modern legal theorists to present "discovery" in terms of irrational and arbitrary factors that are beyond the concerns of jurists helps support the assumption that "discovery" cannot be analysed. However, the work of B. Lonergan on insight suggests otherwise. In fact, his study of insight in theoretical and practical reasoning as a problem-solving process is relevant to questions about both discovery and justification.

Bernard Lonergan was a Canadian Jesuit (1904-1986) who addressed questions regarding philosophy, theology, and economics. Unfortunately, his work is relatively unfamiliar to scholars outside the field of theology and is unknown to most legal theorists. His major philosophic works are **Insight: A Study of Human Understanding**[2] and **Method in Theology**.[3] **Insight** is primarily concerned with analysing the role that questions and insights play in human understanding and in determining its relationship to philosophy, metaphysics, ethics, and theology. In short, his book combines and extrapolates the Aristotelian and European phenomenological traditions. In **Method in Theology**, Lonergan develops the general method of analysis used in **Insight** and discusses its implementation in theology.

Insight is an exploratory study of a neglected region of inquiry - the nature of insight in human understanding and knowing. Despite the efforts of philosophers to study human understanding they have not analysed insight; yet for Lonergan, insight plays an essential role in human knowledge. Insights are the source of knowledge and are also the source of novel rules and practices that can improve or even replace established routines. As such, insights are the source of new discoveries and inventions in human affairs.

The primary reason Lonergan studies insight is that, for him, the critical problem in philosophy is "the question . . . not whether knowledge exists, but what precisely is its nature."[4] As part of that project he analyses acts of insight of people in different fields - mathematics, science, and practical affairs - in order to understand the general structure of insight and to ascertain its significance. Part One of **Insight** is an analysis of insight first as a mental activity and second as an element in the structure of human knowing. Lonergan's analysis of insight focuses on "what precisely it is to understand, what are the dynamics of the flow of consciousness that favours insight, what are the interferences that favour oversight, what, finally, do the answers to such questions imply for the guidance of human thought and action."[5]

Insight is the key part of Lonergan's general theory of human understanding and knowing. It mediates his approach to a wide range of philosophical and theological questions and serves as the basis of his position on issues in philosophy and metaphysics. His philosophy, metaphysics, ethics, and theology are derived from his analysis of insight in human knowing. Insight is related to philosophy in that it is the source of answers to questions that lead to human knowledge and new routines and rules. Hence, in Lonergan's opinion, insight is the most significant activity in his explanation of human understanding and knowing. Insight is related to metaphysics insofar as the nature and ground of specialized methods in various fields are a specialized application of human knowing. Specialized methods of inquiry, such as the scientific method, are answers to questions that seek the best approach to understanding the nature of unknowns in different fields. For Lonergan, "an ethics results from knowledge of the compound structure of one's knowing and doing."[6] Insight is related to ethics to the extent that a person's insight into, or understanding of, a particular situation can lead to the person wondering about and discovering what one can and should do about the situation. When solving practical problems, knowing what to do depends on correctly understanding the situation and correctly identifying problems.

Since his viewpoint is all-inclusive and comprehensive and his arguments complex, a summary of his philosophy would be an inadequate way to introduce his position. However, important aspects of his work can be identified, namely the significance that insight plays in his cognitional theory and his method of studying human knowing. Because insight plays such an important role in knowing, its opposite, the flight from understanding, is also very important in his work. In order to promote and encourage knowing, Lonergan not only studies the conditions that promote insight, but also the conditions that suppress insights.

Lonergan diagnoses various manifestations of the flight from understanding - psychiatric, moral, social, cultural, and philosophic. Although the flight from understanding takes different forms in different contexts, its general nature is the suppression of questioning and the failure of insights to occur. For example, the flight from understanding in its philosophic form "appears to result simply from an incomplete development in the intelligent and reasonable use of one's own intelligence and reasonableness."[7] The flight from understanding is manifest in confused and mistaken theories of knowledge. He argues that insight into oversights will reveal what activities are unintelligent and will explain the existence of a multiplicity of philosophies and a series of mistaken metaphysical and anti-metaphysical positions. He claims that "insight into insight, then, will reveal what activity is intelligent."[8]

Individual bias and group bias are part of the flight from understanding.

Individual bias is illustrated by the person who solves one's own problems, but refuses to consider questions about whether the solutions can be or should be applied in similar situations. Relevant questions that are outside the range of one's own selfish interests are suppressed.[9] Group bias is characterised by loyalty to one group and hostility to other groups. It is a flight from understanding in that the group suppresses questions and fails to have insights that would challenge its own assessment of its well-being and usefulness.[10] In fact, the flight from understanding could be used to characterize the dismissal of the discovery process insofar as it is an oversight or error.

In Chapters One and Two, I argued that (1) the legal positivists have neglected to study the process of discovery and testing in the decision-making process and that (2) the clear distinction between discovery and justification is problematic in that justification seems to involve some sort of discovery. And in Chapters Three and Four, the importance of questions and answers in legal reasoning emerged. Although Lonergan does not discuss law, his analysis of insight is relevant to these issues. He explicitly studies discovery or invention and testing in various fields, particularly science, in terms of puzzling, asking questions, experiencing insights and testing hypotheses. Questions arise when one is puzzled. Insights occur in response to questions. Insights lead to the formulation of new ideas and then one tests them. But as I will explain in this chapter, insights also occur in testing. Because his concern is with insights as discoveries of ideas and also with their role in testing, the distinction between discovery and justification is not as significant for Lonergan as it is for legal positivists. Indeed, a clear distinction between discovery and justification in his work cannot be found, though it is latent in his discussions of judgments and expression. Lonergan's study is not an examination of the process of discovery and justification as they are understood by legal positivists. He neither studies the psychology of decision-making nor attempts to determine the unconscious processes and factors that influence decisions nor does he focus on justificatory expression. But Lonergan's account of human knowing is a philosophical grounding of clarifications in these areas. In the following chapters, I will be using his explanation of insight to help understand the process of discovery and testing[11] in science and in law.

2 Insight as an Act of Discovery or Invention in Solving Problems and Answering Questions

Insight is the mental activity that discovers answers to questions and solutions to theoretical and practical problems. By the act of insight we discover possible answers to questions when we want to understand an unknown and we invent possible answers to our questions when we want to know what to do. According to Lonergan, the act of having insights is a common everyday occurrence in people of all walks of life and circumstances. Insight is involved in both mundane activities such as telling the time and in great scientific achievements such as discovering the molecular structure of DNA.

Lonergan explicitly analyses the essential role of insight as an act of discovery in two modes or dimensions - (1) theoretical reasoning and (2) practical reasoning. In theoretical reasoning, insights can occur when a person is understanding sense-experience and when a person reflects on and discovers the truth or falsity of what one understands. When solving practical problems, insights can occur when a person discovers possible courses of action and when an individual is deliberating about and discovers which possible course of action is sufficiently appropriate to perform in the circumstances.

Lonergan illustrates the distinct nature of insight as an act of discovery by contrasting insight with vision, wonder, or questions that arise when reading a detective story. He writes that

> In the ideal detective story the reader is given all the clues yet fails to spot the criminal. He may advert to each clue as it arises. He needs no further clues to solve the mystery. Yet he can remain in the dark for the simple reason that reaching the solution is not merely the apprehension of any clue, not the mere memory of all, but a quite distinct activity of organising intelligence that places the full set of clues in a unique explanatory perspective. [12]

One can stare at all the clues in a detective story indefinitely and still not be able to solve the mystery because the act of discovery, the insight, has not occurred. The individual cannot discover the significance of the clues by simply looking at them. Moreover, the significance of the clues will not be discovered unless the reader is wondering who the criminal is and asks pertinent questions such as "Who is the criminal?" and "Is so-and-so the criminal?" Insight is achieved after wondering, puzzling, and questioning. Nonetheless, a person may be puzzled and ask questions and still fail to spot the criminal. As yet, insight has not occurred. A supervening mental synthesis of the clues is required if the criminal is to be discovered. Insight is the act of catching on to the identity of the criminal. Insight makes "the difference between the tantalizing problem and the evident solution."[13]

Lonergan portrays insights as acts of discovery that occur in response to wondering and asking questions when attempting to solve problems. As an act of discovery, insight is a distinct activity that can be distinguished from sense-experience, wonder, and questions. Although insight depends on sense, wonder, and questions, it cannot be equated with any of them. Insight is distinct from sense-experience. Sense-experience can be illustrated by imagining a person sitting on a beach staring at the clouds drift by. The individual is doing little more than looking at the clouds. The "looking" is simply sense-experience. One is neither puzzled about clouds nor trying to understand clouds. So far, insight has not been achieved; the act of discovery has not occurred. Sense-experience supplies no more than the raw materials for puzzling and questioning.

Questions are essential to insight. Through questions, an inquiry moves from sense-experience through insight to judgment. The act of insight itself is neither the formulation of an idea or definition nor is it a direct apprehension, perception, or intuition of the truth. It is a prior event that grounds formulation, that grounds the expression of true judgment.

Lonergan analyses the role of insight as a distinct mental operation in terms of its relation to other mental activities in human knowing. Lonergan believes that, in order to understand insight, one must also discover, identify, and become familiar with the other mental elements that compose the recurrent and related pattern of mental activities that constitute knowing. He conceives human knowing to be a structure that is a conjunction of distinct cognitive operations. Lonergan's explanation of human knowing is in terms of cognitive operations that can be grouped according to three dimensions - (1) sensible presentations or imaginative representations, (2) understanding, and (3) reflection. Although his terminology is shared by faculty models of knowing, his conception of knowing is structural; it is not a faculty model. And certainly he rejects theories that consider knowledge to be the intuition of sensible objects.

Individuals are active knowers. Knowing consists of mental acts that constitute experiencing, understanding, and judging. Knowing is illustrated by mathematicians solving equations and testing their answers, scientists understanding their data and verifying their hypotheses, and people of practical affairs finding alternatives and evaluating them. Asking and answering questions is the method by which people are and become attentive, intelligent, reasonable, and responsible human beings. They attend to sense-experience and circumstances, correctly identify problematic issues, actively seek answers to questions, have insights that are intelligent solutions to problems, and critically test the truth and falsity, the value and relevance of their insights.

Lonergan's position includes a normative attitude toward knowledge itself, in that individuals should actively seek knowledge and should not be, for example, passive cloud-watchers. He thinks people should be curious, should wonder, should ask questions, should actively investigate and seek answers to their questions and solutions to their problems until they have insights. They should test their insights to see if they are correct, and should not rest until they have complete answers. In fact, Lonergan thinks knowing is ever-questioning and characterized by an unrestricted desire to understand.

3 Insight in Theoretical and Practical Reasoning

There are two basic types of insight, (1) direct and (2) reflective, and they both occur in two dimensions - (1) theoretical reasoning and (2) practical reasoning. Both theoretical and practical reasoning seek knowledge. Theoretical reasoning seeks knowledge for the sake of knowledge, but practical reasoning seeks knowledge for the sake of knowing what to do. This section develops the basic idea that insight is the activity that discovers answers to questions and invents solutions to problems. I will briefly explain the structure of insight and its role in human knowing not only when a person discovers possible answers to theoretical and practical questions, but also when a person tests and evaluates his or her own answers to theoretical and practical questions. Critical reflection and evaluation occur in both theoretical and practical reasoning. In discovering possible answers, either in theoretical or practical reasoning, there are two distinct orientations. *Direct insight* in theoretical reasoning is analogous to *practical insight* in practical reasoning. Both direct insight and practical insight are oriented toward understanding or discovering possible relations among data. As such, the contents of direct insights are possible answers which could either be true or false and the contents of practical insights are proposed courses of action which may or may not be sufficiently appropriate to perform in a particular situation. In other words, direct insight itself is not concerned with truth, and practical insight itself is not concerned with sufficient suitability. In theoretical reasoning, direct insight is tested by *reflective insight* and, in practical reasoning, practical insight is evaluated by *practical reflective insight*. Insight, in each context, does not occur in isolation. Insight is related to, and depends on, other mental activities such as puzzling, questioning, previous insights and formulations, judgments of fact, judgments of value and decisions. Reflective insight leads to a judgment concerning truth and falsity and practical reflective insight leads to a judgment of value concerning whether a proposed course of action is good or is sufficiently appropriate.

In Lonergan's theory, the crucial activity in theoretical reasoning is *direct insight*. It occurs after wondering and puzzling about sensible presentations, imaginations, or memories. Puzzling in this context can be represented by an individual asking *What-questions* that demand definitions, explanations, or interpretations such as "What is it?" "Why is it so?" For example, a person might ask "What is a circle?" or "What is a cat?" What-questions lead to direct insight. One has a direct insight when one catches on, when the mind clicks, when one grasps the solution. Direct insights are not simply perceptions. They are the consequence of interrogating one's sense perceptions. They go beyond mere perceiving to discovering the relations among what is sensed, imagined, or remembered. Moreover, direct insights are not definitions or interpretations. Rather, direct insights are the mental activities that definitions and interpretations are based upon; thus, such insights are pre-conceptual. Direct insights demand *formulations* and are made explicit as *definitions, explanations,* or *interpretations*. Direct insight is the act of discovery that, for example, leads to formulating the definition of a circle as the loci of a set of points equidistant from a centre in the same plane.

In the theoretical context, just as understanding can be represented as answers to questions such as What-is-it? and leads to direct insight, critical reflection can be represented by questions such as "*Is-it-so?*" that lead to reflective insights involved in testing. According to Lonergan, direct insights occur frequently and are "a dime a dozen". But direct insights do not necessarily discover truth. Some insights may be correct and others may be wrong. Critical reflection in theoretical reasoning is initiated by puzzling and by questions that ask "Is it true?" "Is it so?" These questions lead to reflective insights and judgments of fact. The attitude of the inquiry is characterized by the question - "Is-it-so?" Questioning leads to *reflective insights* which discover the link between prospective judgments and the sufficiency of the evidence for making *judgments of fact* regarding the truth or falsity of direct insights and formulations.

Like direct insight in theoretical reasoning, *practical insight* is the key activity in practical reasoning. As in theoretical reasoning, a person who is involved in practical reasoning wonders and puzzles, asks questions, has insights, and formulates them. However, in practical reasoning one wonders not only about sensible presentations, imaginations, and memories, but also about particular situations and circumstances. The mental attitude in this context is not represented by questions that ask "What-

is-it?", but rather by questions that ask *"What-is-to-be-done?"* This questioning attitude leads to insights that discover the unity of proposed courses of action rather
than the unity in data. Just as direct insights are formulated as explanations or interpretations, practical insights are formulated as possible *courses of action*. For example, a person may arrive at the scene of a gruesome car accident and ask "What can I
do?" Several alternatives such as pulling the people out of the car, calling an ambu-
lance, or stopping other cars for help may be discovered by practical insights. Or a
person who notices that his rowboat is sinking may ask "What am I to do?" and may
consider various options discovered by practical insight such as bailing out the water,
sending a distress signal, rowing to shore, or going down with the ship.

In practical reasoning, testing and evaluating practical insights and proposed
courses of action lead to *practical reflective insights*. Like direct insights that are possible correlations, relations, links or unities that may be correct or incorrect, practical insights discover only possible courses of action. Some of those courses of action
may be impossible or unreasonable to perform. One alternative may be preferred.
The mental attitude of the individual in this context can be represented by questions
that ask *"Is-it-to-be-done?"* and *"Should the course of action be performed?"* When a
person evaluates the alternatives, *practical reflective insight* discovers the relation
between the significant factors of a particular situation, the proposed course of
action, and the consequences and implications of the action. The person at the scene
of a car accident who asks, for example, "Should I first stop the bleeding or give artificial respiration?" then discovers the victim may suffocate before he bleeds to
death. The rower who asks "Should I just row quickly to shore or start bailing out the
water?" discovers that if he does not begin bailing immediately his boat will sink and
he will never reach land. *Practical reflection* or *deliberation* leads to a *judgment of
value* that one course of action is sufficiently suitable. The bystander judges that one
should perform artificial respiration first and the rower judges one should row
rather than bail. A *decision* to perform the course of action ends practical evaluation. For example, "Yes, I will perform artificial respiration first" or "Yes, I will simply row quickly to shore."

Theoretical reasoning (which includes direct insight and reflective insight) and
practical reasoning (which includes practical insight and practical reflective insight)
are related in a number of ways. Practical insights and practical reflective insights
depend on direct insights and judgments of fact about concrete situations. In other
words, knowing what is the appropriate thing to do in a situation depends on knowing what the situation is. For example, a doctor's diagnosis precedes his judgment of
value concerning which treatment should be prescribed. In the legal context, knowing that a situation is a case of nervous shock precedes a judge's judgment of value
regarding what the solution to the case should be. Here, theoretical reasoning precedes practical reasoning insofar as understanding a particular situation leads to
questions concerned with what to do in the concrete situation. On the other hand,
practical reasoning precedes theoretical reasoning when practical questions occur
before the situation is understood. A doctor may ask the practical question "What
should I do to help this patient?" and then realize that a diagnosis must be made
before prescribing a course of treatment. A judge may ask the practical question

"Should I allow this person to recover damages for nervous shock?" and realize that the particular situation and the relevant law must be understood before answering the practical question. In these cases, the person tries to understand the situation through the occurrence of direct insights before judging what is the sufficiently suitable thing to do in the circumstances.

The basic idea which I want to develop in the following chapters is that theoretical reasoning is concerned with interpreting situations and practical reasoning is concerned with discovering or inventing what to do in a situation. By theoretical reasoning one is able to understand the facts of a situation in relation to the relevant law and other cases. But at some point the judge asks "What should I do to solve the problem?" Such a question is a practical question. The judge via theoretical reasoning may judge that the current case and a previous case are similar in relevant ways and then reach the same solution to the current case as the previous case. Here, the judge is using theoretical reasoning to help solve a practical question. On the other hand, the current and previous cases may not be significantly similar and the solution to previous cases may be inappropriate in the current case. Here, the judge must engage in practical reasoning to discover or invent a suitable solution to the current case. Practical reasoning can also lead to theoretical reasoning when practical insights, practical reflective insights, and judgments of value lead to the creation of new situations which are understood by direct insights, which in turn can lead to new questions about what to do, new practical insights, and new judgments of value.

Lonergan's analysis of insight in theoretical and practical reasoning offers a novel approach to examining discovery and testing. The activity at the centre of theoretical and practical reasoning is insight, an activity that discovers or invents possibilities and also tests them. Although it is not surprising that insight, as an act of discovery, is the crucial activity in the creation of ideas and courses of action, one does not expect that insight also plays a key role in testing and evaluating direct insights and practical insights. But for Lonergan, insights are the key activities in discovering new ideas and also in testing them. Lonergan's position is distinct from the realists and legal positivists in that he recognizes that the role of reflective insights and practical reflective insights in testing and evaluating is creative or synthetic insofar as the contents of previous mental activities are considered in a new way. To put it crudely, he examines the role of discovery in justification. In other words, although reflective insights and practical reflective insights test and evaluate direct and practical insights, they are also like direct and practical insights in that they transform the raw materials they work on. Reflective insights synthesize direct insights and what is sensed. Practical reflective insights synthesize practical insights, evaluations, and sense-experience. It is in this sense that discovery is a significant part of testing in theoretical and practical reasoning.

Lonergan's treatment of the nature of, and the relationship between, insight in discovering possibilities and in testing and justifying them further complicates the debate concerning the distinction between discovery and justification that became evident when the realists' and positivists' writings were analysed in Chapter One. For example, in contrast to the legal realists who simply claim that puzzling and brooding lead to hunches, Lonergan explicitly presents what would otherwise be known as "decision-making" as a problem-solving process and argues that particular types of questions demand particular types of insights. Rather than speaking inarticulately of hunches and intuitions, Lonergan analyses the role of insight in human understanding and explains that direct and practical insights discover possible relations and unities in data. Rather than speaking vaguely about the process of discovery and separating discovery and justification, Lonergan explicitly distinguishes between two orientations or phases in reasoning - understanding and testing - and argues that insight is the central activity in *each* context. In marked contrast to legal positivists' explanations of testing and justification, the creative and synthetic aspects of insight constitute a significant part of testing and evaluation.

Lonergan investigates what would otherwise be known by Bankowski as the process of discovery inasmuch as theoretical reasoning includes both procedures of discovery and testing. He also investigates what would otherwise be known by legal positivists as the process of discovery in that he analyses the emergence of direct insights. However, like the legal theorists discussed in Chapter One, Lonergan's use of the term "discovery" is ambiguous. He calls both unverified and verified hypotheses "discoveries". Bankowski, by contrast, would reserve the term "discovery" only for insights that have been tested and found to satisfy the relevant truth-certifying procedures.

It might seem appropriate to call the *understanding phase* in Lonergan's version of theoretical and practical reasoning "discovery" and to call the *testing phase* "justification". And to do so would not be wrong. However, in my opinion, this approach should be resisted. Traditionally, "discovery" has been treated as an intuitive activity that is necessarily distinct from justification. Yet the creative act of *insight* occurs in *both* the understanding and testing phases of theoretical and practical reasoning. "Discovery" could be reserved for the activities involved in having an idea and "justification" could be reserved for the activities involved in testing it. Yet having an idea and testing it are both part of a single comprehensive process, not independent processes. To call the understanding phase "discovery" and the testing phase "justification" would continue to mask the creative role of insight in testing. To analyse reflective insight and practical reflective insight and not to stress that they are acts of "discovery" would mis-represent the creative nature of testing.

4 Lonergan's Method of Examining Theoretical and Practical Reasoning

Lonergan studies the process of discovery from the point of view of those people who are actively engaged in solving problems by asking and answering questions. He explicitly examines the method scientists devise and follow to solve their problems. The person engaged in seeking knowledge for its own sake by asking and answering What-questions and Is-questions is the knowing subject. A scientist searching for the cause of ulcers is a knowing subject. On the other hand, a person seeking knowledge in order to know what to do in a situation is the ethical subject. A judge or jury determining what punishment to give an offender would be ethical subjects.

Lonergan's analysis concentrates on the knowing and ethical subject actively engaged in seeking knowledge rather than on the known. He is concerned with the nature of knowing rather than the existence of knowledge. In fact, the first 315 pages of **Insight** are devoted to the question "What is happening when we are knowing?" which he answers by constructing an account of human knowing. He is not "concerned with the objects understood in mathematics but with mathematicians' acts of understanding, not with objects understood in the various sciences but with scientists' acts of understanding, not with the concrete situations mastered by common sense but with the acts of understanding of men of common sense."[14] His approach is consistent with his conception of knowing as a structure of cognitive operations performed by a subject rather than as some sort of object that can be observed. His notion of the subject as a questioner is apparent in the data he chooses to study; he studies acts of insight, not what is understood. For him, the subject as a questioner is not conceived of as an object. Instead, the knowing and ethical subject is conceived as being constituted by the actual performance of cognitive operations.

The procedure Lonergan uses to study the nature of human knowing is modelled on his understanding of himself as a knower, as a person who experiences, asks questions, understands, reflects, and judges. For Lonergan, it is by attending to his own experiences of knowing that he has come to understand how he understands and judges, and to present his account of human knowing. Similarly, for anyone else to understand the nature of human knowing, one must be attentive to one's own experiences of sense-experience, insights, and judgments. It is in this way that Lonergan understands the structure of knowing to be a conjunction of experiencing, understanding, and judging. Although he refers to the familiar philosophical categories - experiencing, understanding, and judging - they are understood as a unity or a structure constituted by a recurrent pattern of cognitional activities. His procedure of analysis is not to construct catalogues of abstract properties of knowing conceived of as an object. He does not regard knowing as the execution of "this or that operation, but as a whole whose parts are operations."[15] Human knowing is not like taking a look; it is not simply understanding without judging; and it is not judging without experiencing and understanding.

Although one may spontaneously perform the mental activities that constitute knowing, one may not know what they are. Furthermore, a person may be conscious of having insights, but may not have any idea what an insight entails. According to Lonergan, the effort to understand the structure of knowing, which he calls self-appropriation, leads to self-knowledge. Parallels between the activities of knowing and self-knowing can be identified. Just as human knowing "is not some single operation or activity but, on the contrary is a whole whose parts are cognitional activities"[16], self-knowing is also a whole whose parts constitute a dynamic pattern of recurrent operations that are cognitional activities. Just as knowing is not looking or like looking, imagining or intuiting, self-knowing is not inward introspecting, imagining, or a mystical experience. Instead, self-appropriation is a matter of inquiry, of enlarging one's interest, of discerning, comparing, identifying, and naming the operations that compose the structure of human knowing.

Lonergan's procedure to understand human "knowing" is derived from his conception of human knowing. Since he conceives the structure of knowing as a conjunction of experiencing, understanding, and judging, he infers that the procedure used to know human knowing must be a re-duplication of that structure. Thus self-knowledge or knowing "knowing" is "(1) *experiencing* one's experiencing, understanding, and judging, (2) *understanding* the unity and relations of one's experienced experiencing, understanding, and judging. . .",[17] and (3) "*judging* one's experienced and understood experiencing, understanding, and judging it to be correct. . ."[18] Lonergan calls this procedure self-appropriation. His strategy in **Insight** is to invite and lead the reader through a series of strategically chosen instances so that one may personally make explicit one's own "dynamic and recurrently operative structure of cognitional activity."[19]

Lonergan notes that we experience our experiencing, understanding, and judging every time we experience, or understand, or judge. The elements of knowing are conscious when one is experiencing (that is, when one is seeing, hearing, tasting, touching, smelling), understanding, and judging, but as such they are neither understood nor known. Our attention is apt to be focused on the object rather than on the activities of our cognitive operations. In contrast, self-appropriation is finding in oneself the conscious occurrence of the cognitional activities whenever an object is seen, understood, and judged. It is by becoming familiar with one's own performance of these mental activities that one becomes able to understand the mental activities that comprise theoretical and practical reasoning. In this way, the individual's mental activities such as insight become known to that individual.

5 The Elements of Theoretical and Practical Reasoning

Lonergan's efforts of self-appropriation presented in **Insight** and **Method in Theology** reveal thirteen elements or basic operations that are employed in knowing and doing. In the context of human knowing, experiencing involves (1) *sensitive or imaginative representations*. Theoretical understanding includes (2) *What-questions*, (3) *direct insights*, and (4) formulations of *definitions*, *explanations*, or *interpretations*. Testing includes (5) *Is-questions*, (6) *reflective insights*, and (7) *judgments of fact*.

Practical understanding includes (8) *What-is-to-be-done-questions*, (9) *practical insights*, and (10) formulations of *proposed courses of action*. Testing includes (11) *Is-it-to-be-done-questions*, (12) *practical reflective insights*, and (13) *judgments of value*. *Decision*, a separate mental operation, ends practical reasoning. In other words, insight occurs at two levels - understanding and testing - but not at the level of sense-experience.

The relations among the cognitional activities in theoretical and practical reasoning can be illustrated with the following diagram[20]:

PRACTICAL REASONING

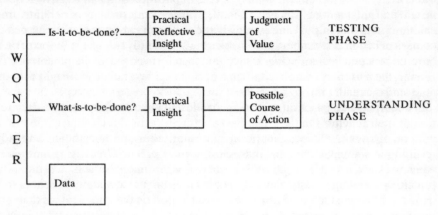

THEORETICAL REASONING

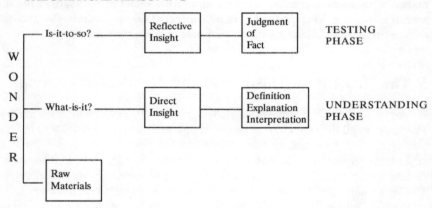

According to Lonergan, these thirteen elements constitute the human cognitive structure. It is materially dynamic since the distinct, irreducible mental activities constitute a pattern that is a particular sequence. One operation follows another and so on. The operations are experienced not only singly but in their relations to each other. Thus, there is a functional unity and relatedness to the extent that, without sense, nothing can be understood and, without sense and understanding, judgment would be rash. The structure of mental activities ". . . is formally dynamic inasmuch as it calls forth and assembles the appropriate operations at each stage of the process . . ."[21] The completion of one operation leads to the initiation of another. The dynamism that promotes or drives this recurrent pattern of related cognitive operations is human wonder. In the inquiring mind, sense-experience provokes wonder. Puzzling shifts the inquiry from sense-experience to understanding, and direct insight goes beyond sense to grasp a synthesis in the data only to call forth, and be called forth, by the exigencies of reflection; this process is completed by reflective insight and judgment of fact. The orientation of one's questioning can shift to practical reasoning, that is, puzzling about what to do. Practical insights discover possible courses of action and deliberation enables the sufficiently suitable solution to be discovered by a practical reflective insight and then formulated as a judgment of value. Finally, the pattern is completed when a person decides or chooses to make the suitable option actual.

Theoretical and practical reasoning are closely linked with respect to the execution of their functions in the cognitive structure. Practical reasoning completes the pattern of cognitive operations insofar as it includes and goes beyond knowing, resulting in action. Theoretical reasoning grounds practical reasoning inasmuch as you must know in order to do. Theoretical reasoning provides the factual data which practical reasoning must take into account. With the question "What-is-to-be-done?", the context of the inquiry moves from theoretical to practical reasoning and the formulation of practical insights is demanded. Once satisfied, the inquiring mind, ever alert, moves to the next context - "Is-it-to-be-done here and now?" Practical reflective insight answers the question only to the point where a decision is made. In **Insight**, the procedure of self-appropriation is also used to analyse the structure of doing. The result of such self-appropriation adds a fourth level to the cognitive structure. Self-appropriation of practical reasoning involves "deciding to operate in accord with the norms immanent in the spontaneous relatedness of one's experienced, understood, affirmed experiencing, understanding, judging, and deciding."[22]

Lonergan wants to promote the operation of knowing in human affairs by explaining its operation and having people know how they understand, judge and decide. His position is normative insofar as he thinks knowing can lead to intelligent and reasonable explanations and responsible actions. For Lonergan, the performance of knowing is good because it can be attentive to circumstances, can discover intelligent answers to questions, can make reasonable judgments, and can discover and execute responsible actions in appropriate circumstances. Moreover, knowing can identify inattention, obtuseness, unreasonableness, and irresponsibility. The operation of knowing is the method that can help arrest the flight from understanding. Through knowing, the occurrence of insights can be promoted and the factors that lead to mistaken insights or suppressed insights can be identified and eradicated. Problems in any field, for Lonergan, can only be solved if their solutions are actively sought.

Lonergan admits that his perspective on cognitional theory is difficult to understand because it requires the reader to familiarize oneself with his terminology, to evoke the relevant operations in one's own consciousness and to discover in one's own experience the dynamic relationships leading from one operation to the next.[23] He asserts that, if one is to understand knowing and doing as he conceives them, one must practise self-appropriation oneself; without doing that, one can no more know knowing and doing than a blind man can know colours.[23]

6 Conclusion

The notion of insight presented so far has been rather static. However, it is necessary to appreciate the nature of insight as an active mental element in theoretical and practical reasoning. The following two chapters analyse insight in detail so that the structure and role of insight in relation to the functions of the other mental activities that constitute theoretical and practical reasoning can be examined. Direct insight, reflective insight, practical insight, and practical reflective insight will be studied in order to understand what it means for each type of insight to say that it "discovers" or "invents" such-and-such a relation. Chapter Six is an analysis of understanding and testing in the process of solving theoretical problems. Chapter Seven is an analysis of understanding and testing in the process of solving practical problems. Lonergan's work raises fundamental questions about the nature of discovery and testing that are not raised by and cannot be adequately answered by examining the writings of modern legal theorists.

1 Throughout this book, I use the term "theoretical" reasoning to emphasize the common structure of direct insight in different contexts and to distinguish between theoretical and practical reasoning. I do not use the term "theoretical", in Lonergan's, more precise sense, to distinguish between the domins or horizons of "theory" and "common sense".

2 B. Lonergan, **Insight: A Study of Human Understanding**, (London: Harper & Row, 1978).

3 B. Lonergan, **Method in Theology**, (London: Darton, Longman, & Todd, 1971).

4 Insight, xvii.

5 ibid., xvi.

6 ibid., xxix.

7 ibid., xii.

8 ibid., xiv.

9 ibid., 222.

10 ibid., 223.

11 I use the term "testing" to refer to the actual process followed by a judge when testing a tentative solution in the decision-making process. On the other hand, while "justification" includes aspects of testing, it also involves the public exposition of the solution or decision.

12 ibid., x.

13 ibid., xi.

14 ibid., xi.

15 B. Lonergan, *Cognitional Structure*, ed. P. McShane, **Introducing the thought of Bernard Lonergan**, (London: Darton, Longman & Todd, 1968), 17.

16 ibid., 18.

17 **Method in Theology**, 15.

18 ibid., 15.

19 **Insight**, xxiii.

20 This diagram is adapted from the diagram in P. McShane, **Wealth of Self and Wealth of Nations**, (New York: Exposition Press, 1975), 15.

21 **Method in Theology**, 13.

22 ibid., 15.

23 ibid., 7.

24 B. Lonergan, **Verbum: Word and Idea in Aquinas**, (Notre Dame: University of Notre Dame Press, 1967), 25.

6

"Discovery" in Theoretical Problem-Solving

1 Introduction

In Chapters One and Two, I noted that the nature of "discovery" in legal decision-making is not settled and, in Chapters Three and Four, I raised further complex questions regarding decision-making, introspection, and expression. The aim of this chapter, and the following chapter, is to provide the context in which such topics can be adequately addressed. I examine the nature of "discovery" in both the understanding and testing phases of theoretical and practical problem-solving.

Conventional accounts of legal reasoning portray legal reasoning in terms of theoretical (empirical) reasoning or, alternatively, as practical reasoning. Theoretical and practical reasoning are presented as each having their own mutually exclusive spheres of operation in the sense that legal reasoning is understood as a specialization of *either* theoretical *or* practical reasoning. In these accounts, theoretical reasoning would be concerned with establishing the facts in a particular case, describing valid law, and predicting the behaviour of judges.[1] Theoretical reasoning also seems to include "decisions on the facts".[2] In such cases, the validity of the rule of law comprising the major premise of the legal syllogism is not in question. Rather the problem is to prove the particular facts of the case or to classify the facts according to a legal category that comprises the minor premise of the legal syllogism.

On the other hand, practical reasoning involves solving practical questions regarding "what should or may be done or not done."[3] It is concerned with establishing the legal validity of universal propositions, ie. "legal rulings or norms". The problem practical reasoning must solve is to decide which rival universal proposition will comprise the major premise of the legal syllogism.[4] Practical reasoning both tests and justifies legal rulings in order to determine which universal legal ruling will be followed in a case and in similar cases that may occur in the future.

Thus, it can be seen that, despite differences in orientation, conventional accounts of the structure of both theoretical and practical reasoning are dominated by analyses of the legal syllogism and universal rules or norms in the context of the process of justification.

In contrast to conventional accounts of theoretical and practical reasoning, in this chapter and the following chapter, I use Lonergan's work to offer an explanation of theoretical and practical problem-solving in legal decision-making that is neither dominated by the legal syllogism nor by universal rules or norms. Rather, questions and answers are the key elements in the analysis. "Discovery", not justification, is the focus of the inquiry. The actual decision-making process, understood from this perspective, involves *both* theoretical and practical problem-solving.

But before analysing "discovery" in legal decision-making, the relation between theoretical and practical problem-solving, as understood from Lonergan's perspective, must be briefly examined. As stated in Chapter Five, theoretical and practical reasoning are concerned with answering different types of questions. In general terms, in the legal context, theoretical problem-solving is oriented to discovering and testing what the particular situation and relevant law, in fact, are. Questions about the interpretation of a situation and relevant law is therefore part of theoretical problem-solving. For example, theoretical reasoning would be concerned with interpreting situations as cases of "manslaughter", "nervous shock", or "pure economic loss" by judging that one case was relevantly similar to other cases of that type or category. On the other hand, practical problem-solving is oriented to discovering and evaluating what should be done in a particular situation. Practical questions are asked in order to find a solution to a case when one cannot be discovered by comparing the case to other cases.

In an effort to minimize confusion between Lonergan's versions of theoretical and practical problem-solving, in Chapter Five, I presented theoretical and practical problem-solving as if theoretical problem-solving always precedes and leads to practical problem-solving in an orderly progression. And in the paragraph immediately above, I portrayed them as distinct methods of problem-solving. However, the interplay between them is much more complex and messy than I have indicated. Not only is practical reasoning involved in cases where rulings compete with each other, but all legal decision-making involves both theoretical and practical reasoning to some extent. Both types of problem-solving complement each other in the decision-making process.

However, understanding precisely the relation between theoretical and practical problem-solving in legal decision-making is problematic. At least three possible general lines of problem-solving can be identified in the legal context. The *first* line is theoretical problem-solving. As mentioned above, it can precede practical problem-solving. A judge may use theoretical reasoning to interpret a situation as a case of manslaughter and then through practical reasoning discover the appropriate punishment. Practical reasoning, then, begins when theoretical reasoning stops. This approach is consistent with the view that, in order to know what to do in a case, one must first understand the situation and the relevant law. *Secondly*, practical questions may guide theoretical problem-solving. A judge may ask the over-arching practical question "What should I decide in this case?" and then use theoretical reasoning to compare the case to other similar cases in order to discover the answer to the over-arching practical question. *Thirdly*, practical problem-solving can be an alternative to theoretical problem-solving. In cases in which a solution cannot be discovered by comparing cases, it may be necessary to discover or invent a solution by practical reasoning.

However, the other possibility is that when a judge is *actually* solving a problem, theoretical and practical problem-solving are inter-related throughout the decision-making process. A judge's attention may shift from theoretical to practical problem-solving and from practical to theoretical problem-solving more or less continuously. Attention would alternate between theoretical questions such as "What is it?" and "Is it so?" to practical questions such as "What is to be done?" and "Should it be done?" This process would lead to a complex inter-related set of insights, judgments of fact, judgments of value, and finally a decision.

But the primary aim of this chapter and the following chapter is to investigate "discovery" in legal decision-making, not to determine the relation between theoretical and practical problem-solving. Despite the apparent complexity of theoretical and practical problem-solving in legal decision-making, they can be examined separately insofar as they each involve different types of questions and answers. Thus, in this chapter, I analyse "discovery" in theoretical problem-solving and, in the following chapter, I analyse "discovery" in practical problem-solving. These two chapters are a more detailed study of problem-solving than that of Chapter Five. I will return to the issue regarding the relation between theoretical and practical problem-solving in legal decision-making.

2 Theoretical Problem-Solving

Lonergan's work can be understood as an investigation of the nature of "discovery" in that he carefully articulates the nature of insight through his explanation of theoretical reasoning. As outlined in Chapter Five, two types of "discovery" occur in the process of solving theoretical problems: (1) *direct insight* and (2) *reflective insight*. Direct insights are the creative and synthetic acts that discover tentative answers to questions; reflective insights are the creative and synthetic acts involved in testing these answers.

In this chapter, I examine Lonergan's explanation of theoretical reasoning as a dynamic problem-solving process. I explicitly distinguish between two phases in theoretical problem-solving: (1) the *understanding phase* and (2) the *testing phase*. In the understanding phase, one has hunches and insights and discovers hypotheses and explanations. The aim of analysing this phase is to explain the nature of hunches and insights. The understanding phase would otherwise be known by legal positivists as the process of discovery. Although calling it the "discovery" phase, rather than the "understanding" phase, would be in line with conventional terminology, as I stated in the previous chapter, using the term "discovery" to refer to untested hunches and insights would mask the fact that "discovery" also occurs in testing. I use the term "discovery" to emphasize the creative nature of *both* direct insight and reflective insight. The understanding phase involves: (a) *sense-experience*, (b) *wondering* and *puzzling*, and asking *What-questions*, (c) having *direct insights*, and (d) formulating and expressing direct insights as *hypotheses, definitions, explanations, diagnoses*, or *interpretations*.

In the testing phase, one is concerned with testing and verifying hypotheses, definitions, explanations, diagnoses, and interpretations. This phase involves (a) asking *Is-questions*, (b) having *reflective insights*, and (c) formulating *judgments of fact*.

Contrary to expectation, "discovery" is a crucial part of the testing phase. The aim of the analysis of testing is to examine the extent that the testing phase involves "discovery".

Unfortunately, Lonergan does not examine problem-solving in the legal context. He investigates discovery and testing in science and other fields. To the extent that various contexts involve direct insight and reflective insight, they can help us understand the general characteristics of insight in the legal context. Moreover, I will suggest that the distinctions that can be identified between insights in different fields are of some significance. Hence, throughout this chapter, I draw analogies between medicine and law in order to illustrate the general procedure whereby theoretical problems are solved. I note the similarities in the problem-solving procedures followed by physicians and judges, especially the similarities among What-questions and Is-questions and the direct insights and reflective insights those questions demand. I would like to stress that I am not analysing Lonergan's explanation of theoretical reasoning to construct a new analogy between science and law. Rather, the aim is to investigate the nature of "discovery" in judicial decision-making.

3 Elements in The Understanding Phase of Theoretical Problem-Solving

Doctors and judges follow the same general method when solving problems or searching for answers to questions. In the understanding phase, they both ask What-questions that call for direct insights and formulations. The understanding phase begins when a doctor or judge wonders or puzzles about *sense-experience*. A physician may wonder about why the patient complains about stomach cramps and a judge may puzzle about the course of events that led to a person's death or whether a situation amounts to a case of murder. The doctor and judge ask questions in order to understand the situation. The type of questions they pose are *What-questions*. A physician consulted by a patient asks the over-arching question "What is the situation?" or "What is the problem?" and then searches for an explanation. Similarly, a judge listening to lawyers' arguments and witnesses' testimony, asks "What is the situation?" or "What is the problem?" and seeks an answer. Such questions lead to *direct insights* into particular situations. The physician's direct insight is into a particular problem experienced by a particular individual. The answer is a direct insight that discovers the connections among the doctor's understanding of relevant symptoms, diseases, and previous diagnoses, and the patient's complaints and symptoms. Similarly, a judge has a direct insight into a particular situation or course of events that occurred at a particular time and place. The judge experiences a direct insight that discovers the relation among the judge's understanding of the situation as potentially defined by legal categories and previous cases, lawyers' arguments, and witnesses' testimony. Direct insight is an act of discovery or invention in that it discovers relations among data that were previously not understood to be related. Direct insight transforms sense-experience and What-questions by considering sense-experience in a new way. It discovers a unity among data that can include sense-experience, imaginations, memories or any raw materials such as direct insights and judgments of fact. Direct insights into concrete situations are formulated by physicians as *explanations* or *diagnoses* and by judges as *interpretations*. The doctor formulates this direct insight as a diagnosis of the situation or problem such as "This person has an ulcer." The judge formulates direct insights as a tentative interpretation of the situation or case such as "This is a case of murder" or "This is a case of nervous shock".

The aims of this section are (1) to analyse the relations among the elements in the understanding phase of theoretical problem-solving, (2) to explain the extent to which direct insight is an act of discovery, and (3) to illustrate the conscious and deliberate nature of the understanding phase.

3.1 Sense-experience

Imaginings, memories, sensible presentations such as colours, shapes, sounds, odours, and tastes are the raw materials of direct insights. According to Lonergan, direct insight depends on sensible presentations and memories for its object. Sensible presentations represent a link between outer circumstances and mental activity. Unlike other mental activities which are not directly dependent on outer circumstances, sensible presentations depend on outer circumstances to the extent that "the occurrence and the content of sensation stand in some immediate correlation with outer circumstance."[5] For example, "unless you are deaf, you cannot avoid hearing, and unless you are blind, you have only to open your eyes to see."[6] As already mentioned in Chapter Five, sensation is distinct from direct insight. A person lying on a beach gazing at the clouds is not puzzled about clouds. Similarly, there is no effort to understand when we are remembering past experiences, imagining other places and times, or telling stories. These examples are simply presentations. No synthetic activity is occurring. The attitude of the curious, puzzled, inquiring mind is not present. Perception by itself, in Lonergan's view, never leads to direct insight. By itself, presentations yield nothing more than uninterrogated sense-experience.

3.2 Wondering, Puzzling and Asking What-questions

But, one can see, hear, taste, touch, smell and also be wondering about what one sees, hears, tastes, touches, smells, remembers, or imagines. One may be puzzled; one may wonder about something; one's curiosity may be sparked. A physician may be puzzled about how a patient's complaints are linked and a judge may be puzzled about how the testimony of witnesses is related. The attitude of the inquiring mind has replaced the passive observer and one may express one's puzzlement as *"What is it?" "Why is it so?"*

According to Lonergan, wonder is the root of all questions, not a question in words or concepts, but just the effort to understand without any formulation.[7] For him, inquiry is the element of intellectual alertness. It is a questioning attitude which is oriented toward understanding. One is trying to get hold of something but as yet one is not understanding anything; one is puzzled. The desire or effort to understand what one sees or remembers is driven forward by the dynamism of the inquiring mind and is represented by questions that seek understanding such as "What is it?" For example, "What is a circle?" "What is cross-eyedness?" "What is a house?" "What is the patient's problem?" "What type of legal situation is this?"

What-questions are posed in two contexts - the context of everyday speech and the theoretical context. Hence two types of answers can be given to the same question. One can ask "What is a circle?" and be satisfied with the answer, "Something round". One can ask "What is the patient's problem?" and be satisfied with naming the patients's problem "a duodenal ulcer" and yet have no understanding of ulcers at all. One can ask "What type of case is this?" and be satisfied with naming the situation "murder" and yet have no knowledge of the elements of the crime of murder or how they are relevant in the concrete situation. Such answers simply involve pointing or naming and are insights into the use of language.

But a person may not be satisfied with answers that simply point or name. What-questions can also demand definitions, explanations, and interpretations. When you ask "What is a circle?" you seek the definition of a circle. When you ask "What is strabismus?" you seek an explanatory account of cross-eyedness. These are what Lonergan would understand as typical "scientific" questions. But even when you ask "What is a house?" you seek an explanation of how the parts constitute a unity or whole. And when you ask "What is the patient's problem?" you seek an explanation of how the symptoms are related. When you ask "What type of legal situation is this?" you seek an interpretation of the situation that relates the facts of the case to previous cases, legal categories, and relevant law. These types of questions, called "What-questions", ask for a cause, a reason, a correlation, a unity, an explanation, or an interpretation.

Sometimes, according to Lonergan, the two questions "What?" and "Why?" turn out to be the same. For example, the questions "What is rain?" and "Why does it rain?" turn out to be one and the same. The answers to both questions involve an explanation of evaporation and condensation. Lonergan writes that Aristotle's example, "What is an eclipse of the moon?" and "Why is the moon thus darkened?" are not two questions, but one and the same because if you "Say that the earth intervenes between the sun and the moon, blocking off the light received by the latter from the former. . .at once you know why the moon is thus darkened, and what an eclipse is."[8] They are the same question because both questions represent the orientation of the inquirer toward understanding the nature of eclipses and because the same answer satisfies each question. In the legal context, the question "What caused this person's death?" and "Why did this person die?" turn out to be the same question. They both demand an explanation of the course of events that led to someone's death.

Unlike sensible presentations which depend on outer circumstances, the emergence of What-questions depends on presentations insofar as a person is attentive to what one sees, hears, etc., but What-questions are also free from outer circumstances in a way that the raw materials of inquiry, sensible presentations, are not. Although sensible presentations have some immediate relationship to outer circumstances, What-questions can occur or not occur. What-questions are concerned with what is sensed, yet they move beyond sensible presentations to ask about what is sensed, imagined, or remembered. The inquirer asking questions arranges particular aspects of the materials presented by sense and imagination in a new way. The creative element in this activity is the emergence or creation of the question itself from the raw materials of sensible and imaginative presentations. Questions focus attention on particular aspects of the data.

Answers will not occur unless questions are asked. For example, if King Hiero had not asked Archimedes to determine whether the crown was pure gold, Archimedes probably would not have thought about the problem and probably would never have reached his insight.

Answers to What-questions depend on the accurate presentation of questions and problems. Questions and answers form a context and until the question or problem is accurately and precisely formulated, an answer, which is a related insight or a related set of insights, will not be immediately forthcoming. Problems will not be solved until the appropriate questions are asked. Insights depend on the particular questions that are asked. For example, the motion of falling bodies was not understood until the impetus theories of the Aristotelians were replaced by Galileo's inquiry into the relationship between the distance and time of falling objects. Galileo's insights depended on him specifically asking "What is the relationship between distance and time when objects fall?" For Galileo, the particular problem was not to describe the trajectory of the object but to correlate the distance and time of falling objects.

But solutions to problems that represent great advances in science are not the only insights that depend on precisely formulated questions. Solutions to familiar problems and questions also depend on questions being accurately formulated. For example, wanting to know the time at this moment depends on posing the question "What is the time?", not on asking "What day is it?" Similarly, wanting to know someone's birthdate is not met by asking "What is your sign of the zodiac?", but by asking "What is the date of your birth?" A physician wanting to understand why a patient cannot read an eye chart will ask specific questions such as "Does the person have cataracts?" and "Does the person have glaucoma?" Asking questions about the patient's teeth will not help the doctor understand the patient's eye problems. Similarly, a judge may ask specific questions about the order in which events occurred in a case in order to understand a particular case.

The fact that direct insight depends on an accurate formulation of the question not only illustrates the fact that the question focuses attention on particular aspects of data that will be considered relevant to answering the question. Framing the question accurately narrows the link between the question and answer to be discovered by direct insight. The question can place limits on the direct insight inasmuch as it focuses attention on particular aspects of the data and creates the context in which answers will be relevant. Questions, then, guide the inquiry toward answers and solutions to problems.

However, the relevance of questions to a problem can depend on the previous occurrence of direct insights. Previous questions and direct insights may be required in order to answer a question or solve a problem. For example, the emergence of questions about molecular formulae depend on understanding the periodic table. The questions asked by a physician about a patient's symptoms depend on a doctor's understanding of disease, similar symptoms encountered in previous patients, and previous diagnoses. Previous knowledge helps a doctor pose the pertinent questions in that an experienced doctor can probably detect what is relevant and what is irrelevant to the inquiry. Similarly, questions asked by a judge about a particular case depend on the judge's knowledge of law and similar cases and their relation to legal categories. An experienced judge is more likely to ask the relevant questions in order to understand the relevant aspects of a specific case.

Insight is not restricted to the raw materials of sense perception. Not only do insights occur in the context of presentations, What-questions, and formulations, but insights are also related to other insights. According to Lonergan, insights do not occur in isolation. In the scientific context, "A single insight yields an object of thought; a conception yields a definition; and from a cluster of insights, one builds up a system of definitions, axioms, postulates, and deductions. . ."[9] According to Lonergan, Euclid's geometry and the periodic table in chemistry are both examples of inter-related sets of insights. He writes that we learn inasmuch as we can add insight to insight, inasmuch as the new does not exclude the old but complements and combines with it. Understanding concrete situations, such as those experienced by doctors diagnosing ailments and judges interpreting situations, also depends on the relation of sets of related insights. A doctor builds on his or her understanding of a patient's complaints by asking questions in order to rule out potential diagnoses and to narrow down the possible diagnoses as much as possible. In this way the doctor adds insight to insight until the doctor has a supervening insight (formulated as a diagnosis) that encompasses the previous insights. Similarly, a judge interpreting a case asks question after question about the law, previous cases, and the events that took place, thereby building on his previous knowledge of the law and the case until a supervening insight that encompasses and synthesizes the previous insights is reached and formulated as an interpretation of the situation.

3.3 Direct Insight - The Act of Discovery in The Understanding Phase

What-questions lead to direct insights. In Lonergan's words, "The insight is the click, the grasp, the discovery, what is added to one's knowledge when one sees the "must" in the data."[10] A doctor's insight into a problem is a discovery of the unity in the symptoms, that is, how the symptoms "must be" linked together. Similarly, a judge's insight into events discovers the unity in the events, that is, how the events "must be" linked together. But the "must" that is discovered is not a "must" that is concerned with truth. Instead, it is a definition, explanation, unity, or interpretation that, as yet, is not known to be correct or incorrect, true or false. The doctor's diagnosis and the judge's interpretation, at this point, are *possibly* correct.

But to what extent is direct insight an act of discovery? The nature of the discovery that occurs in direct insight can be introduced by considering simple examples such as jokes and crossword puzzles. Direct insight occurs when you "get" the punch line of a joke. The act of discovering the relationship between the question and the punch line is the insight. "Do you know why mice have such small balls????????????????? "Because not many of them dance." In this example, "getting the joke" depends on an insight that discovers the link between the ambiguous meaning of the word "balls" and dancing. Put crudely, this section is concerned with what it is to "get" a punch line of a joke. In other words, the goal of this discussion is to explain the structure of the "get" or the "discovery" in human understanding. Similarly, people doing crossword puzzles also have insights. They are provided with clues in the form of obscure phrases, letters they have already filled in, and boxes indicating the length of words. Insights discover possible solutions to a puzzle.

So what does it mean to talk about direct insight as discovering relations immanent in data such as sensible presentations or imaginative representations? The best way to answer this question is to begin by discussing what Lonergan thinks direct insight is not. Just as Lonergan distinguishes insight from sensible presentations, he distinguishes insight from formulations of insight. The activity of insight, according to Lonergan, is pre-conceptual; that is, it occurs before expression. Insight is not expression, ie. stating the contents of the insight. Insight is the basis of concepts; it is not the formulation of what it discovers. The insight is the act of discovery which is prior to stating the content of the discovery as a concept, correlation, definition, hypothesis, explanation, interpretation, or unity.[11]

The difficulty of explaining what it means to discover relations in data or to grasp the "must" in the data is due to the fact that explanations of what insight discovers depend on and occur after insight has occurred, but the resulting explanation of the nature of insight as an act of discovery must be used to explain the discovery that occurred as insight prior to its formulation. So, to explain insight in terms of an act of discovery is to go beyond the insight, the mental activity, to a formulation or explanation of the insight. Hence, defining the structure of discovery or the grasp of the "must" is difficult, but not impossible.

Because the contents of the discovery can only be understood in light of a formulation of an insight, the study of the grasp of the "must" must use particular cases. The notion of "discovering relations" or "seeing the must in the data" cannot be understood apart from particular data since it is meaningless to talk about "discovering relations" in the absence of data. Insights are into data and do not occur unless there are raw materials that can be interrogated. Hence, the search for a universal definition of "what it is to grasp relations" will be in vain. Although some general characteristics of "grasping" can be formulated, the study of the act of discovery is restricted to particular examples and it must be acknowledged that the data for studying what is a pre-conceptual activity are based on and depend on the activity being studied. In other words, to study the activity, the expression of the activity must be examined. The methodological problem lies in the fact that the expression of the insight is not the activity of the insight and yet we want to study the activity of insight itself. Consequently, we must rely on inferences regarding the structure of "grasping" or discovering.

The nature of discovery as "grasping the must"[12] cannot be over-emphasized. Direct insight is into particular data and leads to the expression of particular links and particular relations among data. A doctor's insight into symptoms is a discovery of what the relation among the symptoms "must be". This discovery does not alter the symptoms in any way. The patient still feels ill. A judge's direct insight into legal arguments and testimony is also a discovery of what "must be" the relation among data. A judge's interpretation of arguments and testimony does not alter what a judge has heard. Although insight depends on data for its contents and will not occur without particular data, insight does not change sensible presentations. It does not add anything to the presentations. Rather, insight grasps relations immanent in the data.

Insight can be understood as the nexus between particular What-questions and answers. One can ask "What is strabismus?" which is answered by discovering and formulating a definition or an explanation. From this point of view, the activity of insight - "discovering" - can only be understood and specified if the questions and answers have particular contents. Insight discovers particular relations in data. Consequently, it is necessary to analyse the structure of insight in particular situations to understand the act of discovery that occurs in the act of insight. I have chosen to discuss Lonergan's analyses of geometrical insights, scientific insights, and insights that grasp the concrete unity in data. While both the contexts in which these insights occur and the nature of the discoveries made by these direct insights differ, all three types of direct insight have the same structure in that they all "grasp" or "discover" the *relations* or *links* among raw materials that would otherwise be unknown. Direct insight in geometry discovers the *relations* among the data that are necessary and also the *relations* among the data that are impossible. The scientific direct insight discovers possible *relations* between independent and dependent variables. Direct insights that discover a concrete unity discover how data are *related* to each other to form of a unity or whole. For example, direct insight in medicine discovers how a patients's symptoms are *related* to disease and previous diagnoses. Similarly, direct insight in law discovers how particular events and law are *related* as, for instance, a case of murder.

Lonergan illustrates the *geometrical insight* by explaining how one comes to understand the definition of a circle. In **Insight**, Lonergan considers how one discovers the definition of a circle in detail. He summarizes the process of discovery in **Understanding and Being** in the following manner: "The What-question he answers is "What is a circle?" In his own words,

> We start with the cartwheel and draw the radii. We see that if any of the radii are unequal, there are bound to be either bumps or dents in the perimeter. If one radius is a little too long, we have to bring the perimeter out, and if one is a little too short, we have to bring the perimeter in. However, if one considers that the radii are infinite in number and that they are exactly the same length, then the circle is bound to be perfectly round. That is the insight. What the insight grasps is necessity and impossibility - the necessity of the circle being perfectly round and the impossibility of the circle being perfectly round if any radii are unequal.[13]

Lonergan says that the insight in this case grasps a necessary relation in the sensible presentation. The sensible presentation consists of imagining the perfect roundness of this curve, and supposing an infinity of radii belonging to this curve. The insight adds to the sensible presentation, that in order for the curve to be perfectly round, all the radii must be equal. This is a necessary relation. The impossible relation is that, if any of the radii are unequal, it is impossible for the curve to be perfectly round. The geometrical insight grasps necessity and impossibility immanent in the data. This type of insight grasps that, if a particular relationship among data exists, it is impossible for certain other relationships among the same data to exist.

The *scientific insight* will be analyzed by considering an ophthamologist's desire to understand strabismus (cross-eyedness). This type of insight discovers an explanation, a cause, a reason, or a correlation. For example, an ophthamologist may want to know about crossed eyes and may ask "What is strabismus?" The researcher seeks an explanation of strabismus. He begins his investigation by distinguishing between different types of strabismus and the various degrees of each type, the relative lengths and strengths of opposed sets of eye muscles. The researcher relates his findings to critical periods in eye development and correlates these critical periods to the presence or absence of particular growth factors, chemicals, hormones, environmental factors, and investigates the relationship between strabismus and recessive autosomal genes. For example, he may compare the incidence of strabismus with the occurrence of a particular recessive autosomal gene and find a positive correlation. His insights grasp the possible relations among the two sets of data. Insofar as new developments in technology or research strategies could revise or even supercede his insights, his insights grasp possibilities inherent in the data such as the possibility that there is a positive correlation between the incidence of strabismus and the existence of a particular gene. The relations he grasps are not "necessary" since they could later be revised.

Direct insight can discover a *concrete unity* in sensible presentations. Insight grasps the concrete unity or wholeness in the data. Lonergan notes that an insight into what is a house is not a combination of separate analyses of walls, roof, foundation, windows, and doors. Instead, this type of insight grasps that the relations among these parts constitute a concrete unity or whole - a house. Philip McShane illustrates this type of insight with the tale of Jonah who

> . . . woke up lying on his back feeling sick. The place is pitch dark, smelly, damp. He feels with his hands the damp, mossy surface around him. He gets to his feet and the whole place sways about. He shines his pocket torch around: He is in some sort of cave, reddish coloured, with odd projections and pieces of bone around. Then it dawns on him. . . "I'm in a whale." Now, note that the "dawning" added nothing to the data beyond the unity-identity-wholeness of one thing [that was discovered]. (We speak loosely - obviously it pulls in his understanding of whales.)[14]

Jonah is not the only one to have a direct insight that discovers the unity in sensible data. Doctors and judges also discover the concrete unity in sensible presentations. A physician discovers that the particular symptoms of a patient are related as a disease. Similarly, a judge discovers that particular elements in a case are related to each other as a whole or unity in that they constitute a crime. The discovery that a situation amounts to murder involves discovering the relation among the significant events of the case, the relevant law, and previous cases that amount to murder.

A few observations can be made about these examples. The first is that the relations discovered by the three types of insight are *different*. Geometrical insights discover *necessity* and *impossibility* in the data and are expressed as abstract definitions. Scientific insights discover *possible* relations among the data that are formulated as abstract explanations and definitions. Insights in concrete circumstances discover descriptive relations in data grasped as constituting *concrete wholes*. As I have indicated at various points, legal decision-making primarily involves direct insights that discover the concrete unity in data. But this is not to say that direct insight in law does not resemble scientific insights. Many legal academics are engaged in searching for and formulating legal principles and legal definitions.

However, it is equally important to note that direct insight has the same basic structure in all contexts. The particular relation discovered by direct insight depends on the specific question asked and the type of data that is being interrogated. These differences result in the differences among the three types of insight. Despite the fact that the nature of the grasp of insight is only meaningful in relation to particular questions and data, it seems that the activity of insight can discover relations in data that are very diverse. Insight is an adaptable activity capable of coping with unfamiliar and changing data.

There are no rules that will automatically lead to a discovery if they are followed. Lonergan claims that insight is not reached solely by learning rules, following precepts, nor by studying any methodology. A doctor may have rules of thumb that are followed in order to make a diagnosis, but a problem is not understood because the doctor follows a set of rules. A diagnosis is made if relevant questions are asked. Similarly, while a judge follows rules regarding the order in which testimony can be presented and rules concerning, for example, hearsay evidence, such rules do not guarantee that a judge will discover how the testimony of the witnesses fits together or how the events and the law are related. The judge must ask pertinent questions in order to interpret the situation; these questions are not pre-determined and do not necessarily arise in an orderly fashion. Solving legal problems is primarily a matter of trial and error. In Lonergan's opinion, "Were there rules for discovery, then discoveries would be mere conclusions."[15]

Although the process of reaching direct insights is not determined by following rules or by logical deduction, this does not mean that the process is essentially arbitrary and irrational. On the contrary, the process is conscious and deliberate. Questions are deliberately and consciously asked in order to have direct insights. Moreover, if one wants to understand the nature of something, one identifies the end that is desired and then devises a strategy to reach that end. For example, if a doctor wants to understand the nature of a patient's complaints such as a stomach ache and vomiting, the doctor's strategy might be to feel the person's abdomen and perform an ultra-sound examination. The doctor knows that these methods have successfully led to a diagnosis on previous occasions. If a judge wants to discover if a person is guilty of some crime, the strategy that has been devised is a trial where the evidence and arguments by opposing counsel is subject to strict rules and procedures designed to help the judge or jury reach an unbiased verdict. This trial method is used because it has helped solve legal problems on previous occasions. Although these strategies involve trial and error they are not essentially irrational nor arbitrary, but are conscious, deliberate, and intelligent.

Insight is the source of all learning and knowledge. "Discovery is a new beginning. It is the origin of new rules that supplement or even supplant the old. Genius is creative. It is genius because it originates the novelties that will be the routines of the future."[16] Although Lonergan writes here as if insight leads only to major discoveries that might be considered as representing paradigm shifts in science, he also thinks that insight occurs as a normal activity in science and indeed in all areas of inquiry.

3.4 Formulation

As noted above, insight is different from expression, but it leads to it. Direct insight leads to the distinct mental activity of formulating the insight. The act of direct insight discovers the particular relation that can be formulated or considered and transformed into a general expression. For Lonergan, an insight is distinct from a formulation of a definition or explanation. A direct insight is into a particular case, set of data, or circumstances. In medicine, the doctor's insight is into a particular patient's problem and can be expressed as a diagnosis of one patient's problem. A judge's insight is into a particular case and can be expressed as an interpretation of one particular situation. For example, "This particular situation is a case of murder."

Lonergan writes that ". . .one has to do some further thinking if one wants a conception, an expression, a general formulation of that insight."[17] In science, "One has to take time out to think out a general formula that adequately expresses the insight."[18] Archimedes' insight about weighing the crown in water is expressed in terms of scientific generality as the relation between specific gravity, mass, and volume. Formulation precedes expression. If a doctor wants to formulate a general definition of ulcers, this is done by considering the relevant similarities among ulcers. If a judge wants to express a general definition of murder, the judge must formulate the relevant similarities among cases of murder. Formulating the insight completes the pattern of mental activities involved in the process of discovery in the understanding phase of theoretical reasoning.

Lonergan uses Archimedes' solution to Hiero's problem to illustrate how insight is a pivot between the concrete and the abstract. Lonergan says Archimedes had a concrete problem - "to settle whether a particular crown was made of pure gold."[19] Lonergan says Archimedes' concrete solution was to weigh the crown in water. The abstract part of the procedure includes the abstract formulations of the principles of displacement and of specific gravity that are derived from the concrete problem and solution. The scientific importance lies in the abstract formulations that can be applied to solve other problems. The direct insight was into one particular problem and the solution concerned one particular crown. Archimedes' direct insight was into his particular situation. However, because the formulation of his direct insight as an abstract law can be applied to other situations, Lonergan understands the scientific direct insight, as he does all types of insight, as a pivot between the concrete situation and the abstract formulation.

Lonergan notes that defining what is necessary and sufficient to the insight may be tricky because attention to the general case may not be automatic. The act of formulating the direct insight involves picking out everything that is sufficient and nec-

4.2 Reflective Insight - The Act of Discovery in The Testing Phase

Reflective insight is the mental activity that mediates between Is-questions and judgments of fact. It transforms Is-questions into judgments of fact. As such, reflective insight is an answer to a question, a solution to a problem about whether or not a formulation is correct. Both direct and reflective insights are insights into data. Whereas direct insight is into sensible presentations and imaginative representations, reflective insights are insights into a conjunction of presentations and conceptions, explanations, definitions, diagnoses, and interpretations. Direct insights and presentations are the raw materials for reflective insight. For the doctor, reflective insight grasps the relation among symptoms and the diagnosis. The reflective insight reached by a judge grasps the link among oral testimony, legal arguments, and the judge's interpretation of the situation. The mental attitude of the inquirer in this context can be represented by the questions "Is-it-true?" "Is-it-so?" Is-questions initiate reflection by demanding reflective insight.

Both direct insight and reflective insight involve discovery. As direct insight discovers causes, correlations, definitions, explanations or unities, reflective insight discovers *"the sufficiency of the evidence for a prospective judgment."*[23] The reflective insight itself discovers whether or not the evidence is sufficient as a basis for making a judgment of fact, that is, whether the patient's symptoms or the oral testimony of witnesses are a sufficient basis for making the diagnosis or the interpretation. The questions I want to answer in this section are: "What does it mean to discover the sufficiency of the evidence for a judgment?" "What is the nature of the discovery that occurs?"

An individual begins the process of reflection by formulating a prospective judgment that "Such-and-such is correct" or "Such-and-such is incorrect". This judgment is prospective in the sense that it is a potential or possible judgment. A judgment will be made after a reflective insight has occurred. Hence, at this stage, a judgment has not yet been reached. A judgment that "Such-and-such is correct" has conditions which must be fulfilled if the judgment is to be correct. The judgment must be supported by sufficient evidence.

Both the conditions for making the judgment and whether or not they are supported by evidence must be discovered. Hence, reflective insight involves two types of discovery. First, the individual discovers the link or relations between the prospective judgment and the conditions that are sufficient for making that judgment. In other words, in reflective insight one discovers the conditions or criteria that are sufficient, if fulfilled, for making the prospective judgment. Secondly one discovers whether or not the conditions for making the prospective judgment are actually fulfilled or satisfied.[24]

In a single act, the reflective insight itself discovers (1) the link between the prospective judgment and the conditions for that judgment and (2) whether or not these conditions are fulfilled. Lonergan summarizes the general form of critical reflection as the occurrence of

. . .a reflective insight in which at once one grasps:

(1) a conditioned, the prospective judgment that a given direct or introspective insight is correct,
(2) a link between the conditioned and its conditions, and this on introspective analysis proves to be that an insight is correct if it is invulnerable and it is invulnerable if there are no further, pertinent questions, and
(3) the fulfilment of the conditions, namely that the given insight does put an end to further, pertinent questioning and that this occurs in a mind that is alert, familiar with the concrete situation, and intellectually master of it.[25]

Let's examine a simple example. Suppose I am about to leave my flat and as I gaze out of my third floor window I ask myself "Is it raining today?" The prospective judgment I might formulate is "Yes, it is raining." But I have not yet made this judgment; it is only a prospective or potential judgment.

I must discover the conditions or criteria that, in my opinion, are sufficient for making this judgment. The conditions that, in my opinion, are sufficient for the prospective judgment are: (a) that people on the sidewalk have their umbrellas open and (b) that cars on the road have their windshield wipers operating. I have discovered the first element of reflective insight, the link between the prospective judgment and the conditions that are sufficient for the judgment.

Next I look out the window and see that umbrellas are open and windshield wipers are operating. I discover that the conditions for the judgment are satisfied. The fulfilling conditions are on the level of sense-experience. I have relied on acts of seeing but these sense-presentations are not judgments.[26]

Reflective insight, in a single moment or instant, discovers that the prospective judgment that "It is raining" is correct, that seeing umbrellas open and wipers operating is sufficient for making the judgment that "It is raining", and that the two conditions are satisfied - umbrellas are open and wipers are operating.

A doctor discovers the conditions that are sufficient, if fulfilled, for making the judgment that the diagnosis of a stomach ulcer is correct. The conditions that must be fulfilled, that is, the symptoms that are sufficient, consist in sense-experience and previous judgments. In the "discovery" phase, the doctor listens to the patient complain about stomach aches and vomiting and feels the patient's enlarged stomach. What the doctor hears and feels is sense-experience. A direct insight is reached and formulated as the diagnosis that this patient has a stomach ulcer. But is this diagnosis correct? The doctor tests whether the three symptoms - the stomach ache, vomiting, and enlarged stomach are sufficient conditions for making the diagnosis. Whether the three symptoms are a sufficient basis for the diagnosis is discovered by asking relevant questions such as "Could the symptoms support a different diagnosis?" If the symptoms can also support the diagnosis of a duodenal ulcer, then the three symptoms are not sufficient for diagnosing a stomach ulcer. Further conditions must be satisfied, but what are they? Perhaps an ultra-sound test will resolve the doubt about the diagnosis. The point is that, when there are no more pertinent questions about the conditions for making the diagnosis, then the sufficient conditions (if fulfilled) for making the judgment have been discovered.

But so far the physician has discovered that only three conditions have been fulfilled. The patient has stomach aches, vomits, and has an enlarged stomach. The fourth condition that must be satisfied is that some aberration of the stomach must

Insights are correct as a matter of fact, and the fact exists when there are no further relevant questions. "It is not a question of possibility, 'Could there be some further relevant question?' The question of possibility does not bear upon the judgment that de facto these insights have reached the point of invulnerability."[35]

Although his notion of objectivity is linked to the fact that no further questions arise, he is not stating that invulnerable insights are absolutely correct. He is only saying that the insights may be as invulnerable as you can get or need to get in the circumstances. Good judgment then is relative. In Lonergan's view it depends on:

(1) "[giving] the further questions a chance to arise."[36]

(2) "the previous acquisition of a large number of other, connected, and correct insights."[37]

(3) the fact that insights occur within a self-correcting process of learning in which the shortcomings of insights provoke further questions until one becomes familiar with a situation and masters it.[38]

(4) making a special effort to cope with temperament, ie. rashness and indecisiveness.[39]

Thus, reflective insight depends on inner conditions insofar as one takes one's time before judging, is alert and asks questions, talks things over, and tests hypotheses, explanations, and interpretations.

4.3 Judgments of Fact

Reflective insight leads to the act of judgment. Judgment itself depends on reflective insight. Judgment can be expressed in two basic ways - "*It is so*" or "*It is not so*." Lonergan states that "judgments proceed rationally from a grasp of the sufficiency of the evidence."[40] "One makes a judgment because one grasps the sufficiency of the evidence."[41] In other words, "the act of judgment is caused by the act that grasps the sufficiency of the evidence where "cause" means "because" as rational consciousness, a consciousness that is obligated by its own rationality to judge, by the rational necessity of judging."[42] The act of judgment is not of synthesis, but an act in which one *posits synthesis*. A theory, an hypothesis, an explanation, or an interpretation is already a synthesis. Judgment does not add further synthesis.

A judgment of fact answers the Is-question by expressing what is grasped by reflective insight as one of two alternatives: "Yes" or "No" or in one of a variety of modalities - "I don't know", "Possibly", "Probably", "We'll see", "Certainly". The act of judgment is the act that adds assent to a proposition, that changes a proposition from the expression of an act of conceiving, defining, thinking, supposing, or considering to a proposition that states that the content of the expression is true or that an object exists. A doctor states, "Yes, this patient's problem is a stomach ulcer", and a judge states, "This situation is a case of murder". Thus a judgment of fact is more than an expression or formulation of a reflective insight.

For Lonergan, judgment is a personal commitment. Judgment involves personal responsibility.[43] Unlike memory or insight judgment is under our control, and is a personal act. "One does not have to say "Yes" or "No"; one can say "I don't know." One does not have to say "It certainly is so"; one can say "It probably is so" or "It possibly is so." All the alternatives relevant to human weakness, ignorance, and tardiness are provided for, and one is committed to picking out the right one . . ."[44] He states that "a judgment is the responsibility of the one that judges."[45] "Because it is so personal, so much an expression of one's own reasonableness apart from any constraint, because all alternatives are provided for, it is entirely one's own responsibility, one does not complain about one's bad judgments; one is responsible for them."[46] Yes, No, I don't know, with certitude or only probability; the question as presented can be dismissed, distinctions introduced, and new questions substituted. "The variety of possible answers makes full allowance for the misfortunes and shortcomings of the person answering, and by the same stroke it closes the door on possible excuses for mistakes."[47] A physician is held responsible for a diagnosis, just as a judge is held responsible for a verdict. Both the doctor and the judge are the individuals who discover the criteria that are sufficient for their judgments and also discover whether the evidence is a sufficient basis for their own judgments of fact. If the evidence is considered by the doctor or judge to be sufficient for the judgment, then, according to that doctor or judge, the judgment is correct or justified. Hence doctors and judges are held responsible for their mistaken judgments. Doctors are sometimes sued for mis-diagnosing ailments and judges are sometimes criticized for their interpretations of cases.

Like formulations which depend on the concrete data that are studied and the particular direct insights that occur, the meaning of a judgment depends on its context. It is related to a particular Is-question and a particular reflective insight. According to Lonergan, a judgment is meaningless apart from the question it answers and its content which is supplied by a reflective insight. For this reason Is-questions, reflective insight, and judgment form an integrated whole. It is an integral element of the structure of knowing.

Because the judgment depends on the sufficiency of the evidence it follows that if one does not grasp the sufficiency of the evidence and nevertheless says "It is" or "It is not", one is just guessing. For example, judging that a person has an ulcer without undertaking some sort of investigation is rash, and judging that a person is guilty of murder would be unfounded without relying on relevant forensic evidence. On the other hand, according to Lonergan, if one grasps the sufficiency of the evidence and hesitates, one is being silly because one's rationality demands that one judge. For example, the doctor would be defaulting on his rationality if he grasped that the evidence for the diagnosis of a duodenal ulcer is sufficient, but did not judge. In Lonergan's opinion, defaulting on your rationality is introducing a contradiction within your cognitive structure because what reflective insight discovers or fails to discover does not become explicit in the act of judgment. Another characteristic of rational consciousness "includes the principle of excluded middle, provided the question is fairly put - either it is or it is not, either one or the other. It includes the principle of non-contradiction - it cannot be both."[48] Rationality, for Lonergan, does not lie in logic.

Understanding and testing in theoretical problem-solving are not independent phases. According to Lonergan, because the two previous levels of presentations and understanding provide the content for Is-questions and reflective insights, it is

34 ibid., 152.
35 ibid., 153.
36 **Insight**, 285.
37 ibid., 285.
38 ibid., 286.
39 ibid., 287.
40 **Understanding and Being**, 138.
41 **Insight**, 140.
42 **Understanding and Being**, 137.
43 ibid., 138.
44 ibid., 138.
45 **Insight**, 322.
46 **Understanding and Being**, 139.
47 **Insight**, 272.
48 **Understanding and Being**, 144.
49 ibid., 140.
50 **Insight**, 282.
51 ibid., 282.
52 **Wealth of Self and Wealth of Nations**, 36.

7

"Discovery" in Practical Problem-Solving

1 Introduction

Not only does decision-making in medicine and law involve theoretical problem-solving, it also involves practical problem-solving. Physicians and judges both ask practical questions such as *"What is to be done?"* "What can I do about the patient's stomach ulcer?" and "What can I do with the guilty person?" However, these are only the most obvious examples. Practical questions occur throughout the decision-making process. Practical questions demand the emergence of *practical insights* which are formulated as *proposed courses of action*. The doctor's options could include prescribing drugs, performing surgery, or advising a special diet. The judge's options could include probation, a suspended sentence, or a term in jail. A judge faced with the problem of judging whether parents, who suffer from post-traumatic stress syndrome after watching their children physically injured on television, can recover for nervous shock has two options - either to award the parents damages for nervous shock or not to award them damages.

Nor does the practical problem-solving process end with the discovery of alternatives. Having formulated their options, the doctor and judge go on to ask which alternative they should perform. Doctors and judges both ask *"Is this proposed course of action sufficiently suitable in the particular circumstances?"* "Should I prescribe drugs or perform surgery?" A judge could ask "Should the sentence be probation or 10 years in jail?" "Should I judge that the parents can recover damages due to nervous shock after watching the Hillsborough disaster on television?" or "Should I judge that they cannot recover damages for nervous shock in this case?"

Evaluations of options by a doctor or a judge lead to a *practical reflective insight* and a *judgment of value* that one course of action is sufficiently suitable or more appropriate than others in the circumstances. Finally, the physician or judge *chooses* or *decides* whether or not to perform the course of action that has been judged to be sufficiently suitable in the circumstances.

As in theoretical reasoning, Lonergan does not distinguish between a process of "discovery" and an independent stage of "justification" in practical reasoning. The image that a discrete and essentially irrational "discovery" stage ends with the formulation of courses of action which are subjected to an independent and essentially logical process of justification cannot be found in Lonergan's writings. Rather, the

of watching the Hillsborough disaster on television as having an "instant effect on emotions and a lasting effect on memory" makes the situation similar to previous cases in which parents have seen or heard of the disastrous event or its immediate aftermath and have recovered for damages due to nervous shock. This interpretation of the situation leads to one solution - the parents can recover. But an interpretation of the situation as a case of communication by a third party, not a case of parents being within sight and hearing of the event, and not a case equivalent to the immediate aftermath of an accident, leads to the alternative solution that the parents cannot recover for nervous shock. In all these examples, the courses of action that are judged to be suitable depend on how the situation is understood.

The occurrence of practical insights depends on one's concerns insofar as one is alert to, and concerned with, practical matters and asks questions such as "What-is-to-be-done?" The more familiar a person is with solving practical problems in particular fields, the more likely it will be that practical insights will occur in new situations. Practical insight occurs almost at will in similar circumstances once one has had the initial practical insight. What was once a difficult and vexing problem is no longer so. The solution is simple and obvious after the practical insight has occurred. For example, a doctor who treats ulcers will probably know immediately what the treatment options are when faced with an ulcer in a patient. The options do not have to re-invented each time a doctor diagnoses an ulcer. Similarly, a judge who awards damages in the case in which nervous shock is the outcome of watching a disaster on television will probably not have to re-discover the range of damages that would be appropriate compensation in a similar case. The point is that the entire practical problem-solving process that was required to find a solution in a novel situation does not need to be performed again to solve a similar case. The range of options has already been discovered.

Moreover, familiarity with situations helps a person identify what is different, new, or changed and relevant in subsequent circumstances. In general, experts in particular fields who are interested in, and experienced in, solving practical problems will probably notice deviations from expectations more readily. The doctor who is an expert in ulcers will probably be able to discover what to do when faced with unfamiliar types of ulcers. Similarly, a judge who is an expert on nervous shock cases will probably be more likely to discover or invent a suitable solution in a novel case than a judge who is not familiar with cases involving nervous shock.

2.3 Proposed Courses of Action

In contrast to direct insight, practical insight does not possess the same degree of generality and relevance to other situations. A doctor can formulate a general definition of an ulcer and a judge can formulate a general definition of murder. But practical insights lead to the formulation of possible courses of action that might or might not be appropriate in the particular circumstances. In practical affairs, new courses of action may be required if the situation changes. The old options may not work or may not be applicable. Practical insight lacks the generality of direct insight in theoretical reasoning because in each concrete situation practical insights occur.

Practical insight depends on particular situations. Drugs may be an appropriate way to treat one person's ulcer, but surgery may be required to adequately treat another person's ulcer. Similarly, a two-year sentence may be appropriate in one case of manslaughter, but ten years may be suitable in another manslaughter case. Awarding damages for nervous shock may be appropriate in one type of case such as when parents see their injured children immediately after an accident, but it may not be judged to be suitable when parents have seen the accident on television. Practical insight is universal only to the extent that one situation is judged to be significantly similar to other situations. And what is significant in a particular situation is what the person who is familiar with both situations judges to be significant in the circumstances.

Practical insights do not discover the most suitable option in a situation. In Lonergan's words, practical insight is not concerned with "Whether the unity is going to be made to exist or whether the correlation is going to be made to govern events."[7] For example, a cyclist with a flat tyre could come up with a variety of courses of action to consider. She could phone home and ask for a lift; she could stick out his thumb and hitch hike; she could fix the tyre on the spot; she could walk the bicycle home; or she could throw the useless machine into the lake and revel in her ability to solve problems. After a doctor diagnoses an ulcer, she may ask "What treatment should I prescribe for this patient?" and become cognizant of various possibilities such as drugs, surgery, or special diet. After a judge interprets a situation to be a case of manslaughter, a judge discovers the possible sentences such as one year, two years, or ten years. After a judge interprets the situation of watching a disaster on television to be equivalent to the perception of the actual event or its immediate aftermath, the judge may discover that the possible solutions to the problem are limited to awarding damages, but that the amount of suitable compensation must be discovered. The question concerning which option is sufficiently suitable in the particular circumstances has not yet been posed.

3   Elements in The Testing Phase of Solving Practical Problems

Wondering about possible courses of action leads to asking questions about whether a proposed course of action should be performed. The attitude of the inquirer in the testing phase can be represented by questions that ask "*Is-it-to-be-done*?" or "*Should I perform this course of action*?" These questions, according to Lonergan, demand *practical reflective insight*.[8] The practical reflective insight is an act of discovery. It discovers the relevant issues and their implications. According to Lonergan, questions can be raised regarding the proposed course of action such as the steps required to realize it, its consequences, the feasibility of making the course of action an actuality; the motives for performing the course of action - its agreeableness, its utility, the desirability of the goals, its short-term and long term implications.[9] Practical reflective insight leads to a *judgment of value* that a particular course of action is sufficiently suitable or more suitable than others. Practical reflection or evaluation ends in a *decision* or *choice* to perform the action or not to perform it.

The testing phase involves discovering answers to questions such as *"Which option should be realized?"* and *"Is this course of action sufficiently suitable in this particular situation?"* In this section, I want to examine the actual process of testing and to analyse the extent to which "discovery", in the form of practical reflective insight, is a crucial part of the testing phase in practical problem-solving.

3.1 Is-questions

The raw materials of reflective insight in theoretical problem-solving are the contents of previous mental operations such as sense-experience and direct insight, but the raw materials for practical reflective insight are presentations, direct insights, judgments of fact, practical insights, and proposed courses of action.

Questions for practical reflection can address two issues. One set of questions asks whether a proposed course of action can be reasonably realized. *"Is this proposed course of action feasible in the circumstances?" "Is it possible?" "Is it sufficiently suitable?"* Another set of questions involves a comparison of proposed courses of action in order to discover which alternative is sufficiently appropriate in the circumstances. "Is this proposed course of action more suitable or more appropriate than others?"

For example, from my analysis of practical insight we know that the cyclist has a number of options. Although individuals who are familiar with flat tyres may discover the most reasonable course of action without hesitation, the activity of practical reflection can be illustrated by an analysis from the cyclist's point of view of how she chooses or rejects possible courses of action. The bike rider could phone home for a car ride; hitch hike home; repair the flat on the spot; pump up the tyre and ride on it; or throw the bike away and walk home. Each alternative raises further questions if one is to judge which one is sufficiently suitable. The reasonableness of phoning home and asking for a ride depends on whether it is possible, that is whether a car is available and whether someone will pick her up. These factors may depend on whether she is near or far from home, whether she is prepared to inconvenience someone, or whether she has enough money for the phone call assuming that a phone is nearby. These queries and possibly others must be answered if this particular proposed course of action is to be judged by the cyclist to be both possible and reasonable. The course of action may be possible - someone may be able and willing to pick her up. But she may judge that this particular course of action is not reasonable because she does not want to inconvenience anyone. The option to repair her tyre on the spot may be judged to be impossible if she is on a deserted road and does not have a bike pump, or if she has the equipment but lacks the ability to fix flat tyres. Inflating the tyre to ride on it is possible only if she has a bike pump and the air does not escape as soon as she inflates the tube. Or she may judge that the option is unreasonable because she will bend her rim if she rides on it without the tyre fully inflated. After judging which alternatives are possible and impossible, reasonable and unreasonable, other factors may be relevant to deciding which alternative to choose.

She must judge which option is more suitable than any other. If she has the repair equipment she may judge that fixing it on the spot is more suitable than riding on a flat tyre. If she is a short distance from home, she may judge that simply inflating the tyre, riding home, and fixing it later is more suitable. Judging which proposed course of action is more appropriate or suitable depends on the particular situation and the particular person who assesses one's options in the situation. Each solution in a case has the potential to be a precedent insofar as other cases are judged to be similar to it and the solution is judged to be sufficiently suitable.

A doctor asks whether each option - drugs, special diet, or surgery - is feasible in the circumstances. For example, the doctor asks "Is the patient capable of following a special diet?" "Can I (the doctor) perform the surgery?" "Is the patient allergic to the drugs?" The doctor could ask which course of action is more suitable than others. For example, "What are the side effects of the drugs?" "Will a change of diet cure the ulcer?" "How much does surgery cost?" Similarly, a judge could ask whether the proposed course of action - probation or a prison sentence - are feasible in the circumstances. A judge could ask whether it is possible to perform each particular course of action. For example, "Is the person likely to leave the country?" "Is there room in a prison for the person?" A judge could also ask whether each course of action is reasonable. For example, "Is probation a sufficient punishment?" "Will a prison sentence deter the person from doing the criminal act in the future?" In the case of parents watching a disaster on television, a judge could ask questions such as "Can the police authority pay the damages?" "Can the plaintiffs be accurately identified?" "Is the class of plaintiffs too wide for some reason?" "Is it reasonable to compensate people who suffer nervous shock after watching the disaster on television?" "Was it reasonably foreseeable to the defendant that the defendant's negligence would lead people watching the event on television to suffer injury?"

3.2 Practical Reflective Insight - The Act of Discovery in The Testing Phase

Practical reflective insight discovers the relevant issues and their implications. The aim of practical reflective insight is a *full discovery of the relevant issues and their implications*. The answers to questions of practical reflection resemble answers to questions for reflection in that answers can be "yes", "no", "maybe", "possibly", "certainly", "probably". You may wonder if you can fix the flat tyre and answer that "probably you can since you have the equipment" or that "no, you cannot since you lack the ability". Practical reflection not only demands reasons, but you may also ask yourself ". . . just what the proposed course of action is, what are its successive steps, what alternatives it admits, what it excludes, what consequences it will have, whether the whole proposal is really possible, just how probable or certain are its various features."[10] In this fashion, comprehensive sets of practical reflective insights are constructed that discover the links among particular aspects of the situation or problem and particular courses of action.

Practical reflective insights are concerned with assessing the suitability of proposed courses of action. Practical reflective insight discovers the links between the relevant features of a particular situation, the proposed courses of action, and the reasons for and against the proposed course of action in order to discover whether the course of action is possible or impossible, sufficiently suitable or unsuitable.

The discovery of the appropriate course of action by practical reflective insight depends on one's familiarity with the situation at hand, the seriousness of the consequences of the proposed course of action, the uncertainties and risks it involves, the extent of one's willingness to assume responsibility for the consequences and to run the risks further questions may raise.[11] These factors influence the emergence of questions that would be considered relevant.

As in other types of insight - direct, practical, and reflective - once practical reflective insight occurs, its emergence in identical or similar circumstances is easier and occurs almost at will. A doctor may routinely dispense medicine for common ulcers but in unfamiliar and complicated cases may spend time talking to colleagues about what the most suitable treatment would be. A judge may spontaneously discover what to do in familiar cases but may agonize for days, weeks, or months over what to decide in cases that are unfamiliar.

3.3 Judgments of Value

Practical reflective insight leads to judgments of value that pronounce whether a particular course of action is *possible* or *not possible, sufficiently suitable* or *unsuitable*, or *more appropriate than others* in the circumstances. In other words, the judgment of value pronounces whether or not the action should be performed.

Barden explains the method of testing proposed actions along lines similar to Lonergan. A proposed action is tested by subjecting the reasons for it to questioning. As in theoretical testing, in practical testing the absence of further relevant questions is the criterion for the invulnerability of judgments of value. He emphasizes that the ultimate criterion for a judgment of value is the individual who chooses the reason and the criteria for the action.

As in Lonergan's discussion of practical reasoning, the criteria of action is whether the ethical subject is convinced that a particular course of action is the most appropriate one to perform in the particular circumstances.[12] In other words, the reasons supporting one's judgment of value that a particular course of action is sufficiently suitable in the circumstances must be sufficient for the person making the judgment. The course of action one judges to be sufficiently suitable is correct because the person interpreting the situation and making the judgment of value has asked what are, for that person, all the relevant questions and is satisfied with the answers. Thus, the criteria of action depend on the questions that are asked and answered and the extent that each ethical subject is open to questions.

Barden stresses that judgments of value are not certain or infallible.[13] One can over-look relevant features of a situation. One can give more or less significance to evaluations than one would give on another occasion. One can also mis-interpret the situation and thereby reach a mistaken judgment of value. And one can judge from within a restricted horizon or context thereby suppressing questions that would otherwise be relevant in a broader context.

The particular questions posed and answered depend on one's horizon or context. Barden notes that the variability among people in what amounts to sufficient evidence for a judgment of value is due to the fact that, not only do individuals differ in their evaluations, but they also live within different traditions and experience "different emotional, intellectual, social, cultural, aesthetic, moral, and spiritual" development.[14]

Barden argues that the ultimate criterion for a judgment of value is not a rule or proposition that is accepted because it is fixed, given, innate or due to some authority. This perspective would seem to conflict with the goals of more traditional versions of practical reasoning in which decisions are legally justified by virtue of their relation to legally valid universal rules or norms. But from Barden's point of view, the outcome of a case would not depend on a logical deduction from a universal rule of law plus requisite facts nor on the legal justification of one member of a pair of rival rulings. On the contrary, a particular legal judgment would be judged to be suitable or more suitable than other judgments insofar as that judge asked, and satisfactorily answered, what were considered by the judge to be all the relevant questions. For Barden, a universal legal ruling would express an appropriate solution to a practical problem; it would not in itself be the criterion for a legal judgment.

4 Decision/Choice

In Chapter One, I noted the terminological confusion among legal theorists about how to use the word "decision". Lonergan gives a precise definition of "decision". Decision is concerned with actuality; decision confers actuality upon a course of action that otherwise would not occur. Testing or evaluation in practical problem-solving ends with a judgment of value, but decision ends practical problem-solving itself. A decision is an *act of will* which may or may not follow the judgment of value.[15] It is one thing to know why you should or should not do something, but it is quite another matter to do it. Practical reflection can go on indefinitely. In Lonergan's view, it possesses no capacity to bring itself to an end. "As long as one is reflecting, one has not decided yet. Until a person has decided, the reflection can be prolonged by further questions. But when a decision is made the reflection is over and done with."[16] Decision, then, brings to an end the questions and answers in a single view grounding the choosing of a particular course of action which ends practical problem-solving. For example, practical reflection is ended by the cyclist when she decides to inflate the punctured tyre and ride on it as long as possible and then to inflate the tyre again and again until reaching home. A doctor ends practical reflection when she decides, in accord with a judgment of value, to prescribe drugs for the patient's ulcer. A judge ends the practical problem-solving process when the choice is made to sentence the person to ten years or when the decision is made to allow the parents to recover for nervous shock after watching the Hillsborough disaster on television.

According to Lonergan, decision selects one member of a pair of contradictories. Decision either consents or refuses to perform a specific course of action. Decision is not concerned with rival options or rival rulings. After a doctor formulates a judgment of value that drugs should be prescribed, a doctor either decides to prescribe drugs or refuses to prescribe them. After a judge formulates a judgement of value that the person should be sentenced to ten years, the decision involves sentencing the person to ten years or refusing to sentence the person to ten years. After a judge reaches a judgment of value that the parents who watched their children suffer injuries on television during the Hillsborough disaster should recover for nervous shock, the decision involves awarding them damages or refusing to award them damages.

5 Conclusion

Lonergan offers a plausible explanation of practical problem-solving. It is comprised of a dynamic pattern of six mental activities that involve: (1) *wondering, puzzling*, and asking *What-is-to-be-done-questions*, (2) having *practical insights*, (3) *formulating proposed courses of action*, (4) asking *Is-it-to-be-done-questions*, (5) having *practical reflective insights*, and pronouncing *judgments of value*. Finally, decision ends practical reflection.

A number of significant findings can be summarized. First, the understanding phase in practical problem-solving, which would otherwise be known by legal positivists as the process of discovery, is a deliberate and conscious activity that involves asking and answering relevant questions. Secondly, the extent to which legal decision-making involves "discovery" is further developed by my examination of practical insight and practical reflective insight. Not only is "discovery" a key part of understanding, but "discovery" is also a crucial part of testing. Practical reflective insight is a full discovery of the relevant issues and implications of courses of action.

A brief word must be added about the relation between theoretical and practical problem-solving. My analyses of problem-solving in theoretical and practical reasoning, in the two previous chapters, suggest that the understanding phases involve a single insight and that the testing phases also involve a single insight. However, the actual process is much more complex than I have indicated. Many insights are involved in each phase. The procedure a judge follows to interpret a situation can be understood as the emergence of a complex set of related insights and judgments of fact. Sufficiently understanding a situation involves theoretical reasoning. In the process of understanding a particular situation or problem, the judge must discover the relevant data. In a murder trial, if someone has been killed, the judge will listen to witnesses tell their interpretations of the situation. For the judge, the witnesses' interpretations are data that must be understood and tested for their reliability. If witnesses' stories are judged to be reliable, each story only constitutes the data or raw materials of the judge's interpretation. The judge must discover how the different stories fit together. In other words, the judge must interpret the various stories. The selection of the relevant data will depend on the questions and answers of the judge which, in turn, depend on what questions the judge considers relevant to his ultimate goal of judging guilt or innocence. Through sets of direct insights, the judge discovers possible relations among events. The judge must also test that his interpretation is supported by sufficient evidence. Through sets of reflective insights and judgments of fact, the judge discovers in a supervening reflective insight whether the interpretation of the situation is, in fact, supported by sufficient evidence.

Following an interpretation of the situation, the judge must discover what should be done. This procedure also involves complex sets of insights and judgments. There may be no option; according to law a judgment of "not guilty" leads to releasing the accused person. But the judge may have a range of options, albeit limited and pre-scribed, when the verdict is guilty and must judge which course of action would be sufficiently suitable in the circumstances. If this is the case, practical reflection or evaluation occurs. Questions are asked in order to evaluate the various options. The questions lead to sets of practical reflective insights and a supervening practical reflective insight. A judgment of value, expressing that one option is more suitable than another or aspects of one option are more suitable than another, is formulated. On the other hand, the judge may not know what to do and may compare the case to other cases in order to discover whether the solutions in those cases would be suit-able in the current case. This procedure also involves sets of insights and judgments.

The same general complex procedure would be involved when a judge is judging whether the parents of children injured in the Hillsborough disaster should be enti-tled to recover for post-traumatic stress syndrome suffered as a result of watching the disaster on television. In general terms, the judge discovers the relevant data; the particular situation must be sufficiently understood; possible solutions are discov-ered by comparing the case to other cases; the solutions are evaluated; the more suitable solution is discovered by practical reflective insight and is subsequently for-mulated as a judgment of value; finally, a decision is made. Problem-solving in these circumstances also involves a complex array of questions and insights, not single questions and single insights.

In fact, it is difficult to identify all the mental activities that comprise theoretical and practical problem-solving in legal decision-making due to the complexity of situ-ations and the complexity of the process of theoretical and practical problem-solv-ing. Some insights are spontaneous and relations among sense-experience can be discovered instantly and not be noticed. Insights may be combined with other insights so that new insights may include and mask previous insights. The fulfilling conditions of reflective insights may depend on a lifetime of learning law, identifying issues, knowing when to pursue clues, and exceptional powers of attention to what is seen, read, or heard that may be impossible to make explicit or to analyse. Spontaneous shifts in the types of questions asked and the answers reached may be untraceable because they are not noticed. In Lonergan's opinion, it may be impossi-ble to identify the mental activities accurately in all but the simplest situations.[17]

---

1 G. Barden, **After Principles**, (London: University of Notre Dame Press, 1990), 7.

2 ibid., 9.

3 ibid., 12.

4 ibid., 30, 48, 54, 71.

5 ibid., 79.

6 ibid., 72, 79.

7 B. Lonergan, **Insight: A Study in Human Understanding**, (London: Harper & Row, 1978), 609.

8 See P. McShane, **Wealth of Self and Wealth of Nations**, (New York: Exposition Press, 1975), 49; **Insight**, 614.

9 **Insight**, 610.
10 **Insight**, 610.
11 ibid., 610.
12 **After Principles**, 48.
13 ibid., 83-85.
14 ibid., 51.
15 **Insight**, 613, 709f.
16 ibid., 612.
17 B. Lonergan, *The Form of Inference*, **Collection**, (London: Darton, Longman & Todd, 1967).

8

Legal Reasoning in A New Context

1 Introduction

The previous three chapters aimed at a plausible and elementary presentation of Lonergan's view of discovery, insight, evaluation. To grasp that view and to bring it to bear on issues in legal theory is a major challenge that goes well beyond the bounds of an elementary introduction. Further, to get more than a glimpse of how the pressure of that view in the legal community would mediate a new clarity of discussion and decision is a still more remote task. However, some indications of the power of the new context are a necessary conclusion to the present effort. First, then, I will return to the topics of the first four chapters of this work and locate the pointers, achievements, directions of discovery indicated there in the larger context developed by Chapters Five to Seven. The present chapter aims at creatively and critically reviewing the issues and debates raised in those early chapters. Secondly, I will have something to say on the problem of expression - external formulation - of legal views, judgments, decisions. Finally, I will indicate a fuller context of legal studies and practice that Lonergan's work has articulated.

After a preliminary discussion of the central method of introspection, a first section will focus on the activities of discovery, questioning, and insight - the process of discovery or hunching - and will locate the suggestions of various theorists within the relational structure developed in the previous three chapters. The second section will turn to difficulties with formulation, expression, axiomatization, rhetoric and justification. In the third section the problem of a re-orientation of legal philosophy will be put in a larger context made possible by Chapters Five to Seven.

2 Introspection, Question, Insight

2.1 The Process of Introspection

The process of introspection that I have been engaged in throughout this inquiry has been an investigation into the mental activities involved in my own decision-making activities. This inquiry has not involved the application of a distinct mental process that reveals my thoughts and feelings. I have not been engaged in some sort of inward inspection. I did not create imaginary judges or cases in order to explain decision-making.

In order to explain the process of introspection, let us begin by recalling that the problem-solving process itself is spontaneous and conscious. People wonder about, and pose questions about, what they see, hear, and remember. Questions may lead to insights and further questions. And further questions lead to further insights and judgments and so on until, perhaps, a decision is reached. This process is sponta-neous in the sense that once one activity is completed it calls forth the next activity in the process. Lawyers and judges do not have to be legal philosophers in order to for-mulate problems, to correctly understand situations and to solve legal problems. They successfully solve problems without analysing how, exactly, they do it.

This problem-solving process is a conscious process in that the activities that con-stitute decision-making are not performed when a person is in dreamless sleep or a coma. Seeing, remembering, asking questions, and having insights is being con-scious. The activities that comprise the discovery process are intrinsically conscious. They occur consciously and by them a person engaged in decision-making is con-scious. But there is another sense that we are conscious. Our attention may not be fully devoted to solving the problem at hand. We may also be aware that we are puz-zled about some problem. We may also notice that the problem is solved when everything fits together when we exclaim "Yes, I've got it!". Not only do we sponta-neously solve problems, but we can also attend to ourselves solving problems. We can even identify aspects of our discovery process. The legal realists did this when they identified and named the elements that, according to them, comprised the judging process - brooding about the case, having a hunch or intuition, checking or testing the hunch, reaching a solution or judgment, and then expressing that solution or judgment. Cognitive psychologists also identified elements in the discovery process - preparation, incubation, insight, verification. Wasserstrom and MacCormick notice that judges have insights that must be subsequently tested. And Burton, Alexy and Douzinas & Warrington stress the key role of judgment in legal decision-making. Such noticing of our efforts to solve problems is not another men-tal activity over and above the activities (sensing, questioning, understanding, etc.) that we normally perform. Rather, this 'noticing' is a particular focusing of these activities on ourselves as performers.

Lonergan represents differences in the mode of being conscious by distinguishing four different levels of consciousness. First, we are empirically conscious when we sense, perceive, imagine, remember, speak, move. Secondly, we are intellectually conscious when we inquire, come to understand, express what we have understood, work out the presuppositions and implications of our expression. Thirdly, we are rationally conscious when we reflect, marshall the evidence, pass judgment on the truth or falsity, certainty or probablility of a statement. Fourthly, we are responsibly conscious when we are "concerned with ourselves, or own operations, our goals, and so deliberate about possible courses of action, evaluate them, decide, and carry out our decisions."[1] In Lonergan's words, "On all four levels, we are aware of ourselves but, as we mount from level to level, it is a fuller self of which we are aware and the awareness itself is different."[2]

For most people it probably is easy to become aware of themselves seeing, hear-ing and remembering, and puzzling about a problem. But noticing and identifying one's insights, Is-questions and one's grasp of the sufficiency of the evidence for a prospective judgment may be much more difficult. The methods used by legal theorists and psychologists may have helped identify elements involved in the discovery process, but their efforts have not reached an understanding of the elements themselves or the relations among the elements.

But this noticing, this naming of the activities in one's decision-making process is not, in itself, explanatory introspection. Like legal theorists and cognitive psychologists, we may be able to our identify insights and judgments, but we may not be able to define an insight or judgment. Identifying the mental activities in one's discovery process is only the first step in introspection. The experienced, noticed, named mental activities of the decision-making process are simply the data in the process of introspection. These activities themselves and their relations among each other are, as yet, not understood. So far, we have simply selected the data for our investigation. And in this particular investigation the data which we are investigating are the conscious mental activities themselves operating on the four levels of consciousness.

The second step in this process of introspection involves investigating the relations among the data - namely the relations among the mental activities that have been identified. Again, this step in introspective analysis does not entail some other mental activity over and above the activities we have experienced, noticed and named. We investigate the decision-making process in the same way that we would investigate any unknown that we would like to correctly understand. We ask questions about the data such as "What exactly is an insight?" "What is it that an insights discovers?" "What is a judgment?" "What is the relation between insight and judgment?" To state it another way, we apply our problem-solving process to the problem of understanding our decision-making process.

However, this inquiry into the nature of the decision-making process is not spontaneous. We must deliberately identify and distinguish the mental activities. We must pay attention to acts of experiencing, understanding, judging, and deciding. For example, we must explicitly advert to our activity of seeing when an object is seen. We must attend to, and become familiar with, our questioning, our experience of having insights, and become aware or our judging, evaluating and deciding. In Lonergan's words, "Since sensations can be produced or removed at will, it is a fairly simple matter to advert to them and become familiar with them. On the other hand, not a little forethought and ingenuity are needed when one is out to heighten one's consciousness of inquiry, insight, formulation, critical reflection, weighing the evidence, judging, deliberatin, deciding. One has to know the precise meaning of each of these words. One has to produce in oneself the corresponding operation. One has to keep producing it until one get beyond the object intended to the consciously operating subject. One has to do all this within the appropriate context, which is a matter not of inward inspection but of inquiry, enlarged interest, discernment, comparison, distinction, identification, naming."[3] We must deliberately try to understand the unity and relations among the activities we have identified. We must come to understand, for example, how What-questions are related to sensible and imaginative presentations and to direct insights, how reflective insight is related to presentations, direct insight, and judgment.

The third step in our introspective process is to judge the truth or falsity of our understanding of the relational structure comprising the decision-making process. We must ask "Do these operations occur in me in the manner in which I understand them to occur?" We must discover the criteria for our judgment whether or not such a discovery process exists and we must discover the relevant evidence.

The fourth step in introspective analysis involves decision. We must decide whether or not to operate fully in accord with the mental activities we experience and in accord with our understanding of the relational structure which we judge to be correct.

Lonergan's summary of introspection captures the four steps in the introspective analysis. For him, the process of introspection entails: "(1) *experiencing* one's experiencing, understanding, judging, and deciding; (2) *understanding* the unity and relations of one's experienced experiencing, understanding, judging, and deciding; (3) *affirming* the reality of one's experienced and understood experiencing, understanding, judging, and deciding; and (4) *deciding* to operate in accord with the norms immanent in the spontaneous relatedness of one's experienced, understood, affirmed experiencing, understanding, judging, and deciding."[4] The process of introspection, then, is a very complex self-attentive methodology.[5]

Returning to the arbitrator in Chapter Four, my method of investigating his discovery process was not some sort of special look in at his problem-solving process. It is impossible for me to experience what he saw and heard, the insights he achieved, the judgments he made, and the decisions he reached. It is not possible for me to climb into his mind. I can, and did, however, experience my own sensible presentations and imaginative representations, insights, judgments, and decisions and I can come to understand and judge my own experienced presentations and imaginative representations, insights, judgments, and decisions. My method of studying his decision-making process was to recognize by his spoken words the mental activities that he experienced and, by my own efforts, to reproduce these activities in order to solve the same problem he was given and to attend to the procedure which I followed in order to solve the legal problem.

2.2 Questions and Insights

Instead of the random collection of elements that the survey in Chapters One and Two makes possible - hunches, insights, weighing reasons, questioning, heuristics, incubation, various types of judgment, etc. - we can find an ordering of elements that is clearly suggested by the diagrams arrived at, and the related discussions, in Chapters Five to Seven. The focus in this section is on the nine elements contained in the following diagram. It is different from the previous diagram in Chapter Five. We will return to the other four elements in the next section.

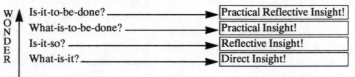

Raw Materials/Data: sense experience, perceptions, imaginations, memories, speech, movements, feelings

Notice immediately the relational structure suggested. It is a pattern one might helpfully place parallel to the periodic table. As oxygen is defined by its relations to other elements within the table, so a type of insight or question is defined by its place in our relational structure. For example, let us consider an Is-question. An Is-question calls for a reflective insight. Further an Is-question draws on direct insight for its content and it draws on data to supply the evidence for a prospective judgment.

Evident is the fact that all these types of hunches or insights are grounded in questions that look to the previous levels of conscious activity. We do not simply go around asking "What?" We wonder about our sensible and imaginative presentations. We ask "What is *it?*" "Why is *it?*" where the *it* is what is seen, heard, felt, tasted , smelled, remembered, imagined. Questions for intelligence look to the level of presentations for their raw materials. Also, we do not go around asking "Is?" We ask "Is *it* so?" "Is *it* true?" where the *it* is an idea, supposition, concept, interpretation, explanation, definition, theory. Questions for reflection look to intellectual consciousness for their content. We understand before we judge.

We do not simply raise the question of planning. One raises it to meet an actual situation. We do not simply ask "What can I do?" We ask "What can I do in this situation as I understand it?" The question of planning looks to the previous level of rational consciousness to supply its context. The *it* in this context is the interpretation of the situation that is judged to be correct. In order to transform a situation you first need to know what that situation is.

Finally, you are not adequately oriented to evaluate plans without the achievement of all the previous levels. You must be attentive to the raw materials. You must reach adequate understanding of the relations among those raw materials. You must assess whether or not your understanding of the raw materials is adequate. And before you ask "Should I execute this plan or that plan in this situation?" and then evaluate the plans, you first have to come up with plans. In our account of the relational structure elements on each level of consciousness depend on sufficient achievements of previous levels of consciousness.[6]

There is a simplification of the diagram above that must be amended. Consider the two types of What-question. They seem evidently distinct, yet in fact, in themselves they both look to possibilities, possible intelligibility of data or situations. They both might be brought into an identical form by expressing the question "What *might* that be?" where *might* can be understood in its two basic senses: one sense, relating to the actual state of affairs or pattern of experience and the other relating to future possibilities. So, for instance, food in a refrigerator may raise the question in a chef "What *might* that be?" And food in a dish may raise the same question regarding the actual achievement. The two questions attain their distinctiveness from their relations to the attitude expressed by their context in the relational structure - their place in the structure as either moving toward fact or from fact towards decision. The concerns in each situation are different. The two questions differ extrinsically. But they are both questions of possibility - either looking to the past or looking to the future. Nonetheless I retain the diagram[7] as it was developed in the previous three chapters since it provides a convenient basis of ordering the suggestions that emerged in the earlier chapters, Chapters One to Four.

It should be apparent that legal decision-making involves more than one great big hunch or insight that is then tested. The explanation of legal decision-making in Chapters Four to Seven illustrates that legal decision-making is comprised of complex sets of related insights. Further, the discovery process in law is not a procedure that moves in a simpïe sequence from puzzling to insight to judgment to decision to expression. It is a recurring pattern in which questions are asked, insights are achieved, judgments are posited, further questions are asked, further insights are achieved, further judgments are posited.

It will also be immediately evident to the reader that in the decision-making process we have developed there is not one type of hunch or insight but, four types. The discussion of hunches and insights in the early chapters can be seen now to focus predominantly on insights that relate to What-questions. For instance, the portrait of insight offered by Wasserstrom and MacCormick presented via the analogy between discovery in Popperian science and law, emphasizes the type of insight that is related to What-questions. Cognitive psychologists focus on insight as related to What-questions in that they limit their inquiries to discoveries in mathematics and science. However, Judge Hutcheson's description of hunching illustrates an orientation to evaluation and decison, to discovering the just solution in a case. His hunches are related to What-should-I-do-questions.

I would note that common experience and reflection upon it reveal that the movement to any type of judgment is by personal hunching and indeed in its successful form it grounds admiration and the attribution of intelligence. We also speak of people as having good judgment, of being shrewd, of being wise. Furthermore, a fuller treatment of these four types of hunching would reveal the fact that different people are talented in different zones of hunching. So there is the judge who is wise. The defence lawyer who is creative of alternate viewpoints. Again, there is the person of scientific bent whose hunches make history, but who is incapable of planning his day. Also, finally one can envisage the person who can accurately assess a situation, but who has poor practical judgment. And there is the opposite personality who is the trouble-shooter.

The next topic is, to what extent all this decision-making activity is irrational. I would contend that, in fact, none of these activities are irrational where rationality is taken in its full sense. All these activities are intelligent and conscious. The grounds for the claim of irrationality comes from a narrow meaning of rationality that would reduce it to logic. Certainly, these activities are illogical and this assertion will become more precise in the following section.

But there is indeed an irrational component in the process through questioning to insight on any level. That irrationality has its grounds in sensibility, both in its receptive and its conative operations. The act of seeing is irrational in its receptive operation in that it has a bodily basis. What is seen depends on whether your eyes are open or closed, which way your head is turned, what your gaze is focused on, whether or not you have your glasses on.[8]The act of seeing in its conative operation is irrational in that seeing occurs in some dynamic context that unifies acts of seeing. What one sees depends on one's interests, alertness, experience, feelings[9] purpose. Take a police officer and an ordinary citizen who both see a robbery. The officer's seeing should be such as to lead to the "taking in" of what the perpetrators wore, what they looked like, and the model and year of their getaway car, whereas the citizen may actually see only the colour of the car.

Particularly important to note here is the manner in which patterning of sensibility - a patterning which occurs from above as well as from below - can be conducive to insight on various levels.[10] Patterning from below is sufficiently illustrated by recalling the famous dreaming of Kekule which led him to the structure of benzene. The image of a dancing snake led to insight. Here the sub-rational yielded a clue, a pattern, the missing link. This patterning is clearly sub-rational. Unconscious process can also aid insight by making their contents conscious if they have some plausible relevance to conscious mental activity. In rational consciousness memory can provide instances that would run counter to a prospective judgment and imagination can devise contrary possibilities. A negative facet of this patterning is a topic for psychology which Lonergan calls the flight from insight or scotosis. In one manifestation of scotosis images that suggest insight are repressed.[11]

The patterning from above, clearly, is rational. Its primary illustration is the good teacher who has organized the elements of a problem to help students achieve insight or a good courtroom lawyer taking a jury through a case one step at a time in order to help them reach a desired judgment or decision. Indeed, we all appreciate the strategies of posing a problem and presenting its solution and we all recognize the strategies of body language and dress code, voice tone, and timing that are relevant in courtroom presentations.

I would also like to emphasize the precision our structure gives to the notion of weighing, particularly the key role of insight in weighing. We can distinguish two types of weighing. The first type is oriented to agreeing or disagreeing with, affirming or denying, assenting or dissenting to, a proposition. Weighing in this context involves a reflective insight that in a single moment discovers the relations among (1) a prospective judgment, (2) the conditions for its assertion and their link with the prospective judgment, and (3) whether or not the conditions are satisfied. The second type of weighing is oriented to evaluating the suitability of plans. Weighing in this context involves practical reflective insight - an insight that in a single moment discovers the relations among the current situation, the proposed plans, and the pros and cons of each plan, and the sufficiency of the suitability of each plan in the circumstances. The explanation of weighing in either of these contexts can be seen as having far greater precision than Burton's vague discussions of congeries of reasons and action thresholds. What I mean by weighing is the performance and achievement of a reflective insight or a practical reflective insight.

Our relational structure also offers an explanation of the ground of judgment. The ground of judgment of fact is the discovery or grasp of the sufficiency of the evidence for a prospective judgment. The ground of a judgment of value is the discovery or grasp of the sufficiency of the reasons to judge that one plan is sufficiently suitable or more suitable than others. The ground of judgment, then, can be understood as these particular activities in our relational structure.

But the ground of judgment involves more than reflective insight and practical reflective insight. These activities are elements in a relational structure. A reflective insight is correct if it is invulnerable and it is invulnerable if there are no further relevant questions. So, judgments depends on questions. Reflective insight and practical reflective insight also draw on previous levels of consciousness and they complement and complete prior levels of consciousness. The level of sensible presentations and imaginative representations provide the raw materials for direct insight, which in turn provides reflective consciousness with its content. But reflective consciousness also relies on sensible presentations when assessing whether or not the conditions for a prospective judgment are satisfied. Finally, as mentioned in the previous section there is a contextual aspect to judgment. Judgments are grounded on previous judgments in that present judgments can build on previous judgments, can conflict with other judgments, and can complement other judgments. Hence the ground of both judgments of fact and judgments of value can be understood as the attentive, intelligent, reasonable, responsible person operating at his or her best.

In this perspective, the ground of judgment is not extrinsic as Douzinas & Warrington suggest when they argue that justice will be achieved by listening to the demands and needs of "the other" or, as Alexy argues in his discussion of the rationality of judicial decisions, in terms of special rules and forms of legal argumentation.

In a fuller discussion of levels of consciousness, the orientations of each level of consciousness would be identified as transcendental orientations that reach towards beauty, understanding, truth, value. Such a context would enable one to treat more precisely the place of aesthetic judgment in general and in the field of legal presentation. It is best to leave Douzinas & Warrington's account of aesthetic judgment for a future time. But at any rate, the primary focus in law is not on the aesthetic dimension of behaviour or presentation, no more than elegance is central to mathematics or science. But it is certainly a feature of all human endeavour.

The relational structure of the full diagram can be brought to bear on the main topic of Chapter Two, MacCormick's analogy. Then a quite different critique emerges from the descriptive criticism given there. A full development of that critique would be considerably larger than Chapter Two, but some pointers may help the reader to glimpse the power of the basis developed here. So, while all the basic elements are called into play both in science and in law, the focus of question in science is the three lowest levels of conscious operation: the reach for fact. The focus of attention in law is on the higher levels: the reach for evaluation. However, the relational structure helps us point to a deeper criticism. Popper's account of science is massively truncated[12]: the elements of questioning and insight find no thematic place. Likewise, there is a truncatedness about MacCormick's consideration of law that has to be relieved by the full thematic of questioning, discovery, formulation, and expression in the general field of evaluation.

3 Formulation, Expression, Rhetoric, Axiomatics

Four elements of the original diagram in Chapter Five were omitted in the previous section.[13] They are the focus of this section. However, that diagram requires extension if our discussion is to be sufficiently suggestive. One must distinguish clearly in one's own experience between the inner coherent perspective to which one some-times aspires, and occassionally reaches, and the expression of that perspective in written or spoken words and in actions. The emphasis in the present section will be on written expression. In order to discuss this distinction we enlarge our diagram[14] as follows:

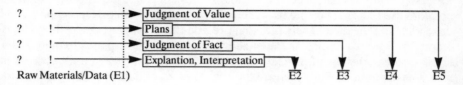

The straight line on the level of data indicates the sensible expression of the inner perspective. So for example, E2 is the expression of a hypothesis. It can be as brief as the hypothesis $E = mc^2$ or as complex as the total presentation of the prosecution in a murder trial. E3 is the expression of a factual judgment. The cluster of evidence accepted by the court - the facts of a case - would illustrate this type of expression. E3, the expression of a factual judgment, is not normally a single sentence, but a suf-ficient constellation of sentences.[15] The manner of constellating (particularly axiomatic and rhetorical constellating) will occupy us later in this section. E4 is illus-trated most easily by recipes and guidelines in a cook book which are expressions of things to be done. E4 expresses a plan. Sentencing proposals would also be an exam-ple. E5 is best illustrated in the field of our concern as the final expression of penal-ties and prescriptions - statements concerning what is to be done or not to be done and the procedures to be implemented. Chapter Four focused on the arbitrator moving to this type of expression. He ended his inquiry by expressing what is to be done.

Here I am indicating clear distinctions of types of expression. The reality of nor-mal expression, however, is that it flows on all four levels. The presentation of a case by a lawyer can include precise suggestions of future behaviour (E4), innuendoes that scarcely merit the title of hypotheses (E2), noise (E1). Variations of expression, for instance, can give rise to courtroom intervention. For example, the efforts of a lawyer to introduce evidence may be objected to on the grounds that it is hearsay (E2), that the statement is speculative and is not the expression of a judgment of fact (E3). We can identify different levels of expression in Wilson's written opinion dis-cussed in Chapter Three. When Wilson initially states that the real or deeper issue in the case is whether or not a woman has the right to decide to have an abortion she is stating a hypothesis (E2). When she writes that men cannot understand the abortion issue she expresses it as a judgment of fact (E3). When Wilson writes how she will attempt to solve the abortion issue, namely by defining the right to liberty in the con-text of the Charter in general and in the context of abortion in particular, she is expressing a plan (E4). When she stipulates the outcome of the case - that s. 256 of the Canadian Criminal Code violates s. 7 of the Charter she is expressing a decision (E5). More broadly, one might consider the variety of fallacies and rhetoric that relate to variations in expression. An expression can shift from the factual to the evaluative by the mere introduction of the word "good" within a sentence.

This explanation of levels of expression gives precision to categorization of statements by lawyers, judges, and legal theorists. We would be able to distinguish, in written legal opinions, whether a proposition expresses a hypothesis, a judgment of fact, an option or a decision. Such an analysis provides us with a context in which to understand and evaluate legal expression. In this context, aspects of written legal opinions can be seen as elements in a relational structure - as corresponding to, and depending on, the mental activities that precede them - rather than as the primary feature of legal reasoning. As stated above, expression corresponds to one of four levels of consciousness of a speaker or writer, but the expression itself consists in marks on paper or sounds which are the raw materials or data for a listener or reader's inquiry and, as such, are sensible presentations. Hence expression in any field will be on the level of sensible presentations. This perspective suggests that the writings of legal positivists are limited insofar as they portray legal expresssion on a single level and it grounds the distinctiveness of legal decision-making in expression.[16]

The diagram above helps make the relation between mental activities and expression more precise. The phrase "Take him down", stated by an English to conclude a criminal trial, corresponds to the level of evaluation and decision (E5). The word "Guilty" corresponds to the level of reflection and judgment (E3). An oral or written description of a sequence of events in a case by the prosecution or defence corresponds to the level of insight and interpretation (E2). Statements by a witness expressing what he or she saw or heard correspond to the level of sensible presentations (E1). It must be stressed that expression is not equivalent to mental activity. A person may present a plan so that it sounds like it would be the best possible plan for all concerned, yet know that the plan only advances his or her own interests. A person might say that they affirm a proposition, but that person may be lying. Expressions are never true or false. Truth and falsity pertain to the judgment, the mental event. They reside in the judgment as assent or dissent to a proposition. Also, a person might understand experience, yet be unable to capture sufficiently that understanding in words or sentences. A person might be rich in experience, yet may not be able to speak or write. Experiencing, understanding, judging, deciding are distinct from their expression.[17]

The perspective of our relational structure provides a context in which to analyse the writings of legal positivists on legal justification. Justification and expression can be understood now as distinct activities. In our relational structure whether a legal decision is justified can be seen as depending on the judge performing at his or her best on all four levels of consciousness - being attentive to raw materials, being intelligent, being reasonable, and being responsible. Expression, then, is a subsequent activity. The work of legal positivists who study legal argumentation as a form of legal justification can be seen as not distinguishing sufficiently between mental activity and expression and as giving priority to expression to the extent of neglecting the performance of mental activity.

We can distinguish, in expression, between two extreme forms of its patterning. There is the form that is patterned in accord with the discovery process. This patterning was illustrated by Wilson's presentation of her viewpoint sketched in

Chapter Three. The other extreme is found at its best in the axiomatic presentations of mathematics. In the legal context we may think of MacCormick's portrait of deductive justification discussed in Chapter Two. These two types of presentation are not independent. The presentation through discovery tends to be inadequate insofar as identification and formulation have not been adequately pursued. Identification involves precision with regard to the data that is being understood.[18] Formulation regards the proper ordering of the understanding achieved. The form of presentation patterned through axioms tends to be inadequate insofar as it ignores the educational level of the reader. I will discuss these topics in the context of rhetorical expression and axiomatic expression.

The most common type of expression is the rhetorical - the expression that pivots on the process of discovery. Moreover, that type of expression normally occurs without the backing of full formulation. Formulation is the process of working out the implications of an insight and its relation to other insights in an effort to reach sufficient understanding and adequate expression. As this point is of some importance, it is best to illustrate it on each of the levels of formulation and expression. The arbitrator's concluding report and Wilson's decision that s. 256 of the Criminal Code violates s. 7 of the Charter illustrate expression associated with the discovery process which corresponds to the level of decision (E5). They both portray the case as a solution to a problem. Such expressions occur without the full backing of formulation inasmuch as the implications and reasons for the steps in the decision-making process are not fully worked and/or the consequences of the outcomes may not be fully considered. Statutes, legal principles, and precedents correspond to the level of planning (E4). Here expression occurs without the full backing of formulation insofar as statutes, legal principles and precedents are often expressed without considering all the characterized situations that they would cover. This is evident by the fact that judges must work out why a statute or legal principle or precedent would or would not cover a situation. During a court case if a lawyer objects to a question a lawyer asks a witness, the judge would probably make a judgment on the issue immediately (E3). The judge would jump to a conclusion and then tell the lawyers whether or not he permits the witness to answer the question. If the judge was subsequently asked to give reasons for his judgment, he would have to formulate them and then express them. The conclusion he jumped to would have been made prior to the full formulation of the issues. An example of a definition that does not have the full backing of formulation is Wilson's definition of the right to liberty as a woman's right to decide whether or not to have an abortion. (E2). She expresses the definition, but it is apparent she has not worked out the data to which this definition is related and the situations in which it holds. Again, expression occurs without the full backing of formulation.

The normal inadequacy of expression is summed up in the cautionary proverb "Don't jump to conclusions!"[19] But the reality of human hunching, in fact, is that there is no other way to arrive at conclusions - definitions, interpretation, (E2), factual judgments (E3), statutes, legal principles, precedents (E4), or legal decisions (E5). It is worthwhile to pause over this in a simple diagram[20]:

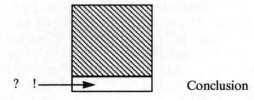

? !————▶   Conclusion

The shaded area is the area of potential formulation, normally left shady or vague in common discourse.

Many legal theorists discuss the problem of justification and expression without an adequate conception of the distinctions I have made here. So it is difficult to interpret their writings with accuracy. In light of the distinction between mental activities and expression, the ideal of legal justification that legal positivists *would seem* to have in mind is the ideal of adequate expression acceptable to the profession. But in the context of the current discussion what they *should* have in mind, however, is the perspective, the cluster of definitions and judgments that give rise to this adequate expression.

Not noticing the basic distinction between the performance of mental activities and expression gives rise to problems about expression and hides problems relating to the adequacy of definitions and judgments themselves. Legal positivists stress the form of the expression that would be adequate and hence legally justified. The problem with focusing primarily on the adequacy of expression is that it may lead a reader to dispense with relevant questions about the implications and suitability of the outcome of a case. The focus on expression and the neglect of mental activity is unlikely to help judges achieve sufficiently suitable insights, judgments, decisions or to help readers towards understanding and evaluating judicial decisions.

Bluntly, definitions, judgments and formulations are inner events. Their external expression is always in a fundamental sense inadequate. A written decision cannot capture the educated attentiveness of an experienced judge, the ease with which the judge understands familiar situations, the way in which the judge homes in on the relevant aspects of unfamiliar situations, the feeling a judge has when someone is lying that is followed by just the right questions that expose lies, the unbiased and thorough evaluation of proposed solutions in the reach for a sufficiently suitable solution. Also, legal decisions will always be inadequate due to the nature of how we learn. No matter what we say or write there are presuppositions. For instance, complex expression is restricted to specialized audiences who have learned the prerequisite pre-suppositions. A lay person may have to spend a year learning about the duty of care, the standard of care, causation, and remoteness before having an educated opinion on the line of cases concerned with nervous shock. Expression, then, is never complete expression. Complete expression would require us to express everything we know. But we know that the achievement of one insight depends on the achievement of previous insights which depend of previous insights and so on.

Expressions, of course, are classified according to adequacy. They are adequate, relatively adequate, inadequate. The adequacy of expression corresponds to what a speaker or writer intends to communicate to a listener or reader. A speaker or writer can communicate noise, thoughts, judgments, decisions. The crucial point is that a speaker's or writer's thoughts, judgments, decisions themselves are not passed on, transferred, or given directly to the listener or reader. The listener or reader must discover and achieve his or her own thoughts, judgments, decisions. Again, it is worth stressing that from both the writer's and reader's perspectives the words, phrases, sentences are not true or false, wise or immoral. The writer's words may express judgments and decisions, but the words themselves are the raw materials, the sensible presentations, the data for the reader's insights, judgments, decisions.[21]

Consider rhetorical expression. Rhetorical expression illustrates the writer's direct concern with the reader's insight. The aim of this type of expression is to provoke insight, judgment, decision. In Lonergan's view, communication proceeds by the writer discovering what the listener or reader has yet to discover and then identifying what sound or sign (E2, E3, E4, E5) would lead the reader to the desired thoughts, judgments, decisions. Communication, then, "is effective only insofar as the writer correctly estimates the [educational] development of the listener or reader and chooses just the words that have a meaning for them."[22] Aristotle's analysis of rhetoric, particularly his discussion of appealing to the audience discussed in Chapter Three, captures this attitude. Wilson's presentation of her legal decision in terms of questions and answers, in the same chapter, illustrates a concern with the reader's insights, judgments, and decisions.

On the other hand, axiomatic expression illustrated by scientific treatises and, in the legal context, by the deductive justification of decisions and by the rational reconstruction of decisions is not directly concerned with leading a reader to understanding, judgment, decision. This pattern of expression disregards what a reader already knows and the elements that would provoke insight. The primary purpose of this form of expression is to set forth clearly and exactly the terms, relations, implications that proceed from understanding and provide materials for judgment and decision.[23] Axiomatic expression consolidates what appears to be permanent and static [24] in the form of a system.[25]

The astute reader will note that the two types of presentation - rhetoric and axiomatic - relate to the two types of reasoning - deductive and inductive reasoning. Induction is a discovery process that is quite different from what is called induction by enumeration. Induction in the discovery process can occur from one adequately comprehended instance. "All swans are white" is not a scientific induction (an incorrect one, of course). The scientific induction regarding white swans is contained in the answer to the question "Why is this swan white?" Answering this question involves all the levels of consciousness operating at their best in a range of sciences. In the legal context, we appeal to precedents, not because it is an implicit appeal to enumeration, but because it is an appeal to the empirical basis of generalisation: "Similars are similarly understood". It is not an appeal to uncritical partial enumeration of authorities, but to the prior exercise of intelligence and wisdom. One looks for situations sufficiently similar to warrant a conclusion without going through a laborious problem-solving procedure. Appealing to precedents is an intelligent short-cut, not the avoidance of sufficient inquiry.

The character of deductive reasoning can best be appreciated by returning to our simple illustration from geometry. That illustration can lead to an enlightening view of the nature of the simple syllogism. The process that leads to the structuring of a syllogism is regularly a process of discovering the middle term, the middle term that lies between a What-question and formulation, and between an Is-question and a judgment. That is what that illustration is. The question "Why is the moon round?"[26] can be answered insofar as one grasps in insight the significance of phases. Consequent to that grasp is the syllogistic formulation and expression:

> The moon has phases.
> What has phases is round.
> Therefore, the moon is round.

Insight, then, in this context discovers the relation among presentations. That insight can be expressed as a syllogism. This type of expression, associated with a What-question, can help a reader toward understanding.[27] It is structured so as to facilitate the reader's understanding of the relevant relation among the data. The key point is that this type of syllogism represents the possibility of understanding. It does not prove anything is true or false.

We also know that insight discovers the sufficiency of the evidence and the fulfillment of the conditions for a prospective judgment. This type of discovery can also be expressed as a syllogism. Here the expression helps the reader toward reflection.[28] The syllogism represents the possibility of reflective insight. It does not prove a proposition is true or false

The function of logic is to make explicit all the elements essential to understanding, judgment, decision whether or not they are obvious.[29] Consider the law that whoever kills someone with intent is guilty of murder. The problem in a case is to discover whether or not this particular case is an instance of that class. Aspects of space and time and the characteristics of the accused are relevant aspects of the discovery process. This case can be categorized by a deductive expression. Axiomatic expression aims to articulate all the elements relevant to insight. Such expression may also reveal inattention, misunderstanding, unresonable judgments, and irrational decisions. If you have an implicit postulate such as "He is black, so he must be the murderer" adequate logical expression would make this assumption apparent. But just as in the case of the phases of the moon, the real crux of the matter is not the deductive expression, but the discovery of the nature of the instance in the question "Did this person kill the victim?" "Did this person intend to kill the victim?" And that discovery is grounded in reflective insight.

The adequacy of the axiomatic expression depends on the competence of the reader to retain all the propositions within the fundamental form of inference: "If... Then." For example, the function of a jury discussion is to bring the jury to that state. When you jump to a conclusion, you have implicitly the entire set of insights. The function of a legal process would be to make explicit all the relevant insights and judgments whether obvious or not.[30]

Axiomatic expression is inadequate to a reader because the reader must return to the process of discovery to grasp the unity of a single internal formulation, the total expression. Sufficient insight occurs when the total expression becomes unified as the luminous antecedent to the conclusion.

In fact, axiomatic expression is never adequate without rhetorical expression. Justification without rhetorical expression will not bring the reader to adequate understanding to make a stand on the final conclusion. Rhetorical expression, in its turn, lacks the control of the ordering to insights given by the deductive presentation. So we arrive at the complementarity of deduction and induction. The expression adequate to a community of informed judgement/judges must be adequate to generate comprehensive insight. The expression must be one that finds the relevant balance between rhetorical and axiomatic presentation. That relevant balance is particular to each instance.[31] There is not going to be an axiomatics of balance.

Our reflections on the complementarity of axiomatic and rhetorical presentation can also, of course, be used to throw an organising light on work such as that of Wilson. That organising light, however, requires for successful exploitation the larger controlling context that I wish to sketch in the final section. The balance, the quality of axiomatization, the rhythm of relevant rhetoric are all functions and topics of historical criticism. A discussion of them therefore calls for a larger historical consideration of sequences of formulations in history, and of levels and sequences and lags of expression. To this we will shortly turn, but our sketch is already sufficient to warrant the suspicion that the strategies of Wilson can be adequately understood by our schema. Two issues remain regarding Wilson: the distinction between reasoning in men and women, and the claim that certain types of data are out of the reach of one sex's reasoning ability.

First, then, there is the implicit claim in our discussion and in our relational schema that reasoning in men and in women is adequately explained by the relational structure developed in these four final chapters. Certainly the field of presentation or data vary in the two sexes, but then that field is a general variable. Each individual's physics and chemistry grounds variations in the neurological potential for representation, which in turn is meshed into a linking of memories, emotions, aspirations. And in this context we can turn to Wilson's question in a blunt fashion: is it the case that a man cannot understand abortion, that a woman cannot understand vasectomy?

I would suggest that the solution calls for a broader reflection on the reach of human inquiry and understanding, and the character of sensible representation. Such reflection, a lengthy affair, would reveal that the reach of human inquiry is not limited to the actual conscious experience of the human subject, that the field of representation can include symbolically, analogically, even anagogically, sufficient data on anything that is real. I would hold, then, that Wilson's tendency to exclude certain areas of female reality from male inquiry and understanding is just a particular instance of a general, more evidently mistaken, tendency to consider human inquiry, male or female, as incapable of reaching an understanding of other types of reality. Such a tendency, pushed to its logical conclusion, would exclude the manifest achievements of physics, chemistry, botany, zoology, etc.

What is valuable about the feminist perspective[32] is that it calls attention to a truncated view of knowing, that has dominated the western tradition of male reflection, since the time of Scotus.[33] Concept is considered as prior to insight. Judgment is taken to be some type of synthesis. Gradually expression becomes the focus of attention, as in so-called linguistic analysis. So, the real procedures are thrown into obscurity. And of course there is no chance of the discovery of "If *all* this . . .. Then".

By contrast, the adequate expression of a unified perspective by a written legal decision would invite the reader to share that unified perspective. Adequate expression aims to generate a unified and conclusive perspective in the reader. A unifying insight grounding the adequacy of expression is central to axiomatic justification.

It is now possible for me to relate our relational structure to reflections on discovery and justification, particularly the rigid distinction between discovery and justification. The process of introspection reveals that the actual decision-making process is intelligent and conscious. The process of discovery is not an essentially irrational, arbitrary, unconscious activity. Also, the analysis of our relational structure reveals that the central activity in legal decision-making is not one big insight. It is four different types of insight that are part of a relational structure.

Our introspective analysis suggests that the argument that discovery is an independent process distinct from a process of justification must be revised. The discovery or actual decision-making process can now be seen as including the thirteen elements that comprise our relational structure. Justification, in this fuller context, is understood as involving the discovery of the sufficiency of the evidence and the discovery of sufficient reasons, activities that are part of the actual decision-making process. Testing or justifying insights does not involve a further process that occurs over and the actual decision-making process. Further, it turns out that the performance of the mental activities concerned with testing direct and practical insights involves discovery.

In our relational structure, achieving insights and testing them are both essential activities in the decision-making process. Of course, insights must be tested, but without insights there would be nothing to test. And even though reflection and decision complement and complete prior activities they draw on these prior activities for their content. Hence, it no longer makes sense to say that the process of justification is more important than the process of discovery.

It is perhaps worth noting at this stage that no one (Alexy, Burton, Douzinas & Warrington, cognitivie psychologists, MacCormick, & Wilson)[34] distinguishes between inner perspective and outer word. The discussion of expression indicates that legal theorists' efforts to define adequate expression in the legal context and to equate expression with justification miss the key point that emerges from introspective analysis, namely that the suitability of a legal decision rests primarily on the adequacy of mental events, not on the adequacy of the expression. In the relational structure we draw a distinction between testing and expression. Now what we would call justification is related to the mental activities concerned with reflection and deliberation, whereas the expression of judgments of fact and judgments of value are associated with the level of sensible presentations - words, phrases, and sentences. Expressions themselves do not justify legal decisions. Moreover, the form of expression, whether rhetorical or axiomatic, simply invites or facilitates insight. Expression, then, represents the *possibility* of a reader understanding and evaluating a legal decision.

4 Functional Specialties

The two previous sections brought the cluster of pointers of earlier chapters into the perspective of Chapters Five to Seven. But this perspective is incomplete. A further problem, a further ordering is needed: the concluding reflections of the previous sections bring to the surface larger issues of legal philosophy and legal practice. The various confused descriptions of legal decision-making in Chapters One to Three illustrate the disorder in explanations of legal reasoning. But Jurisprudence itself is in a disorderly state. Legal theorists concerned with Marxism, Realism, Critical Legal Studies, Post-modernism, positivism, natural law, feminism, semiotics, autopoesis offer competing and conflicting accounts of law.

Disorder is manifest in other legal activities. There is discontent, perhaps even resentment or contempt, among some practitioners and legal theorists regarding each others' work. Some legal writers would even have us believe that law is a field distinct and independent from politics, economics, sociology, etc. By contrast, the Lord Chancellor's Advisory Committee on legal education asserts that legal education should promote an understanding of the historical, social, economic, political context of law. The law reports reveal additional disorder. Although there are report series that collect the cases on particular subjects such as the **Criminal Law Reports** and **Lloyd's Reports**, cases on administrative law, contracts, torts, company, and crime can all be found mixed together in law reports such as the **All England Law Reports**, **Weekly Law Reports**, and **Dominion Law Reports**. The legal journals reflect this disorder. Journals such as **The Criminal Law Review**, **The Tort Law Review**, **Journal of Contract Law**, **Public Law** publish articles dealing with a particular field, but other legal journals such as the **Oxford Journal of Legal Studies**, **Canadian Bar Review**, **Dalhousie Law Journal** do not make such distinctions among subjects and publish articles on virtually any topic related to law. Law is portrayed as a unified field. Still other journals such as **Law and History**, **Socio-Legal Studies**, **Ratio Juris**, and **Law and Critique** seem to be cut off from traditional legal scholarship and practice.

In summary, collaboration in the legal context is in a disorderly state. There is little collaboration between legal theorists and practioners. Collaboration among legal academics is focused on subject specialisation, while collaboration among people in different subject specializations is haphazard. There is no coherent collaborative structure in legal activity. Yet, there is a need for all members of the legal community to appreciate what they are doing, to reflect on a division of labour that would enable them to solve problems more effectively and efficiently. But how is collaboration to occur? How are diverse problems and topics to be ordered? The need, then, has emerged for reflection on an adequate integration for the future.

The need and urgency for such reflection on collaborative efforts is manifest in the recently acknowledged failure of the North Atlantic ground fisheries off the east coast of Canada. In a recent paper on the crisis Cynthia Lamson writes that "In 1991, there was resistance in certain agencies and industry sectors towards co-operative problem-solving. There were few incentives to develop working relationships among and between members of private industry, government, academia and scientists working in government research institutions. However, circumstances have changes quite dramatically in the intervening years and the requirement to find new approaches to living resource management is now urgent."[35]

She notes that the National Advisory Board on Science and Technology released a report called *Opportunities from Our Oceans* which "highlighted the importance of moving from reactive, crisis management towards a proactive, planning model." It advocated an integrated and comprehensive oceans strategy particularly with regard to wealth creation, risk management, scientific research, technological development, and the enactment of laws as a necessary framework for managing ocean resources.[36] The Canadian Fisheries minister also released a discussion paper *A Vision for Ocean Management* on the topic. It called for legislation and a comprehensive management framework to promote development that was economically sustainable and environmentally acceptable.

These two reports demand a solution that calls for a total view and the organisation and co-ordination of efforts of fishermen, fish processors, scientists, lawyers, politicians, and government officials. But what sort of collaborative structure would be effective in dealing with this crisis? How are these people to move from the past to the future in some critically and creatively organised fashion?

A plausible way to proceed is to list the problems and activities that are disorderly and to try to discover some way to order them. Consider the fisheries crisis. Reports on aspects of the problem have been commissioned and collected. Fishermen and fish processors have released their own interpretations of the problem. Scientists have written their explanations of the crisis. Histories of the crisis have been written by different groups. There are political histories, scientific histories, social histories and general histories. Mistakes in the past management of the fishery have been identified by various interested groups. The need to develop general norms to face the future has been recognised. The urgency of developing a fisheries policy has been identified. A policy that promotes risk management, technological development, and economically sustainable and environmentally acceptable fishery has been released by one group. The fishermen and fish processors have offered their plans for the future fishery. But so far, nothing has been done except to close entire fisheries in particular geographic areas.

Clues to discovering a plausible ordering of the activities and materials relevant to the fisheries crisis can be identified in the disorderly materials themselves. There seems to be an obvious concern with the past: with **Research** - collecting relevant materials, with **Interpretation** - settling the meaning of written reports, with **History** - determining how and in what context, in fact, the problem emerged. There is a concern with **Conflicts**. It is evident that there is a need to evaluate interpretations and histories so that mistakes are not repeated and that desirable practices can be identified. An orientation to the future is also obvious. It is not difficult to order that concern in terms of the slogan **Policy**, **Planning**, and **Executive Reflection**. A division of concern, then, can be identified in the efforts to cope with the fisheries crisis by learning from the past in order to deal with the problems of today. The division is made not in terms of distinct subjects, but in terms of the performance of specialised tasks.

Can a similar ordering of law be discovered by observing the division of interests and problems within the legal context? The short answer is "Yes". A direction to the ordering can be had by merely observing the division of interests within the legal context. It is not difficult to order legal activity in terms of **Research, Interpretation, History**. There is a massive enterprise throughout the legal world to collect, select, edit, and record cases. Para-legals, lawyers, and judges all dig up cases and statutes. Tort lawyers commission medical reports and contract lawyers ask to see their clients' contracts. Lawyers initiate discovery proceedings to obtain details. Witnesses swear affidavits to provide information. Historians uncover manuscripts and share their contents with colleagues. Comparatists provide us with the law from foreign jurisdictions. And discourse theorists find their texts. **Research**, then, is an essential activity in law.

The results of research activity provide interpreters with the raw materials for their work. It is apparent that the performance of **Interpretation** is a crucial activity in the legal context. Lawyers interpret their data in light of their clients' statements, other cases, and statutes. Academics write interpretations of statutes and provide interpretations of whole areas of law when they write their textbooks. Socio-legal scholars and feminists provide their interpretations of the current state of legal affairs. And we have Marxist, Post-modern, positivist, realist, autopoetic, communitarian, black-letter interpretations of law. Legal academics make interpretation itself an object of inquiry when they articulate rules of statutory interpretation and analyse the nature of legal interpretation itself.

We can also identify a historical dimension in law. Specialists in Roman Law and Common Law can be identified. Some historians trace the development of subjects such as Property, Contracts, and legal education. Others trace the development of law throughout Europe. Still others write "Marxist" histories, feminist histories, critical histories. Even lawyers, judges, and juries are concerned with history, with settling what, in fact, happened in a case or with establishing the continuities and transitions among related cases. **History** can be seen as an essential aspect of legal activity.

Identifying and settling **Conflicts** is a crucial part of legal activity. In litigation lawyers endeavour to specify the conflict among parties, to identify the mistakes and oversights in the other's presentation, and to stress the strengths of their own argument. Judges and tribunal members, for example, evaluate the merits of arguments in order to settle disputes. Discussions of what is called "policy" by the legal profession are often presented in legal decisions when conflicts among values are identified and resolved. In Jurisprudence there are conflicts between various interpretations of law. For example, natural law and critical legal studies are seen by many scholars as conflicting with legal positivism. And post-modern interpretations of law, for example, can be seen as conflicting with most other interpretations of law. But these are mainly illustrations of what I might call short-term conflictual analysis. Long-term analysis aims at deeper roots. Histories can conflict. "Marxist" histories and Whig histories can be seen as conflicting with more systematic and comprehensive views. Although conflicts of this scope between interpretations and histories can be identified, few public attempts have been made to identify, and to settle, them.

There seems to be an obvious ordering of legal activity that is oriented to the future, a concern with **Policy**, **Planning**, and **Executive Reflection**. The European Convention on Human Rights, nations' constitutions, principles of natural justice, and the principle that people harmed by others should be compensated are examples of **Policies**. They express policies in the sense that they declare general "truths".

It is evident that **Planning** is a crucial part of legal activity. Judges articulate general principles to deal with types of cases. Legal academics propose their solutions to types of cases in textbooks and journal articles. Politicians come up with plans that they hope will be transformed into statutes. Interest groups fight to have their own plans enacted as law. Comparative lawyers forage through foreign law to find laws that can be used in the domestic scene. International lawyers meet to negotiate perspectives or plans that underpin or contextualize treaties.

Finally, **Executive Reflection** is called for. Plans are implemented in concrete situations. Someone or some group must decide which plan would be appropriate and must communicate decisions. Judges, tribunal members, arbitrators, tax auditors, building and banking inspectors, water and energy regulators, politicians, etc. select creatively from plans (rules, principles, precedents, legislation, proposed solutions) so they can adequately meet problematic situations.

I have identified, in the performance of legal activity, the direction of an ordering of concerns. Different activities were identified. **Research**, **Interpretation**, **History** are concerned with revealing the past. A concern with identifying, evaluating and settling **Conflicts** among interpretations and histories was also recognised in legal activity. Even though this concern in the main was short-term, it pointed towards the need for a broader conflictual analysis. The further activities of **Policy**, **Planning**, **Executive Reflection** are concerned with transforming the present to meet the future.

However, these activities occur haphazardly in no particular order and are performed more of less adequately depending on the particular individual or school of thought. The different concerns are not seen or performed as specialised activities with their own aims and specialised procedures. Rather, these activities are all performed by individuals or groups focused on some aspect of their own specialised subject such as contracts, legal theory, comparative law. Current legal writing is a composite result of the performance of all these activities. There is little concern for methodology in law. In law, there is little collaboration among investigators engaged in these activities. A further ordering of these concerns seems to be called for. However, the larger problem comprises the issues raised in Chapters One to Four, the crisis in the fisheries, and the division of legal interests in institutions. How is collaboration to occur? How are diverse problems and topics to be ordered?[37]

Lonergan has written about these problems in relation to our problem-solving structure. His answer is that each of the different concerns identified above should be explicitly distinguished in terms of its proper achievement and end and that each activity should be performed by a group who specialise in that particular concern or type of analysis. Such distinctions and division of labour would enable investigators to know that the proper procedures and ends of each specialty are quite distinct.

Investigators would be clear about their procedures and their limitations. They would know how their responsibilities are related to their immediate goals and to the ultimate goal of the inquiry. Subjects would no longer be closed off to each other. For example, the roles of **History** and **Policy** in the legal context would be explicitly recognised and placed under deliberate guidance and control in that they have a clearly defined function in a collaborative structure.

How, then, are we to discover the proper achievements and ends of Research, Interpretations, History, Conflicts, Policy, Planning, Executive Reflection? Our relational structure provides the clues. The line of solution involves specifying the correspondence between the four levels of consciousness and the activities or concerns identified in the legal context. Lonergan's view is that each of the activities identified above corresponds to a particular level of consciousness, and it is by specifying that correspondence that the proper functions and procedures of the activities can be made explicit, thereby enhancing their performance.

Recall the four levels of consciousness - experiencing, understanding, judging, deciding. Perhaps a diagram[38] will help.

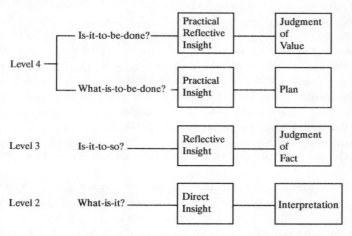

In spontaneous decision-making we do not explicitly distinguish between levels and we do not seek the end of any particular level itself. We do not treat the activities of a particular level of consciousness as a specialised type of inquiry. A decision, for instance, relies on the adequate performance of all four levels of consciousness. Further, the performance of mental activities does not necessarily occur in an orderly sequence beginning with experience and moving to understanding, judging, deciding. Attention may shift spontaneously from one level to another. Also, problem-solving may suffer from inattention, mistakes, oversights, poor judgment, and irrational decisions. But if we explicitly distinguish between each of the four levels of consciousness and make the search for, and discovery of, the proper achievement and end of each level the aim of legal activity does it provide the collaborative order of legal activity we seek?

4.1 The Past Phase

The field called **Research**, in its strictest sense, focuses on the expression of the past - particularly written expression in the legal context. According to Lonergan, the specialised function corresponding to the level of experiencing would be the proper achievement and end of this first level of consciousness. So, the specialised function is to attend to the raw materials or data. If the performance of these activities is considered, and is performed as, a specialty itself by a group of people rather than performed spontaneously by one individual its function would be to collect data. Its task would be to uncover available data, and to make available what is written. In the legal context, people, in fact, are engaged in this specialised task. The function of the people engaged in this specialty is not to understand the materials collected. Their function is **Research** - to assemble the materials that will be subsequently interpreted by a separate group of specialists. Of course, at the present time, the performance of such research activities in law is not considered a distinct functional specialty.

Consequent on the previous specialty is **Interpretation** of documents. The proper achievement and end of the second level of consciousness - understanding - is insight into the data or raw materials provided by sense, memory, imagination. These activities would become a distinct functional specialty when they are performed deliberately and that if understanding the data provided by Research is considered the proper achievement and end of a particular group. The specialised function or principal concern of this group would be to understand what was meant in its proper context and in accord with its proper mode, and level, of thought and expression. The specialised function, then, of **Interpretation** is to settle what was meant.

Not only does Interpretation involve understanding, but it also involves experiencing, judging and deciding. Even though this group makes judgments and decisions, the key function of this group is limited to providing interpretations of texts, to presenting what authors' meant. Their responsibility does not include ordering sequences of interpretations or their effects. That task is the specialised function of a subsequent group.

Interpretation leads to the **History** of interpretations and their application in law and in the general culture. The proper achievement and end of the third level of consciousness - judging - is "accepting or rejecting the explanation put forward by understanding to account for the data." If the performance of these activities is seen as the focus of attention of a group, the group would be primarily concerned with judging, with settling matters of fact, with setting forth what really happened. The concern, then, of **History** is with what really happened. This group would be concerned with discovering the course of events. The object of their inquiry is knowledge - historical knowledge - what was going forward in particular groups at particular times and places that, for the most part, contemporaries did not know.

The performance of the activities of this specialty is manifest in the work of legal historians. Legal historians can be seen as the group who have incipiently promoted the activities comprising the third level of consciousness to a specialty. Again, it must be stressed that the group engaged in this specialty are primarily concerned with judging, with settling what was going forward in a group. It is the specialised function of the following group of specialists to evaluate what happened.

The fourth level, in which the focus is on value, may at first seem unfamiliar[39], yet it is the level that has been the focus throughout this book. It is the level at which contrary results of Research, Interpretation, and History have to be assessed in order to move forward with some communal perspective. People in this specialty take a stand on obtuseness, stupidity, dishonesty, and immorality. The proper achievement and end of the fourth level of consciousness - deciding - is to acknowledge values and to select the methods to settle conflicts among them. The aim of a group which makes the performance of these activities their primary concern is a comprehensive viewpoint. The function of people in this specialty would be to unravel the conflicts between values, facts, meanings, and experiences represented by conflicting research, interpretations, histories, policies, plans. These specialists would also be working to discover the best history in light of human aspirations, what could have happened if only such and such was done. Lonergan calls this functional specialty **Dialectics.** In the legal context, such concerns are currently dealt with haphazardly and inadequately by politicians proposing legislation, by judges deciding cases, and by legal academics criticising or affirming outcomes of cases.

4.2 The Future Phase

The effort to transform the spontaneous and disorderly legal activity into explicit and discrete functional specialities concerned with Research, Interpretation, History, Dialectics has been concerned with the past. But the past points us to the future. Attending to the past is a crucial part of an effort to learn from the past, to avoid heading mindlessly into the future without reflection. Such reflection on the past grounds the question "Is there a better way?" "Is there a more adequate perspective that would promote a more refined reflection on future possibilities?

Again, the four levels of consciousness offer a clue to answering this question. Legal activity concerned with the future can be presented in terms of explicit and discrete specialities that correspond to the four levels of consciousness. The order of the performance of Research, Interpretation, History, Dialectics in the past phase of legal activity corresponds to the order in which we spontaneously solve problems. As experiencing calls forth understanding, judging, and deciding, Research leads to Interpretation, History, and Dialectics. In this phase, oriented to the past, inquiry begins with the specialities that correspond to the first level of consciousness and progresses to the specialities concerned with the second, third, and fourth levels of consciousness. But in the future phase of legal activity the order of concern is reversed. Inquiry begins with the specialty that corresponds to the fourth level of consciousness and then progresses to the specialities corresponding to the third, second, and first levels of consciousness. Perhaps a diagram will help explain this ordering.

Levels of Consciousness	Past	Future
4. Deciding	4. **Dialectics**	5. **Foundations**
3. Judging	3. **History**	6. **Policies**
2. Understanding	2. **Interpretation**	7. **Planning**
1. Experiencing	1. **Research**	8. **Executive Reflection**

The entire project relating to the past is of course a project committed to the movement forward and that movement forward is the movement of the community of levels of consciousness. Already we have noted the accepted division between Policy, Planning and Execution which a little reflection revealed as being activities, of the third, second, and first levels of consciousness respectively, in their drive towards the future. What our grounding schema adds is a fourth level of future orientation which can conventionally be named **Foundational**. It asks for a specification of the fundamental orientations that would ground progress within the legal and the larger world. The group that is primarily concerned with this specialty is fundamentally focused on the grounds of evaluation and decision. Their task is to provide **Foundations** for reflection on future possibilities. This group would take the best elements from the previous specialty Dialectics to identify fundamental needs of a community and to formulate general norms for progress. They would affirm what worked in the past to help provide a basic orientation to the future. In Dialectics the concern was judgments of value and expressions such as "This is good" or "This is bad." In Foundations the concern is also with judgments of value, but now the judgment of value is oriented to the future, with judging what would be good and with expressing "This would be good." A group specialising in this function cannot be found in the present legal context.

If the performance of the activities comprising the third level of consciousness - judging - is the specialty of a group, they would be concerned with developing **Policies** from the general norms articulated by specialists concerned with Foundations. In both History and Policy the primary concern is with judgments of fact. In History the concern is to judge what, in fact, happened in the past. By contrast, in Policy the concern is to provide the direction for what is to happen in the future. It involves affirming that we hold particular policies as "truths". The aim of these specialists is to develop policies and to affirm them. In the current legal context, the pressure on judges is to avoid and/or ignore "policy" issues.

Policies lead to planning. A group concentrating on the performance of the activities of the second level of consciousness - understanding - would be specialists in **Planning**. They would be "concerned with promoting an understanding of the realities affirmed in Policy."[40] They would develop and structure sequences of plans in the light of the work done in conflictual analysis. They would integrate developments in systematic planning in the light of the results of specialists in Policy. Their specialty would be the understanding of good plans and working out the optimal use of existing resources for attaining the ends articulated in Policy. This group would be primarily concerned with understanding and presenting hypotheses, understandings of what the future could be. This task is done haphazardly by judges when they create new principles or rules of law.

Executive Reflection corresponds to the first level of consciousness - experience - in that the primary concern is with implementing plans - producing action and expression. Judges and other decision-makers currently perform this role sponta- neously without the backing of the results of specialists in the previous seven special- ties.

Eight explicit and separate stages in the process of inquiry, each with its own spe- cialised function and procedures, have been identified. McShane summarises them in the following way:

1. Research: finding relevant data, written or other.
2. Interpretation: reaching the meaning of such data, the meaning of those that produced it.
3. History: figuring out the story, connecting the meanings of the writings and the doings, etc.
4. Dialectics: coming up with a best story and best basic directions. . .
5. Foundations: Expressing the best fundamental (in the sense that they are not tied to age, time, etc.) directions.
6. Policies: Relevant basic pragmatic truths, somewhat like the core of national constitutions or of tribal legends.
7. Planning-Systems: drawing correctively and contrafactually on the strategies of the past to envis- age ranges of time-ordered possibilities.
8. Communizings: local collaborative reflection that selects creatively from ranges of possibili- ties.[41]

This perspective is foundational: it underpins and informs. It reaches into history and it has a perspective on the future. Research, Interpretation, History, Dialectics are concerned with revealing the situation and Foundations, Policies, Planning, Executive Reflection are oriented to the future.

5 Conclusion

I have suggested that a plausible ordering of legal activity would be in terms of the performance of eight functional specialties. In fact, such an ordering of legal activity would amount to a paradigm shift. For instance, topics in Jurisprudence would be assigned their proper place rather than considered, by some people, as a subject that is, for the most part, irrelevant to, or in conflict with, legal practice. Take the subject- matter of this book - legal decision-making. It is in the area of Dialectics and Foundations that the fuller consideration of the topics raised, almost anecdotally in the present book, would find their adequate discussion. In particular, the area of Dialectics would have to be developed with serious full scientific intent, thus order- ing what at present is the random debate of which Chapters One, Two, and Three are representative.

It is of interest to note the precise description of the dialectic enterprise given by Lonergan. (Dialectics is not concerned with conflicts among intepretations or histo- ries that can be settled by more research.) Regarding the proper procedures of Dialectics he writes:

Before being operated on, the materials have to be assembled, completed, compared, reduced, classified, selected. *Assembly* includes the researches performed, the interpretations proposed, the histories written, and the events, statements, movements to which they refer. *Completion* adds evaluative interpretation and evaluative history; it picks out the one hundred and one "good things" and their opposites; . . . *Comparison* examines the completed assembly to seek out affinities and oppositions. *Reduction* finds the same affinity and the same opposition manifested in a number of different manners; from the many manifestations it moves to the underlying root. *Classification* determines which of these sources of affinity or opposition result from dialetically opposed horizons and which have other grounds. *Selection*, finally, picks out the affinities and oppositions grounded in dialecticaly opposed horizons and dismisses other affinties and oppositions.[42]

Let us consider six people who are serious about dialectic issues. Imagine that six books emerge that are explicit about their foundational perspective. The results of the six analyses will not be uniform as each investigator will be operating within a different horizon. Differences in horizon, and hence differences in evaluations of interpretations and histories, may be due to differences in the investigators' more or less explicit theories of knowledge and decision-making. Mistaken theories of knowledge and decision-making can affect an investigator's evaluations of interpretations and histories insofar as the investigator relied on them to guide analyses and to ground judgments and decisions. Hence, in Dialectics, not only is there a need to evaluate interpretations and histories, but there is also a need for self-criticism, a need for the person engaged in dialectic operations to discover one's own decision-making activities and procedures in order to take a stand on what others have written.

It is worth considering Chapters One to Four in light of the operations called for in Dialectics. It is in that context that discussions in those early chapters would find their own foundational perspective. Dialectic analysis would constitute a novel relocation of the discussions of legal decision-making. An adequate treatment of legal decison-making would not proceed in a random manner of constellating views. Rather, it would involve performing the operations outlined above in a full explanatory context. Further, the relevance of understanding the nature of "discovery" in legal decision-making in legal activity would be revealed in this fuller context.[42] In the context of the eight functional specialties, my study of legal decision-making, then, is not simply an effort to order a problematic jurisprudential issue, but is a crucial part of efforts to discern what was good and bad in the past so that we do not mindlessly create the future. Finally, a larger presentation of the authors discussed in earlier chapters would reveal even more massively the need for self-criticism. The task for initiating, developing, and sustaining that communal self-criticism in a manner that would give rise to constantly refreshed foundations is a task not for a single book, but for a community committed to luminous self-determination

1 B. Lonergan, **Method in Theology**, (London: Darton, Longman & Todd, 1971), 9.

2 ibid., 9.

3 ibid., 15.

4 ibid., 14-15.

5 The results of such an introspective inquiry are illustrated by the analysis of decision-making in Chapters Five to Seven.

6 In the present context it would be beside the point to contrast Lonergan's position with that of Scotus, Descartes, Kant, and Hegel. However, such analyses can be found in B. Lonergan, **Insight** and **Verbum**.

7 The diagram is in Chapter Five.

8 Sensibility, the receptive function of sense, is active. For instance, the hearing of a musician would be patterned to the extent that an attentive musician hears notes, chords, phrases, whereas a tone deaf person would not hear the patterning of the music.

9 A more elaborate treatment of feelings would enter into such topics as the detachment of the scientist and the relation of feeling to judgment and the relation of feelings to evaluation. See: **Insight**, 185-186 on the intellectual pattern of experience and **Method in Theology**, 30-34, 65 on feelings.

10 For more on this topic see **Verbum**, particularly Lonergan's summary of the Thomist description of the disposition of the phantasm on 25-33.

11 Lonergan discusses this topic in **Insight**, 191-203.

12 Lonergan distinguishes between the neglected subject and the truncated subject in *The Subject*, **A Second Collection**, (Darton, Longman & Todd, ?), 73. "The neglected subject does not know himself. The truncated subject no only does not know himself but also is unaware of his ignorance and so, in one way or another, concludes that what he does not know does not exist. Commonly enough the palpable facts of sensation and speech are admitted. Commonly also there is recognized the difference between sleeping and waking."

13 I conclude this section by suggesting that the issues and debates associated with the distinction between discovery and justification in Chapters One and Two should be considered in a new light.

14 This diagram was invented by Philip McShane.

15 Expression of a judgment is often complex because there is a contextual aspect of judgment. We have seen how judgment is related to an Is-question, but judgments are also related to each other. Lonergan identifies three ways in which this contextual aspect of judgment appears. First, a present judgment is related to past insights and judgments in that past insights and judgments stand ready to elucidate the judgment just made. Secondly, judgments can be related to other judgments in that the present judgments may conflict thereby releasing the discovery process. Or present judgments may be complementary and the person may strive to organize coherently these judgments. Thirdly, judgments are related to the future in the sense that the process of discovery is an incremental process. Although we can only make one judgment at a time "... all we know lurks behind the scenes and reveals itself only in the exactitude of each minor increment." **Insight**, 277.

16 Our relational structure also suggests that law differs from other fields inasmuch as the contents of presentations, insights, plans, decisions in the legal context differ from the contents of mental activities in other fields.

17 By differentiating between mental activities and expression I am not denying that there is an interpenetration of mental activity and expression. My aim only has been to stress the distinction, a distinction that does not seem to be sufficiently developed by legal theorists and cognitive psychologists.

18 A good teacher is able to add identification to his or her insight. Then the teacher "... is able to select and arrange and indicate to others the combination of sensible elements that will give rise to the same insight in them. One is able to vary the elements in different circumstances. One is able to ask questions that reveal the pupil's blind-spots and proceed to prior insights required to understand the lesson." **Insight**, 559.

19 The difficulty of achieving adequate formulation can best be appreciated by noticing the failure of Euclid to achieve such a formulation. So, for instance, in Euclid there is no definition of a straight line. On this topic see: B. Lonergan, *A Note on Geometric Possibility*, **Collection**, (London: Darton, Longman & Todd, 1967), 98-101.

20 This diagram ws provided by Philip McShane.

21 For Lonergan's discussion of views that equate mental activity with expression see **Insight**, 557.

22 **Insight**, 544.

23 **Insight**, 573-577.

24 ibid., 560.

25 Of course, logical systems can be understood by readers. To do so they engage in a discovery process - selecting data, discovering the relations among the data, and grasping the sufficiency of the evidence for the prospective judgment that the reader correctly understands the relations among the data.

26 **Verbum: Word and Idea in Aquinas**, 11-16.

27 P McShane, **Wealth of Self and Wealth of Nations**, 69-70.

28 ibid., 70.

29 *The Form of Inference*, 6.

30 On the relation between insight and syllogism see *The Form of Inference*, 3-16 and P. McShane, *In Tune with Timely Meaning*, unpublished manuscript.

31 This complementarity in expression corresponds to a complementarity between induction and logic. The human mind works inductively and then orders insights to find what is missing. Inductive reasoning pursues discovery, but at some time a point is reached and the person wants to organize his or her insights, judgments, decisions. Such a job is the task of logic.

32 For example, C. Gilligan, **In a Different Voice** (London: Harvard University Press, 1982) and S. Harding, **Whose Science? Whose Knowledge?** (Ithaca: Cornell University Press, 1991).

33 See **Verbum: Word and Idea in Aquinas**, 25, footnote 101
34 Strictly speaking this is not correct. The realists did write that once a decision is reached it is then expressed in the time-honored fashion.
35 C. Lamson, *The Gound Fisheries*, ed. P. Mushkat, H. MacPherson, F. Crickard, **Canada's Ocean Strategies Project–The Atlantic**, 375-6. I am grateful to P. Mushkat, PWM Consulting, Halifax, Nova Scotia for bringing this paper to my attention.
36 ibid., 391.
37 For a discussion of the ordering of other areas of inquiry see: On theology see B Lonergan, **Method in Theology.** On musicology see P. McShane, **The Shaping of The Foundations**, (New York: University Press of America, 1977), Chapter Two. On literature see P. McShane, **Lonergan's Challenge to the University and the Economy.** On economics see P. McShane, *Systematics, Communications and Actual Contexts*, **Lonergan's Challenge to the University and the Economy**, (New York: University Press of America, 1980); **Economics for Everyone: Das Jus Kapital**, unpublished manuscript, Chapter Five; **Process: Introducing Themselves to Young (Christian) Minders**, unpublished manuscript, Chapter Four.
38 This diagram is adapted from P. McShane, **Process: Introducing Themselves to Young (Christian) Minders**, unpublished manuscript, Chapter Two, 57.
39 Earlier in this section, I described the orientation of the activities of this specialty as a concern with identifying and settling **Conflicts**.
40 P.McShane, **Economics For Everyone: Das Jus Kapital**, Chapter Five.
41 **Economics for Everyone: Das Jus Kapital**, (unpublished manuscript) Chapter Five, 16.
42 **Method in Theology**, 249-250.
43 A fundamental reason for investigating decision-making can be offered. In legal practice, the object of analysis is the adequacy or legitimacy of judgments and decisions. In criminal cases, judges assess whether or not accessed persons made conscious decisions in order to judge whether or not actions are voluntary. The decision process of accused persons is traced from the action back to how the decision was made. Judges assess whether or not accused persons intended to perform their actions and whether or not they were aware of the risks of an action when they carried out their actions. In torts cases, judges assess whether or not a defendant owes a duty of care by assessing the foresight and reasonableness of defendants decisions to act. In contract law, judges say that they interpret the intentions of the parties to a contract. In cases involving judicial review, the adequacy and legitimacy of a decision process itself is scrutinised. And, of course, the most obvious example where the adequacy and legitimacy of the decision process operates is when a judge reaches a decision in a case. The decision process is, in fact, a central topic in legal practice. Yet the decision process itself is left unscrutinised. Judges make assessments and evaluations about the decision-making processes of defendants, plaintiffs, and other judges, but no one understands the nature of the decision-making process itself. My point is that to ignore how decisions are "actually" reached is to neglect what is the key activity in the legal context.

Law and Philosophy Library

1. E. Bulygin, J.-L. Gardies and I. Niiniluoto (eds.): *Man, Law and Modern Forms of Life*. With an Introduction by M.D. Bayles. 1985   ISBN 90-277-1869-5

2. W. Sadurski: *Giving Desert Its Due*. Social Justice and Legal Theory. 1985
                                                                                   ISBN 90-277-1941-1

3. N. MacCormick and O. Weinberger: *An Institutional Theory of Law*. New Approaches to Legal Positivism. 1986   ISBN 90-277-2079-7

4. A. Aarnio: *The Rational as Reasonable*. A Treatise on Legal Justification. 1987
                                                                                   ISBN 90-277-2276-5

5. M.D. Bayles: *Principles of Law*. A Normative Analysis. 1987
                                                            ISBN 90-277-2412-1; Pb: 90-277-2413-X

6. A. Soeteman: *Logic in Law*. Remarks on Logic and Rationality in Normative Reasoning, Especially in Law. 1989   ISBN 0-7923-0042-4

7. C.T. Sistare: *Responsibility and Criminal Liability*. 1989   ISBN 0-7923-0396-2

8. A. Peczenik: *On Law and Reason*. 1989   ISBN 0-7923-0444-6

9. W. Sadurski: *Moral Pluralism and Legal Neutrality*. 1990   ISBN 0-7923-0565-5

10. M.D. Bayles: *Procedural Justice*. Allocating to Individuals. 1990   ISBN 0-7923-0567-1

11. P. Nerhot (ed.): *Law, Interpretation and Reality*. Essays in Epistemology, Hermeneutics and Jurisprudence. 1990   ISBN 0-7923-0593-0

12. A.W. Norrie: *Law, Ideology and Punishment*. Retrieval and Critique of the Liberal Ideal of Criminal Justice. 1991   ISBN 0-7923-1013-6

13. P. Nerhot (ed.): *Legal Knowledge and Analogy*. Fragments of Legal Epistemology, Hermeneutics and Linguistics. 1991   ISBN 0-7923-1065-9

14. O. Weinberger: *Law, Institution and Legal Politics*. Fundamental Problems of Legal Theory and Social Philosophy. 1991   ISBN 0-7923-1143-4

15. J. Wróblewski: *The Judicial Application of Law*. Edited by Z. Bańkowski and N. MacCormick. 1992   ISBN 0-7923-1569-3

16. T. Wilhelmsson: *Critical Studies in Private Law*. A Treatise on Need-Rational Principles in Modern Law. 1992   ISBN 0-7923-1659-2

17. M.D. Bayles: *Hart's Legal Philosophy*. An Examination. 1992   ISBN 0-7923-1981-8

18. D.W.P. Ruiter: *Institutional Legal Facts*. Legal Powers and their Effects. 1993
                                                                                   ISBN 0-7923-2441-2

19. J. Schonsheck: *On Criminalization*. An Essay in the Philosophy of the Criminal Law. 1994
                                                                                   ISBN 0-7923-2663-6

20. R.P. Malloy and J. Evensky (eds.): *Adam Smith and the Philosophy of Law and Economics*. 1994   ISBN 0-7923-2796-9

21. Z. Bankowski, I. White and U. Hahn (eds.): *Informatics and the Foundations of Legal Reasoning*. 1995   ISBN 0-7923-3455-8

22. E. Lagerspetz: *The Opposite Mirrors*. An Essay on the Conventionalist Theory of Institutions. 1995   ISBN 0-7923-3325-X

23. M. van Hees: *Rights and Decisions*. Formal Models of Law and Liberalism. 1995
                                                                                   ISBN 0-7923-3754-9

24. B. Anderson: *"Discovery" in Legal Decision-Making*. 1996   ISBN 0-7923-3981-9

KLUWER ACADEMIC PUBLISHERS – DORDRECHT / BOSTON / LONDON